World Heritage   *Monumental Sites*

A joint co-publication by

The United Nations Educational, Scientific and
Cultural Organization (UNESCO),
7, Place De Fontenoy, 75007 Paris, France
and
Skira Editore spa, Palazzo Casati Stampa,
via Torino 61, 20123 Milan, Italy

World Heritage

Monumental Sites

Skira

Cover
The Palace of Caserta, Italy

Pages II-III
The Temple of the Sun at Koṇārak, India

Page VII
The Sphinx of Giza, Egypt

Pages VIII-IX
The Palace of Caserta, Italy

Pages X-XI
The Cathedral of Chartres, France

Page XII
Alhambra at Granada, Spain

Design
Marcello Francone

Editing
Marco Abate

Layout
Serena Parini

Translations
Antony Shugaar

Iconographical Research
Alessandra Montini
Massimo Zanella

First published in Italy in 2003 by
Skira Editore S.p.A.
Palazzo Casati Stampa
via Torino 61
20123 Milano
Italy

© 2003 Skira for the texts
© 2003 Banca Intesa
© 2003 UNESCO for their own images
© 2003 Skira/UNESCO

Printed and bound in Italy. First edition
Skira ISBN 88-8491-557-0
UNESCO ISBN 92-3-103919-9

Distributed in North America and Latin America
by Rizzoli International Publications, Inc. through
St. Martin's Press, 175 Fifth Avenue, New York,
NY 10010.
Distributed elsewhere in the world by Thames and
Hudson Ltd., 181a High Holborn, London WC1V
7QX, United Kingdom.

This book was first published
exclusively for Banca Intesa

In 1972, UNESCO founded the Convention concerning the Protection of the World Cultural and Natural Heritage – an international convention and a fundamental tool for the identification and safeguarding of the cultural, artistic and environmental heritage of humanity. Over the course of thirty-one years of work, a non-partisan list has been developed of some 700 sites, a list that is constantly being expanded to include cultivated natural settings, archaeological areas, small and large urban settlements, monumental complexes, individual artistic monuments and uncontaminated natural areas, all of which combine to create an ideal catalogue, but also a virtual route, through the history, cultures and multiform creative expressions of the civilizations of humanity.

Skira, in collaboration with the executive leadership of UNESCO and IntesaBci, has undertaken to devote its efforts towards the creation of a rich and intelligently structured collection of information and images, which describe an emblematic selection of locations drawn from this World Heritage List developed by UNESCO. In order to better structure and justify the selections, the sites were chosen, not by country of location or chronological order, but rather by typology. The first volume, *World Heritage: Archaeological Sites and Urban Centres*, published last year, offered a review of significant archaeological areas, exploring religious sites, urban settlements and palace complexes, as well as important historical and city centres. This year's volume is dedicated to a deeper study of individual monumental structures of varying degrees of complexity, all of which stand as autonomous and complete entities.

The organization of themes in this volume calls for a series of larger presentations offering an account of each monument's history, its structural and stylistic stratifications, and its most emblematic and salient points in historical and artistic terms. These are assisted in many cases by detailed sidebars that examine historical figures, critical problems and individual artworks. The wealth and variety of illustrations presented alongside the main text are offered as a potentially independent photographic essay, and are supported by thorough full-length captions. The index, meanwhile, features the list of sites identified by UNESCO – excluding those sites discussed within this volume – with specific descriptions and characteristics relating to each noted typology.

The identification and selections were made from among a wide and extremely diversified patrimony, extending over vast expanses of time and space, in which each individual entry holds valid claims to uniqueness and importance, all worthy of being analysed, described and appreciated. The choices were difficult and made carefully, even though the limitations of space meant that painful sacrifices were sometimes necessary. All the same, the justifications for the forty-seven monuments described in this second volume are fully grounded in the objective of documenting the variations in style and methods of construction employed by different cultures as they assembled forms and symbols tied to the sites chosen for these exercises in political power, social prestige, luxury, religious worship and collective memory.

For certain sites, protected from the hostility of the outside world, the sense of belonging of entire communities was particularly acute. These sites became points of reference for the collective memory as within their boundaries the daily life of an entire people was lived. This was the case for both the simple and archaic forms of the Pueblo of Taos in New Mexico, and the magnificent extension of the Great Wall of China; the latter a human creation that deeply altered the natural environment and which marked an ideal boundary between civilization and barbarianism, but never constituted a real obstacle to the migrations of peoples. To the category of monumental complexes belongs also, by right, the places wherein political and administrative power was exercised. These later evolved into settings where sovereign power was held, and in time became both courts and places 'of delight', that is, residences in which political power and social prestige evolved into a taste for living and an everyday existence of great elegance, right down to the present day.

While Castel del Monte, one of the favourite residences of the Emperor Frederick II of Swabia, appears in spite of its stern, repeated octagonal forms, as a place devoted to the pleasures of hunting as well as an emblematic site of imperial power, the Tower of London appears as an intricately structured architectural complex in which we find a continuum of royal suites, treasure chambers, prison cells and defensive areas. On the other hand, the typology of the fortress as a site enclosed by powerful defensive walls, has been given magnificent and stratified interpretations in the various regions of the world. This is in evidence from the royal huts of Abomey in Benin, where African architecture using natural materials is further enriched with pictorial and plastic decorations, to the exceptional stratification of buildings

that comprise the palaces of the Potala of Lhasa in Tibet – the residence of the religious and political authority of the Dalai Lama; and again from the Kremlin in Moscow, where from the fifteenth century, the fusion of imperial palaces, administrative offices and Orthodox cathedrals resulted in the creation of a fortress resembling a small city with streets, squares and buildings, to the Forbidden City, the site of Chinese imperial power from the Mongol dynasty to the last Manch emperor.

There was a different development in Europe regarding the typology of palace and villa, beginning with the prototypes codified in the classical era and the metamorphoses induced by the culture of the Renaissance. Let us consider four equally exceptional cases: the palaces of the Alhambra in Granada, Villa d'Este at Tivoli, the Chateau of Fontainebleau and the residence of El Escorial, not far from Madrid.

The Alhambra represents one of the very rare examples of Arabic culture still present on European soil, in which is found an extraordinary synthesis. This site, built as a representation of the power of the caliph, incorporates private apartment suites, gardens and fountains, in a harmonious array of man-made structures and natural environments.

The close link between architecture and garden is again made manifest, although in different ways, at Villa d'Este, a masterpiece of the culture of the Italian Renaissance. At this site, the various itineraries mapped out by the designer of the park were conceived as pathways of symbols and knowledge. However, at the royal residence of Fontainebleau – where Italian artists of the Mannerist school such as Benvenuto Cellini and Rosso Fiorentino worked – the need to represent

the grandeur of royal power overwhelmed all other equilibriums, giving absolute space to architecture and decoration in respect to its relationship with nature. In this sense, the design of the residence of Philip II of Spain was even more virtual and abstract. The palace of El Escorial in fact closes itself off entirely from any relationship with the landscape, opting instead for the typology of the monastery, in which religious symbols and royal symbols merge in a single dynastic exaltation.

This volume also reserves extensive space in its itinerary for the magnificent royal and imperial residences of the seventeenth and eighteenth centuries which codified in a definitive way the typology of the courts of Europe. Among the first sites to be listed and documented by UNESCO were the palaces of Versailles, a veritable prototype and point of reference; Schönbrunn in Vienna, built at the behest of Marie Therese of Hapsburg; Potsdam, the elegant retreat of Frederick II of Prussia; and Caserta, the Neoclassical masterpiece of Luigi Vanvitelli. More modest structures are also visited, which are significant both in terms of architecture and the art collections they contain: the castles of Kronborg in Denmark, Kromeriz in the Czech Republic, Drottningholm in Sweden and, above all, the residence of Würzburg in Germany, which preserves the extraordinary celebratory frescoes by Giambattista Tiepolo, which were executed between 1750 and 1752.

The World Heritage List also includes buildings that are considered emblematic of single moments of European architectural taste and culture between the nineteenth and twentieth centuries: these are represented here by the buildings designed by Victor Horta, which made Brussels one of the capitals of Art Nouveau.

The investigations and explorations offered in this second volume devoted to the heritage of humanity also feature the development of monumental complexes linked to places of worship of special significance and prestige. The history of ecclesiastic and temple architecture is examined, running from the High Middle Ages to the heart of the nineteenth century. Beginning with the monastery of Haghpat in Armenia, a genuine prototype of European Romanesque architecture, the text ranges on to that masterpiece of both ancient and modern architecture that is the Palatine Chapel of Aachen, built by Charlemagne as a symbol of his newly won imperial power. But the great eras of Romanesque and Gothic architecture also provide offerings: for the former, the monumental church of Saint Michael at Hildesheim, with its exquisite bronzework inspired by Roman antiquity, and the more modest church of Münstair, with its lavish cycle of paintings, and on to the splendid church of Saint Mary Magdalene in Vézelay in Burgundy; for the latter, the cathedral of Chartres, the church of San Francesco in Assisi, with the cycles of paintings by Cimabue, Cavallini, Giotto and the Lorenzettis, and Westminster Cathedral in London – the beating heart of the English monarchy and a site devoted to the collective memory of British culture. A place of special importance is held by the monumental complex of Santa Maria delle Grazie in Milan: masterpiece of Solari's Gothic architecture, transformed into a Renaissance array as a ducal mausoleum for the Sforza family by Donato Bramante and decorated with the *Last Supper* by Leonardo da Vinci. At the same time in other sites around the world, the transformation or the continuity of structural typologies of places of worship has resulted in such absolute masterpieces as the mosque of Isfahan in Iran and the Golden Mosque of Dambulla in Sri Lanka, as well as the Hindu temple dedicated to the Sun at Konarak in India, with its exceptional sculptural decorations, the temple of Borobodur in Indonesia, the rigorous and traditional monumental complex of the Himeji-jo temple in Japan, and the remarkable interplay between sacred itinerary, temples and nature that has been preserved in the area of Wudang in China. On the other hand, European culture has also thrived in interaction with Eastern influences, acquiring structural and decorative elements or standing as a barrier to the anti-iconic culture of Muslim origin: the monastic complex of Mount Athos in Greece or the complex of Rila in Bulgaria offer substantial examples of this phenomenon, as do the complex of Tomar in Portugal and, to an even greater degree, the sanctuary of Congonhas in Brazil and the hospital of Cabaña at Guadalajara in Mexico. All these sites illustrate the potential of metamorphosis of European architectural idioms – between Mannerism and the Baroque – when they enter into contact with different cultures. Special attention is also devoted to the German sanctuary of 'in der Weis', located at the foot of the Bavarian Alps, which forms one of the most exquisite and entrancing examples of the Rococo style.

Finally, the itinerary includes those monumental complexes erected for funerary or celebratory purposes, yet which have become over time meta-historical symbols and have thus won places of their own in the collective memory of humanity. While the Royal Hill of Ambohimanga in Madagascar represents the sole symbol of cohesive identity for the local civilization, the typology of the pyramids of Saqqara, Dashur and Giza are not only synonymous with Egyptian civilization, but have entered into the world heritage as funerary symbols and symbols of antiquity. Similarly, the temples built by Ramesses II at Abu Simbel have become for contemporary culture both symbols of the power of one of the greatest sovereigns of antiquity and of his love for his wife Nefertari. Furthermore, they have come to symbolize UNESCO's commitment towards the safeguarding of the heritage of humanity. UNESCO organized and supported in 1968 the titanic undertaking of dismantling and moving this monumental complex that would otherwise have been forever lost beneath the Nile, the waters of which had swollen into Lake Nasser following the construction of the Great Aswan Dam. Separated by many thousands of years and miles, but a veritable monument and symbol of European civilization is the Statue of Liberty located in New York Harbour. A work of the French sculptor Bartholdi, this monument represents the rights and duties of all human beings. A special place, lastly, has been accorded to one of the masterpieces of civilization at large and one of the pearls of world heritage: the Taj Mahal in Agra, India. This splendid funerary monument, midway between a mosque and a royal palace and surrounded by gardens and fountains, was built between 1632 and 1654 at the behest of Shah Jahn, the Moghul emperor, to commemorate his beloved wife. This structural and decorative event engendered by the emotions of one man, has become over the centuries a point of reference for all human civilization.

Contents

EUROPE

Austria
4
The Palace and Gardens
of Schönbrunn
Roberta D'Adda

Belgium
18
Victor Horta's Brussels
Roberta D'Adda

Bulgaria
24
The Monastery of Rila
Cecilia Gibellini

Denmark
28
The Kronborg Castle
Cecilia Gibellini

France
32
The Cathedral of Chartres
Cecilia Gibellini
44
The Palace and Park
of Fontainebleau
Roberta D'Adda
56
The Palace and Park of Versailles
Roberta D'Adda
70
The Church of Sainte Madeleine
at Vézelay
Cecilia Gibellini

Germany
76
The Cathedral of Aachen
Cecilia Gibellini
82
The Cathedral of Saint Mary
and the Church of Saint Michael
at Hildesheim
Alessandra Montini
86
The Palace and Park of Potsdam
Massimo Zanella
96
The Sanctuary in der Wies
Massimo Zanella
100
The Castle of Würzburg
Massimo Zanella

United Kingdom
110
The Tower of London
Roberta D'Adda

116
Westminster Abbey in London
Roberta D'Adda

Greece
122
Mount Athos
Cecilia Gibellini

Italy
130
The Basilica of San Francesco in Assisi
Cecilia Gibellini
142
The Palace and the park of Caserta
Massimo Zanella
154
Castel del Monte
Cecilia Gibellini
160
The Church of Santa Maria delle
Grazie and the refectory in Milan
Massimo Zanella
168
Villa d'Este at Tivoli
Roberta D'Adda

Portugal
178
The Convent of Christ in Tomar
Roberta D'Adda

Czech Republic
184
The Castle of Kroměříž
Cecilia Gibellini

Russia
188
The Kremlin of Moscow
Cecilia Gibellini

Spain
202
The Monastery of San Lorenzo
at El Escorial
Roberta D'Adda
214
The Alhambra in Granada
Roberta D'Adda

Sweden
224
The Palace of Drottningholm
Cecilia Gibellini

Switzerland
228
The Abbey of Saint John the Baptist
at Müstair
Cecilia Gibellini

ASIA

Armenia
234
The Monastery of Haghpat
Sergio Basso

China
236
The Great Wall
Sergio Basso
242
The Potala in Lhasa
Sergio Basso
250
The Forbidden City in Beijing
Sergio Basso
262
The Wudang Mountain
Sergio Basso

Japan
268
The Castle of Himeji-jo
Sergio Basso

India
274
The Taj Mahal in Agra
Cecilia Gibellini
288
The Temple of the Sun
at Konarak
Sergio Basso

Indonesia
298
The Temple of Borobudur
Sergio Basso

Iran
306
The Mosque of Isfahan
Sergio Basso

Sri Lanka
316
The Golden Temple
of Dambulla
Alessandra Montini

AFRICA

Benin
322
The Royal Palaces
of Abomey
Alessandra Montini

Egypt
326
The Temples
of Abu Simbel
Alessandra Montini
336
The Pyramids from Giza
to Dashur
Alessandra Montini

Madagascar
342
The Royal Hill
of Ambohimanga
Alessandra Montini

AMERICA

Brazil
348
The Sanctuary of Bom Jesus
do Matosinhos at Congonhas
do Campo
Alessandra Montini

Mexico
354
The Hospicio Cabañas
at Guadalajara
Alessandra Montini

United States
358
The Statue of Liberty
in New York
Cecilia Gibellini
362
The Pueblo of Taos
Alessandra Montini

Unesco
369
World Heritage Sites

383
Photo credits

ICELAND

NORWAY

SWEDEN

FINLAND

RUSSIA

Drottningholm

ESTONIA

DENMARK

Helsingør

LATVIA

LITHUANIA

Moscow

Northern
Ireland

IRELAND

UNITED
KINGDOM

NETHERLANDS

Hildesheim ◆ *Potsdam*

BIELORUSSIA

London

BELGIUM

Aachen

POLAND

Brussels ◆ *Würzburg*

Versailles

GERMANY

CZECH

Kroměříž

UKRAINE

Chartres ◆ *Fontainebleau*

REPUBLIC

SLOVACKIA

Schönbrunn

FRANCE

Wies

Vézelay

SWITZERLAND

AUSTRIA

Müstair

HUNGHARY

ROMANIA

Milan

SLOVENIA

CROATIA

YUGOSLAVIA

BOSNIA

PORTUGAL

Tomar

El Escorial

SPAIN

Assisi

HERZEGOVINA

BULGARIA

Tivoli ITALY

Rila

Granada

VATICAN CITY

MACEDONIA

Mouns Athos

Caserta

*Castel
del Monte*

GREECE

TURKEY

EUROPE Europe

The Palace and Gardens of Schönbrunn

The Castle of Schönbrunn, located 10 kilometres to the south-west of Vienna, was first built in the sixteenth century as a hunting lodge, and it later became one of the residences of the Habsburg Imperial Dynasty, reflecting over the years their political role and their varying fortunes. The present-day image of the palace, apparently characterized by a uniform style of Baroque influence that would appear to indicate that the building was an exceptional total work of art (*Gesamtkunstwerk*), in fact acquired its final appearance through a series of progressive modifications that extended well into the nineteenth century.

At the origin of the long history of Schönbrunn was the decision on the part of Maximilian II to set aside the forest of Katterhölzel (which extended over the area now occupied by the palace and the hill behind it) as an imperial hunting preserve: in 1573, the enclosure that the emperor had ordered was completed, and a programme of stocking the preserve with wildlife was undertaken. In 1622, the water from a spring that had been discovered near the preserve was deviated towards the royal park, and before long the more level sections of the estate were transformed into a simple pleasure garden, with an adjoining two-storey castle.

In 1683, the building, which in the meantime had been named, along with the estate itself, Schönbrunn ('beautiful spring'), was seriously damaged in the battle fought against the Turks during the Siege of Vienna, and it became necessary to rebuild it; the project was assigned to Johann Bernard Fischer von Erlach, an Austrian architect who had studied in Rome, following the styles of Carlo Fontana and, especially, Bernini and Borromini. At a time of special prestige and expansionism for the Viennese ruling house, the castle was conceived as a monumental palace, inspired by the great models of the Italian Renaissance, and capable of rivalling Versailles.

A first design by Fischer von Erlach was rejected, probably for economic considerations or possibly because it was too daring; in fact it had the castle standing on the top of the hill, at the steepest point, as the ultimate and final culmination of a gigantic series of artificial steps and terraces that made it, visually speaking, a nuanced and distant objective, almost unattainable. It is possible that with such a layout the architect had meant to illustrate the role of the imperial institution, which from its serene residence controlled the newly secured territories and, especially, the neighbouring capital, which was expanding in accordance with very specific regulations. In this context, the palace of Schönbrunn stood outside the outermost sector of the city, establishing itself as a crucial point of reference for the landscape at large.

In 1699, after the architect presented a second plan, construction began and was completed in 1701. Although he maintained the monumental scale of his earlier idea, Fischer von Erlach gave up the idea of a dominant placement high atop the hill, placing the new building instead on the lowlands and joining the high ground behind it through the development of the park. The original core of the present-day construction, the imperial residence consisted of a rectangular *corp de logis*, structured by a giant order of supports set upon a false-ashlar basement; added to this central element during construction were two lateral wings, corresponding to the new residential requirements of the Emperor Joseph I, who had married in the meantime. The building, which was two storeys tall, was covered by a roof with the slightest inclination to its pitch, which did not emerge behind the line of the balustrade, punctuated in turn by statues which corresponded to the pilaster strips. The central structure was marked by the presence of a loggia that served as a filter towards the vast rear garden; in the drawings of the architect (pub-

Garden parterre, seen from the Fountain of Neptune (1780).

On the facing page
Detail of the central structure of the palace and the eastern wing, seen from one of the fountains in the French-style gardens.

*The monumental
structure of the Gloriette,
Italianate in the style
of its pediments, arches,
and twinned columns,
provides a theatrical
backdrop for the prospect
of the park, with two
broad staircases adorned
with ancient-style
triumphs, with weapons
and armour.*

lished in Vienna in 1721) this garden was meant to be rectangular in shape and culminate in a semi-circular structure comprising a backcloth of niches, separated by twinned columns and surmounted by a balustrade with statues, and situated along the symmetrical axis that ran out from the palace's loggia. From this line of demarcation, the main boulevard of the garden ran in a straight line along the slope of the hill, ending in an open loggia that overlooked the surrounding countryside; the last-named construction, which was never built, was clearly a holdover from the very first design. The work on the garden began in 1695 under the supervision of Johann Trehet, who initially worked on the waterworks needed in order to implement the fountains that had been designed by Fischer von Erlach; he had planned out for the park a clear gridwork plan, devoid of oblique angles or great open spaces, and defined by the sole presence of parterres adorned with flowers and yew trees. This decision could be understood as an attempt to delineate an open

spatial system, potentially extendable to all the surrounding territory, and thus returning to the basic motif expressed symbolically in the first design. The physiognomy of the seventeenth-century garden, in any case, was profoundly modified over the course of the century, when under Maria Theresa massive restructurings and modernizations were undertaken in order to rectify the state of neglect into which the palace had fallen after the reign of Joseph I. The modifications undertaken during her reign reflected the new requirements of courtly life, which had changed radically in the meantime, and which now reflected specific cultural and stylistic orientations typical of the era of the enlightened empress.

The first restorations done in the eighteenth century concerned the buildings' roofs which were replaced by high pitched roofs, thus undercutting the effect of ample linear extension that had been sought by Fischer von Erlach. In 1740 a more far-reaching building campaign was commissioned under the supervision of

MARIA THERESA

The daughter of the Emperor Charles VI, Maria Theresa (1717–80) secured her rights to the throne through the law endorsed by her father and widely known as the 'pragmatic sanction' (1713), which established the hereditary succession of the Habsburg territories through the female line as well as the male. In 1736 Maria Theresa married Francis of Lorraine, and in 1740 she became the ruler of her hereditary domains (Austria, Hungary, and Bohemia). At first, her attention was fully absorbed by the War of Succession and the Seven Years' War, but from the 1760s the empress devoted herself to decisive internal policy, pursuing the reinforcement of the state and, at the same time, improvements in the living conditions of her own subjects; in this way following her own conceptions of the enlightened despot and founding, among other things, a vast network of public and affordable schools. Under her rule, which relied upon the collaboration of her able Prime Minister, Kaunitz, Austria was transformed from a feudal state into a bureaucratic and centralized state, in which the bourgeoisie was entrusted with important administrative responsibilities and the traditional privileges of the aristocracy were restricted. Her son Joseph II (co-regent and emperor, who often stayed at Schönbrunn with his wife Elizabeth) gradually took her place at the head of the government, undertaking a policy of reformation that was far more radical than his mother's had been.

Under the patronage of Maria Theresa, two Italian artists enjoyed great success: the Roman painter Gregorio Guglielmi (1714–73), who worked on Schönbrunn and on the University of Vienna, and the poet and librettist Pietro Metastasio (1698–1782); the latter, summoned to Austria by Charles VI to serve as imperial poet, wrote the texts for numerous operas and introduced into the Habsburg Court the Arcadian culture of Rome, intertwined with the bucolic themes taken from the classical tradition.

Martin van Meytens, the Younger, Portrait of the Empress Maria Theresa, *oil on canvas, c. 1760. Vienna, Palace of Schönbrunn.*

On pages 8–9 *Panoramic view from the Gloriette of the long side of the palace.*

View of the façade with the renovations done during the reign of Maria Theresa, when the original entrance stairway was replaced by

two symmetrical flights of stairs in a pincer configuration, converging on a broad terrace set on a line with the rusticated socle.

View of the Fountain of Neptune (1780) and the Gloriette, crowned by the imperial eagle.

On the facing page The Milionenzimmer, with its rosewood walls, adorned by over sixty Indo-Persian miniatures set in Rococo frames.

THE BOTANICAL GARDEN AND THE GREENHOUSES

In 1753 Francis I, a passionate follower of natural science, acquired a parcel of land to the west of the park with the intention of creating a botanical garden there, later known as the Dutch Garden. Organized in keeping with a geometric layout, the garden was subdivided into three parts and adorned with a fountain: in it, fruit trees, vegetables, and flowers were cultivated. The successors to Francis I enlarged the Dutch Garden by purchasing more parcels of land and creating, among other things, an arboretum, with exotic American trees and small greenhouses. At the end of the eighteenth century, the botanical garden of Schönbrunn contained 4,000 plants representing almost 800 species; later transformed into a landscape garden on the English model, this section of the imperial park still preserves some of the exotic trees that once belonged to the original collection.

In 1881 on the area originally purchased by Francis I a greenhouse was built, a massive structure made of iron and glass, by Franz Xaver Segenschmid; composed of a central pavilion standing 28 metres tall and two lateral structures that were slightly shorter, the Palm Greenhouse extended over a length of more than 110 metres and reproduced, in its interior, three different climatic zones.

Palm Greenhouse. Built in iron and glass by Franz Xaver Segenschmid in 1881, the greenhouse stands on the former site of the old botanical garden.

The Palace of Schönbrunn seen from the garden in a watercolour print, as it appeared in the first half of the nineteenth century.

On the facing page Detail of the frescoes portraying the Glories of the House of Austria, *done by Gregorio Guglielmi, in the Grosse Galerie. In the central medallion are illustrated the* Advantages of Peace, *with the figures of Francis Stephen and Maria Theresa, surrounded by allegories.*

Martin van Meytens, the Younger, Official Banquet for the Wedding of Joseph II and Isabella of Parma on 6 October 1760, *oil on canvas. Vienna, Palace of Schönbrunn.*

Bernardo Bellotto, View of the Palace of Schönbrunn, *oil on canvas, 1759. Vienna, Kunsthistorisches Museum.*

On the facing page *Chinese Cabinet. Overlooking the Kleine Galerie, this room was reserved for private conversations and for entertainment, and it is decorated with elegant lacquered chinoiseries set in white wooden frameworks.*

Nikolaus Pacassi, an Austrian architect, who worked to adapt the palace to the residential requirements of Maria Theresa's court, which was far more numerous than the courts that had previously resided at Schönbrunn. In order to increase the space available, the architect introduced a mezzanine into the side areas of the central structure, thus profoundly altering the harmony of the original elevation and interrupting the trabeation which separated the two storeys and marked distinctly the horizontal distribution of the mass of the castle. The great entry staircase was replaced by two symmetrical pincered flights of stairs, converging in an ample balcony that was set on a line with the rusticated plinth; a similar system of flights of stairs was also built on the façade overlooking the garden, so as to create on the ground floor a passageway which served as a covered atrium, but which destroyed the effect of lightness created by the loggia that had originally been set on the first floor. The interior layout of the central structure was entirely revised: the existing double-height main hall was replaced by two small parallel galleries, the Grosse Galerie, which overlooked the courtyard of honour to the north, and the Kleine Galerie, which overlooked the garden. In the context of the structural renovations done during the reign of Maria Theresa, the entire decorative array of the palace was also redesigned, thus eliminating almost every trace of the previous seventeenth-century decorations; all that survives of the building's first phase is a ceiling painted with an *Allegory of the Princely Virtues,* frescoed by Sebastiano Ricci in the old dining hall, later transformed into the atrium of a staircase. The Rococo decorations from the era of Maria Theresa have been preserved in many major rooms, beginning with the two galleries where the ceilings were frescoed by Gregorio Guglielmi with the *Glories of the House of Austria,* framed by white and gold cornices. Among the most original and interesting ornamental motifs we should mention the chinoiseries, which adorn two cabinets set at the extremities of the southern gallery. There are also numerous rooms decorated with landscapes, in keeping with the taste for the picturesque that spread throughout Europe in the eighteenth century: Joseph Rosa painted romantic views of mountains and crags at Schönbrunn, while Johann Wenzel Bergl preferred exotic and tropical motifs. A number of rooms

The Hall of Lacquers is decorated with portraits of the members of the imperial family, painted by Pompeo Batoni, alternating with Chinese lacquered panels.

On the facing page Hall of the Tapestries. The eighteenth-century tapestries that adorn the walls were woven in Brussels, and they depict harbour and market scenes; the hall was arranged as it is today in 1873, on the occasion of the Universal Exposition of Vienna.

Detail of one of the rearing horses which adorn the Fountain of Neptune.

present original and quite excellent features: the Porzellanzimmer takes its name from the white and light-blue coverings of its walls, in imitation of the effect of porcelain, while in the Milionenzimmer the walls are adorned with Persian miniatures from the Moghul period.

The restructuring ordered by Maria Theresa affected the park as well, which was almost entirely redesigned by a number of different artists, some of them linked to the House of Lorraine and to Francis I, husband of the empress. On the hill a number of diagonal axes were traced, running from the tops of the flower-beds and from four open plazas created along the slopes of the hill to the avenue that runs along the top of the hill. In the gridwork that defined the lower flat land were inserted a number of *bosquets* and small buildings, artistically constructed in keeping with the atmospheres and the images of the Arcadian and bucolic literature of the time, which found its most representative expression in the operas of Metastasio (often performed in the gardens

of Schönbrunn). In a later intervention, Ferdinand Hohenberg built the so-called 'Roman ruin' (1778), a monument composed of intentionally decrepit structures, to symbolize the decay of all things and the destructive action of the passage of time, and the Fountain of the Obelisk, which served as a pendant to the other fountain, and celebrated the Habsburg genealogy. The climb up the hill was redesigned, beginning with the central Fountain of Neptune, with a double system of curving ramps, arranged along the central axis constituted by a rectilinear waterfall; the spring from which the water gushed forth, set on the top of the hill, was emphasized by the Gloriette, a belvedere with loggia designed by Hohenberg in solemn forms, set where Fischer von Erlach himself had imagined a structure of the same sort. The definitive plan of the park, which called for the deployment of a series of imperial symbols and insignia, was only partially implemented.

Victor Horta's Brussels

The buildings constructed in Brussels by the architect Victor Horta, one of the founders of Art Nouveau, provide documentation of a stylistic revolution that profoundly marked the history of European art in the early twentieth century. His architecture is marked by the use of large apertures and open plans (plans, that is, that were free of regular geometric forms and that were adapted to the various functions to which the structure responded) and for the perfect marriage between the building's structure and its decoration, largely undertaken with the most innovative material of the time: iron. In the Belgian city, which was the chief site of his work, there are still four renowned buildings which constitute the most important documents of his style, since other major buildings by Horta have unfortunately been destroyed. These are the Hôtel Tassel, the Hôtel Solvay, the Hôtel van Eetvelde, and the Maison-Atelier Horta.

The first piece of architecture in which Horta displayed his own innovative style, after a few modest youthful attempts, was the Hôtel Tassel (1892–93), an elegant residential building constructed in the Rue de Turin: on the street in question, then newly built, the building had to be erected on a very deep lot that had a very narrow frontage (7.2 metres), and had to respect the height of the adjoining buildings between which it would be set. Making use of traditional architectural elements (columns, brackets, cornices, and architraves) arranged on a symmetrical plan, Horta created in the façade a plastic continuum enlivened by contrasts and tensions and embellished by the juxtaposition of stone (in two colours, ochre and dark blue) and iron. The front of the house consists of two lateral stone wings that run as a single element along the building's four storeys, flexing slightly outward so as to halt the dynamic movement of the central structure. Here, above the powerful cornice set

on a level with the first attic, the eccentric curve of the two lateral elements develops in a concentric counter-curve, along which are placed the windows of the mezzanine, the important loggiaed bow-window of the main floor, and the balcony on the highest floor, internally resolved into a three-light window. On the main floor, the structure of the central portion of the building is made entirely of iron, transforming the casement into a load-bearing structure of the house: in this structural gridwork we find the decorative elements, executed in flat forged iron and bent to form elegant and slender curls. The façade concludes by returning to its own plane of normal standing, marked by a tall and massive cornice. As if to underscore the interruption of the centrifugal movement of the central structure, we see two stone curls, which project from the side wings on a line with the balustrade on the second floor. All of the elements of the façade, both structural and decorative, respond to a single formal language marked by an absolute stylistic unity, utilized as well in the interior treatments, which however over the years have been remodelled fairly heavily. Here the most significant part is the staircase, which occupies an elongated octagon and follows a slightly spiralling direction; the mahogany steps are set in an iron structure, itself transformed into an ornamental motif with curls and scrolls. The pictorial decoration designed by Horta for the walls of the staircase involved airy motifs with curved lines, similar to those on the iron balustrade and intertwined and nuanced so as to repeat its undulations. This linear motif, known as the 'whiplash', follows the same sinuous, twisted, and spiral-shaped forms that inform the entire construction (from the structures to the decorations down to the smallest details) and would become one of the distinctive elements of Horta's architectural lan-

View of the main façade of the Hôtel Tassel, built between 1892 and 1893.

On the facing page
A landing on the staircase on the main floor of the Hôtel Tassel, decorated with emblematic plant-like motifs in the Art Nouveau style, seemingly creeping up along the walls.

*Street frontage
of the Hôtel Tassel,
distinguished by the large
bow-window and
the apparent simplicity
of the marble surfaces.*

*Octagonal space on the
ground floor of the Hôtel
Tassel. At the centre,
notice the metal grate
that covers the heating
duct, while the mosaic
floors and the windows
depict enveloping plant-
like motifs.*

*On the facing page
Staircase of the Hôtel
van Eetvelde, built
between 1895 and 1897,
and marked by
the display of exceedingly
elegant metal structures.*

guage, beginning with his next major project, the Hôtel Solvay (1894–1900). Commissioned by the chemicals industrialist Armand Solvay, this house was probably the most sumptuous among those executed by the master, and it still preserves all its original furnishing, also designed by Horta. The long symmetrical façade, whose distinctive element is to be found in the central bow-window, and which joins the sidewalk with a highly accentuated curve, and seamlessly, is built out of two different kinds of grey stone, juxtaposed with subtle colour effects. In the interior, the huge reception rooms are marked by the open display of the metal structures and by the total diffusion of light, which comes from the sky-

lights in the roof and spreads down along the staircase, passing through the folding glass doors which allow the intriguing overlapping of points of view along the various rooms.

In a later project, the Hôtel van Eetvelde (1895–97), the façade, one of Horta's most modern, is an articulated array of jutting and recessed elements, in which particularly noteworthy are the curves of the lintels of the windows and the mosaics with spiral motifs. In the interior, marked by a free sense of space that forebode Modernism, what dominates is the octagonal space of the staircase, faced with mosaics that form an exquisite continuum of pink and orange decorations on a green background. Among the houses built by the Bel-

*Portrait of Victor Horta
(Ghent 1861 – Brussels
1947).*

*Dining room of the Hôtel
Solvay, in a photograph
from 1901.*

*View of the main storey,
looking towards
the smoking room
in the Hôtel Tassel.*

VICTOR HORTA

First trained in Ghent, his native city, Victor Horta (1861–1947) studied first at the Conservatory and later at the Academy, focusing his interests upon architecture. He moved in 1878 to Paris and worked in the atelier of the architect and decorator Jean Dubuysson, then resumed his studies in Brussels at the Royal Academy of Fine Arts. He joined the studio of Alphonse Balat, a neo-classical architect, where he worked on the design of a number of greenhouses for Leopold II, thus becoming familiar with the use of iron and glass, materials that would characterize his later work.

In 1890, he opened his own studio, and also began to teach at the Free University of Brussels. In those years, the city was undergoing great cultural ferment, and there was widespread interest in the research then being done in France (Exposition Universelle of 1889) and in England (Pre-Raphaelite painters and the Arts and Crafts movement). One fundamental point of reference for Horta's education was the theoretical work by Eugène-Emmanuel Viollet-le-Duc (*Dictionnaire raisonné de l'architecture française*, 1854–68), in which, among other things, he maintained the validity of the modern technology of iron frameworks which, with aesthetic effects comparable to those of Gothic architecture, made it possible, according to the author, to replace masonry walls with vast apertures.

Between 1890 and 1903, the most fertile period in his career, Horta designed in Brussels twenty-four homes and a number of non-residential buildings such as the Maison du Peuple (1895–99, destroyed in 1964) and the department store À l'Innovation (1901, demolished in 1966). His later activity, marked by the two major public works of the Gare Centrale (Central Train Station, designed in 1910) and the Palais des Beaux-Arts (Palace of Fine Arts, designed in 1914), show a sharp retreat from Art Nouveau (which he himself had helped to found) towards more traditional and academic forms.

*On the facing page
Interior of the dining
room, looking towards
the music room,
in the Maison Horta.*

*Detail of the entrance
with the staircase
in the Maison Horta,
1898. The column on the
left conceals a radiator.*

gian architect, we should mention, lastly, his own (1898–1901), which now, with the adjoining studio, is the site of the Musée Horta: here, according to his own words, he reached the apex of his career. His most prestigious project, however, should certainly be considered the now-lost Maison du Peuple, the monumental headquarters of the Socialist Party, set at the intersection of two radial streets; the irregular configuration of the land on which the building was to be designed determined the lively shape of the façade, articulated in a concave central structure flanked by two rectilinear fronts, set at angles. Among the various service rooms and meeting rooms that occupied the four ample floors, the auditorium, which was located on the top floor and which could seat 1,500 people, constituted a fullfledged engineering miracle. The hall, consisting of a gridwork iron structure that could barely be perceived in the vastness of the room, jutted out and was supported by a trusswork with a span of some 15 metres; on the walls were two iron galleries, one with seating and one with technical functions.

The Monastery of Rila

The Rila monastery, the oldest in the Slavic world and still the largest active religious centre in Bulgaria, is first and foremost an extremely fine artistic complex, in which architecture and painting merge harmoniously. Aside from this, it has been for centuries the seat of the development, preservation, and diffusion of Slavic religious culture in all its various manifestations, even literary and artistic, becoming the symbol of a Bulgarian cultural identity that has been continually threatened by Turkish domination.

The monastery stands about 120 kilometres from Sofia, in the heart of the Rila Massif, located at the north-western extremity of the Rodopi Mountains, a mountainous system with peaks that rise to almost 3,000 metres of elevation. In this area, still covered by a forest of beeches and pines, between A.D. 876 and 946 lived the hermit Ivan Rilski, Saint John of Rila as he is known in English, the evangelizer of the Slavic peoples. He was responsible for the construction of the earliest nucleus of the coenobitic community, just a few metres from the cave in which he lived as an anchorite. The early nucleus was, however, completely destroyed in the thirteenth century by a fire, the first among the many fires that marked the history of the complex. A new building was constructed just a few kilometres away from the site of Ivan's foundation, and it was completed in the fifteenth century thanks to the donations of Stefan Hrelyu, a powerful local prince, who ordered in 1335 the construction of the tower that still bears his name and a church dedicated to John of Rila, who had in the meantime been canonized as a saint.

In the period of the Ottoman Turkish domination of Bulgaria (1396–1878), the monastery took on the role of bulwark of national identity in the face of a foreign occupation, and it became a destination for pilgrimages from all over the Balkans region, especially after 1469, when the relics of the founding saint were brought there. The complex continued to serve this function in the centuries that followed, especially in the eighteenth and nineteenth centuries, when it became one of the powerhouses of the so-called Bulgarian Renaissance, a movement that witnessed an exceptional flowering of the arts and sciences. That extraordinary cultural period is documented by the splendid cross that is still preserved in the museum of the monastery, executed and decorated with more than 100 biblical scenes by one of the leading figures of the movement, the monk Raphael.

A first building project in 1816–19, which resulted in the completion of the northwestern section of the monastery, was destroyed in 1833 by a fire, and was followed, between 1844 and 1847, by the reconstruction of the same buildings and the creation of the southern wing. The existing structures, with the exception of the Hrelyu Tower, date back in fact to the nineteenth-century building project. They occupy a vast area (some 32,000 square metres) which forms an irregular square, provided with two entrances, both decorated with frescoes. The buildings that surround it contain four chapels, a refectory, and some 300 cells, to which the monks returned from 1968 on, as well as a library and rooms for the guests of the monastery. The complex has an exquisite interior courtyard overlooked by three- and four-storey constructions, embellished by orders of arches set upon stone columns which unify their façades and form airy loggias. These, like the arcades of the main church itself, are enlivened by the chromatic interplay between the white of the plaster and the red and black hues of the bricks, an example of the typical decorativism of Eastern art.

The Hrelyu Tower is a compact building that stands 23 metres tall, with a square plan. The last of its five storeys, jutting out from the

The interior courtyard of the monastery, surrounded by airy loggias on several floors, and the main church.

On the facing page
Detail of the frescoes at the base of the main dome.

The arches of the main church are enlivened by the chromatic interplay between the white of the plaster and the black and red tones of the bricks.

Behind the apses of the main church stands the massive fourteenth-century tower, built at the behest of Stefan Hrelyu.

line of the others and supported on each façade by three exterior pillars, contains a chapel dedicated to the Transfiguration and decorated by a series of frescoes that were done in the second half of the fourteenth century: in the nave are depicted the *Stories of Saint John of Rila* while in the narthex is the great concert of voices praising the Lord (accompanied by Bulgarian musical instruments) with which David concluded the Psalms. Not only does the building in which the chapel is located owe its existence to Stefan Hrelyu, but so do the two carved wooden doors and the exquisite throne originally located there, now on exhibit in the museum of the monastery.

Of the buildings constructed in the nineteenth century, the most important is the Cathedral of Our Lady of the Assumption, built in 1833 on the structures of the preceding building. The church, which echoes in its layout the model of the monastic churches of Mount Athos, houses a magnificent carved wooden iconostasis, executed in 1842 by Athanasios Taladuro of Thessalonica, and frescoes painted by Zakhary Zograph, Stanislav Dospevski and Toma Vishanov.

The cultural heritage contained in the monastery is not limited to its buildings, but extends to the astonishing number of artworks and documents that constitute a priceless testimonial to the Bulgarian civilization, chiefly found in the museum and in the library: hundreds of icons, the first books about the history and geography of Bulgaria, a papier mâché globe dating from 1836, letters from Ivan the Terrible and from the Romanovs.

Outside of the principal nucleus of the monastery we find numerous churches, among which we should mention the Church of Saint John of Rila, built in the eighteenth century to house the tomb of the saint.

A figure of the prophet Jeremiah, frescoed in the pendentive of the dome of the Cathedral of Our Lady of the Assumption.

Detail of the frescoes with Stories of John the Baptist.

View of the frescoes adorning the triumphal arch and the dome, with God the Father.

The Kronborg Castle

The Castle of Kronborg stands on the point that closes off to the east the port of Helsingør (Elsinore), overlooking the Øresund, the stretch of sea that separates the coast of Denmark from the southern coast of Sweden at its narrowest point (just 5 kilometres). On this site of great strategic importance, there already existed a fortress in the Middle Ages, known as early as 1230 by the name of Ørekrog, which was destroyed by the Hanseatic League in the fourteenth century. The castle was rebuilt in 1420 by Henry VII of Pomerania, who accorded extensive privileges to the city of Helsingør, including the right of demanding a tax from all the ships that sailed through the strait, a benefice that was not abolished until 1857. In the medieval fortress of Kronborg, Shakespeare took the liberty of setting his tragic tale of Prince Hamlet, who supposedly lived here in the fifth century, even though the historic events experienced by the Danish Prince Amled took place on the island of Mors in Jylland.

The castle, surrounded by a double ring of walls and moats, was utilized over the centuries as a military stronghold more than as a residence. Its original nucleus was in fact constituted by the central fortress with its square plan, built between 1574 and 1577, to designs by the Dutch architect Jan van Pæschen, at the orders of Frederick II, who funded it with the revenue from the tolls charged for passage through the Øresund. The building was completed in 1585 by the Flemish architect Anthonis van Opbergen, who continued the use of brick for the fortifications, while he sheathed the exterior of the main structure with sandstone, and replaced the original terracotta roof with a copper roof which is still in place. In 1629 a fire destroyed everything except for the perimeter walls and the furnishings of the chapel. The reconstruction began immediately, once again funded by the rev-

enue from the tolls paid for passage through the Øresund. In 1658–60 the castle was occupied by Swedish troops who plundered most of the furnishings and, especially, the rich art collection for which Kronborg had rivalled important Danish castles such as those of Copenhagen or Hillerød. During the seventeenth and eighteenth centuries, work was done to enlarge and reinforce the double ring of walls.

You reach the fortress by crossing the first outer moat over a bridge and passing through the first ring of walls through the monumental gate in sandstone, built by Lambert van Haven. You thus enter into the perimeter of the castle proper, enclosed by another moat and by a second curtain wall of brick, renovated and extended by Frederick IV during the eighteenth century. In the northern zone of this ring of walls you will find the Mørkeport (the dark gate), which leads to the Renaissance structure. The external appearance of this building, extremely sober and austere, is embellished by large windows that punctuate the façade at regular intervals and by the great pointed-arch windows in the chapel at the south-eastern extremity, and enriched by the south-eastern façade (the Kakkelborg), with its large windows adorned with statues and an octagonal corner tower, as well as the Renaissance portal of honour. This last feature is composed of four columns and two niches with statues; if you pass through it, you will enter the inner courtyard of the fortress, a large square space punctuated by the large windows arranged with geometric regularity on the three different registers and surmounted by the tall octagonal tower known as the 'Tower of the Trumpeters'. Built in 1777 on the site of an original, earlier tower destroyed in the fire of 1629, the tower is crowned with an elaborate multi-storey spire roofed in copper.

The Castle of Kronborg was built as a military fortress at a strategic location: the easternmost point of the port of Elsinore, or Helsingør, overlooking the Øresund, the stretch of sea that separates the coast of Denmark from the coast of Sweden.

On the facing page
The medieval fortress, surrounded by a double ring of walls and moats, was almost totally rebuilt during the Renaissance and underwent substantial renovations in the seventeenth and eighteenth centuries, taking on the appearance of a sumptuous late Baroque palace, crowned by slender towers.

From the courtyard you can reach, in the southern wing, the Renaissance chapel of the castle, whose main hall, divided into a nave and two side aisles, preserves the sixteenth-century wooden furnishings, including the magnificent royal tribune, carved and painted. In the western wing you will find the entrance to the fortifications, with subterranean rooms used to quarter the garrison. On the first floor are the apartments of Frederick II and the so-called 'cabinet of the queen'; on the second floor are the reception halls. These rooms preserve the furnishings, the fireplaces, the paintings, the decorated ceilings, and the exquisite tapestries that embellished the building from the sixteenth to the eighteenth century. In particular, the vast Hall of the Knights (Riddersal) has a precious ceiling made of Pomeranian red-deal beams and a splendid Baroque door made of carved and intarsiated ebony, leading to the Tower of the Trumpeters. The hall was originally adorned with forty-two large tapestries, of which the seven that survived the fire of 1629 are now visible in the adjoining Lillesal (small hall). Along with the great tapestries of hunting scenes woven by the Brussels craftsman Jan Raes to cartoons by Rubens and Antonio Tempesta (1625–35), now hanging in an adjoining hall, they document the wealth and luxury that once characterized the castle of Kronborg.

The chapel of the castle, divided into a nave and two side aisles, preserves the sixteenth-century wooden furnishings, including the magnificent royal tribune, gilded and painted.

On the facing page
The original military function of the Kronborg complex can be immediately seen in its double ring of walls and moats.

The monumental Hall of the Knights (Riddersal) measures 62 metres in length by 11 metres in width and has a ceiling made of Pomeranian red-deal beams.

The Cathedral of Chartres

Dedicated to Our Lady, the Virgin Mary, the Cathedral of Chartres stands in an area where the practice of religious cults dates back to very ancient times. In particular, on the site now occupied by the cathedral, there was in the first century A.D. a sacred oak grove where the ancient Celts worshipped a spring and, in all likelihood, a female idol of fertility, made of dark wood. With the advent of Christianity, perhaps as early as the fourth century, a church was built over the spring, the miraculous waters of which had long attracted pilgrims and invalids in search of a cure; there flourished a cult around an image known as Our Lady Underground, the first of a series of Black Madonnas venerated on the site.

The only traces that remain of the sacred buildings that stood on that site before the construction of the cathedral are found in documents; the last of the buildings, according to the chronicles, was entirely destroyed by a fire that broke out in the year 1020. Reconstruction was then undertaken under the leadership of Fulbert, Bishop of the city from 1006 to 1028, and the lead figure in a school that constituted one of the most important episodes of the 'renaissance', of classical, philosophical and scientific studies of the entire Middle Ages. In the immense crypt of the cathedral, you can still see the ruins of this building, which was a determining factor in establishing the width and length of the cathedral's aisles and bays.

Fulbert's successors completed the main façade of the cathedral with its three portals, adorned with sculptures, and its two side towers, still present, which replaced the original elevation, and included a portico dominated by a tower. In this phase of construction, alongside the two towers of the façade, there had been plans to build seven more, but none of them was ever built. These towers were intended to give the Cathedral of Chartres a magnificent appearance, similar to the appearance of the neighbouring cathedrals of Tournai and Laon.

The two existing towers were conceived and built separately, over a fairly long span of time. The construction of the north-west tower, mentioned in documents as early as 1140, entailed the demolition of the portico and tower built under Fulbert; originally isolated, with clear links to the Romanesque style, this tower led, via a long passageway, to the crypt. Its wooden crown was replaced, between 1507 and 1513, by an elegant stone spire in the 'flamboyant' style by Jean de Beauce. A few years later, the south-west tower was built, and the western façade was pushed forward until it reached its present-day location, incorporating the two towers. This phase of construction – during which, if we leave aside the transepts, the cathedral attained its present-day dimensions – extended until the year 1150, triggering an explosion of religious fervour that led thousands of worshippers to volunteer to haul carts loaded down with building materials.

When, on 10 June 1194, the church once again fell victim to a fire, all that was saved was the crypt and the western façade with the two towers, and it was decided to include them in the plans for new construction. And so fire gave Chartres the

Detail of the southern portal of the cathedral.

One of the monumental figures that adorn the splay of the southern portal.

On the facing page
The exterior of the cathedral's apse area is marked by the volumes of the six radial chapels, surmounted by flying buttresses and slender spires.

unexpected opportunity to include the new developments of Gothic architecture, which had emerged in the Church of Saint-Denis and in the building sites of Noyon, Senlis, Sens, and Laon. The new architectural developments were grafted on to what remained of the existing building, which preserved the size and the layout of the elevation.

The new cathedral was rebuilt with astonishing speed, thanks primarily to donations from the faithful. The main aisle of the nave was completed before 1210, the choir was built before 1220, and the arms of the transept were finished just after 1230; and in 1260 the church was finally consecrated by Louis IX, the future Saint Louis.

Over the course of the construction, the original plans of 1194–95 underwent some modifications, due to the alternating influences of a number of anonymous architects, even though the general conception of the cathedral remained faithful to the principles of the Gothic artistic style that was sweeping everything before it.

Built of limestone, the magnificent cathedral combines, in fact, the floor plan of Notre-Dame of Paris and the floor plan of Saint-Denis: its longitudinal structure (130 metres in length), broken down into a main nave and two side aisles, extends from the block of the western façade to the zone of the choir, which is tripartite and consists of four bays, culminating in a double ambulatory with six radial chapels. Attached to the main body of the church is the transept, which instead borrows the model of the Cathedral of Laon, also broken down into a nave and two side aisles and monumental in size and proportion.

The interior develops vertically over three levels: in the lowest level are large pointed arcades and pilaster strips, constituted by a central nucleus surrounded by four columns that rise up, extending – on a line with the abacus

On pages 34–35
Aerial view of Chartres,
dominated by
the structure
of the cathedral.

On the facing page
The western façade,
built of limestone like
the rest of the church,
incorporated the triple
royal portal, built
in the years 1090–1116.

View of the ribbed
cross vault of the nave,
which soars to a height
of 40 metres.

THE ROYAL PORTAL

An educational intention was present in the conception of the triple portal in the western façade of the Cathedral of Chartres, built during the campaign of decorations undertaken by Yves, Bishop of Chartres from 1090 to 1116. It is called the Royal Portal because many of the characters that adorn its jambs wear crowns and, although it has not been possible to identify them, it is supposed that they were biblical kings and queens. Though it does appear to hark back to Romanesque styles, this portal is considered the point of departure for Gothic sculpture: the three spaces that open in it are in fact linked by a precise mathematical relationship (7:10:7), represented by the modillions above each door and by the number of column-statues that occupy the splayings, originally twenty-four, the sum of the three numbers. The statues depict the world of the Old Testament and therefore, from a doctrinal point of view, prefigure the images arranged in the upper strips, that is, the salient episodes of the lives of Jesus Christ and the Virgin Mary (narrated in the continual strip of capitals that runs from the centre outward in both directions), leading in turn to the depiction, in the tympana, of the three epiphanies of Christ: the one whereby he appeared to the shepherds (the Nativity, carved in the southern tympanum), the one whereby he appeared to the Apostles after his resurrection (the northern tympanum), and in the middle the epiphany of Christ the Judge at the end of time, revealed in the *Apocalypse* according to Saint John. This last epiphany explains the presence, in the architraves and archivolts, of the Elders, while the figures that illustrate the activities and seasons of human life – the signs of the Zodiac, the Labours of the Months, the seven liberal arts and their chief exponents – have an eminently pedagogical and encyclopaedic nature.

The magnificent relief depicting Christ the Judge, surrounded by the symbols of the Evangelists and, in the small loggias beneath, the twelve Apostles.

The Royal Portal of Chartres can be considered one of the fundamental monuments of French Gothic sculpture.

Detail with the Nativity in the southern portal.

Detail of the figures that adorn the splay of the Royal Portal.

– into the ribbings of the ample elongated vaults. Above the arcades, horizontally for the entire length of the church, runs the triforium, a narrow corridor with a continuous order of arches, surmounted by the exceedingly high clerestory, that is, the wall space above the longitudinal arches, entirely occupied in each bay by two windows surmounted by a multi-lobed rose window.

On the exterior, the thrusts and loads of these dizzying structures are balanced by flying buttresses. At Chartres, these static structures were developed in new forms when compared with the models; they were, in fact, built with two stacked arches linked by a small arch, and they were entirely separate from the roofs of the secondary aisles. This innovation, besides becoming a formal element that was capable of enlivening the external mass of the building, made it possible to base the cross vaults of the roof at a height never before attained by Gothic architects: 40 metres.

The system of flying buttresses made possible the most original and ambitious innovation found at Chartres: the tripartite vertical layout. The earliest Gothic cathedrals, such as the Cathedral of Saint-Denis or the Canterbury Abbey, were split up vertically into four strips: at the bottom, the arcades, above them the tribune, then the triforium, and finally the windows, which by this point were necessarily relatively small in size. In order to increase the amount of light entering the building, in keeping with the goals of Gothic architecture which reflected the mystical conceptions of medieval scholastic philosophy, the designers of Chartres decided to sacrifice the tribune and to reduce dramatically the size of the triforium, so that all of the space that was thus saved was filled with vast windows, occupying two orders. And so, freed from its traditional load-bearing function, the wall structure became essential at Chartres, practically a scaffolding that allowed light to penetrate into the sacred space, elevated to dizzying heights.

Eugène-Emmanuel Viollet-le-Duc saw in this cathedral the embodiment of his idea of Gothic architecture, that of a limpidly rational construction based on the combination of pointed arches, ribbed vaults, and flying but-

On page 40
Detail of the stained glass window with Stories of Charlemagne.

On page 41
Stained glass window known as the 'Notre Dame de la Belle Verriere'.

THE STAINED GLASS WINDOWS

With the exception of the ogival windows in the western façade (late twelfth century) and the window of Notre-Dame de la Belle Verrière (thirteenth century), in the southern section of the choir, most of the stained glass decorating the 176 windows of Chartres Cathedral was executed between 1200 and about 1235. The decorated and figured glass, which covers a surface area of more than 2,000 square metres, constitutes a priceless documentation of the exquisite refinement that had been attained in this art form in the period when Gothic architecture made it possible to expand the surface area available for windows, creating on the interior of the cathedrals unprecedented lighting effects. The subjects depicted, however, demonstrate that these windows were not merely decorative in function but were intended to serve as religious messages as well. The five windows of the hemicycle are all united by their Marian theme. They show the Annunciation, the Visitation, the Virgin Mary with the Christ Child, and the figures of the Prophets announcing the birth of the Virgin. The themes of the stained glass windows of the western façade and the transepts harken back to the themes found in the sculptures of the corresponding portals: on the façade we note the warm and profound colours of the twelfth-century stained glass windows, depicting the Jesse Tree, the Nativity, the Passion of Christ and, above all, the Last Judgement; in the rose window of the north transept (after 1223) we see figures from the Old Testament, the Twelve Kings of Judea and the Twelve Prophets; in the pointed arch window beneath them we see Saint Anne with the Infant Mary, while on the right are Solomon and Aaron and on the left a symmetrically composed pair, with a king and a priest, David and Melchisedech. The stained glass windows of the south transept (c. 1217–25) feature in the rose window a scene of the Apocalypse and, in the ogival windows underneath, the Evangelists, the Prophets, and the Virgin Mary with the Christ Child.

These stained glass windows could be created only if someone agreed to assume the financial burden associated with them. The southern rose window, for example, was donated by Pierre Mauclerc, Count of Dreux, as is shown by the presence of his aristocratic symbols in the decoration; the northern rose window was donated by the Royal House, whose insignia were depicted in the mosaics in the floors. But these masterpieces were also donated by guilds which had their trades and vocations portrayed. The stained glass windows thus provide a vivid reproduction of life in cities that were just awakening from centuries of torpid slumber and considered the cathedrals a symbol of their renewed vigour.

tresses. In effect, from its very construction, this cathedral became a model to be imitated. The tribune disappeared from French Gothic churches, which from then on adopted the tripartite vertical structure. The construction yards of Soissons (from 1197–98 on), Reims and Amiens, but also other buildings which were already in full and advanced construction, like those of Meaux and Rouen, followed the example of the Cathedral of Chartres, including Paris's Notre-Dame, when the upper sections were entirely rebuilt around 1225.

Much less care, compared with the attention and focus that was devoted to the stained glass windows, was lavished on the stone and masonry work on the interior of the cathedral. The capitals of the pillars, adorned with plant motifs, are in fact rather rudely made, probably because it was assumed they would not be fully visible in the penumbra of the lower section of the church.

The importance of the Cathedral of Chartres is not entirely based on its architectural structure, but also upon the images, painted and carved, which provide exemplary depictions of the medieval conception of life in its spiritual and moral manifestations, as well as in its quotidian and material forms. Moreover, the figures carved in the main portal and in the portals of the transepts served an important religious purpose: to prepare pilgrims to enter the holy space and to take part in rites and prayers. The Royal Portal, on the cathedral's façade, welcomed the faithful with a series of images dedicated to the theme of the manifestation of the divine (theophany), while the images in the transepts focused on the role of the Church in the history of the world: they corresponded, then, despite the chronological and stylistic distance between the western reliefs – more rigid and hieratic – and the looser and naturalistic figures in the transepts, to a specific and consistent iconographic programme.

While the Royal Portal was sculpted at the end of the twelfth century, during the first phase of the construction, the portals of the transept were modelled when the cathedral was reconstructed after the great fire of 1194. It was then, in fact, that Chartres was conceived as the destination of pilgrimages, and for this reason the cathedral was endowed with two monumental transepts, each of which had three portals in its elevation, just like the main façade. For the reliefs of these portals, the theme chosen was the role of the Church in the history of the world. Indeed, although the fame of Chartres had always been linked to the cult of the Virgin Mary, She was celebrated not in and of Herself, but as a symbol of the Church and as a link between Christ and his forerunners from the Old Testament. Moreover, the reliefs of the transepts were for the most part executed during the papacy of Pope Innocent III (1198–1216), that is, in the years when the papacy reached the culmination of its temporal power.

The history of humanity was thus broken up among the two transepts: the northern one featured the world *ante Cristum natum*, while the southern one celebrated the era of the Church. And so, in the north transept, we see the figures of the forerunners of Christ (Melchisedech, Simeon, Saint John the Baptist), those of the ancestors of Christ (characters from the Old Testament, such as Job, who foreshadowed the infallible knowledge of the Church and the sufferings of the martyr), and fi-nally, through Saint Anne and the Virgin Mary (whose coronation is depicted in the central tympanum), the depiction of the Nativity of Christ Himself. Certain images that vary from this iconographic scheme, or from the style of the others, lead us nevertheless to suppose that there must have been some modifications from the initial programme.

The south transept, with its depiction of the history of the Church, has a greater thematic uniformity: at the centre of the middle portal, the figure of Christ dominates in the *trumeau* (the central support), and is surrounded, in the side splays, by the Apostles and the martyred saints from the western portal and the Doctors of the Church from the eastern portal. That created a perfect equilibrium and a significant correspondence between the great martyrs and the local saints in the north transept, depicted with the specific intent of identifying Chartres as the centre of the universal Church.

The statues in the transepts, sculpted between 1205 and 1260, do not follow the structure of the columns as is the case in the Royal Portal, but are naturalistically portrayed, with more flexible poses. All the same, they are entirely devoid of the dramatic animation that characterizes the contemporary works at the Cathedral of Reims, and with their didactic intent, they appeal to reason more than to emotion.

Figure of a prophet in the southern portal.

The interior of the cathedral is divided into a nave and two side aisles by clustered pillars, each formed by a central pillar flanked by the columns that rise until they merge with the ribbing of the vaults.

On the facing page
Through the tripartite articulation of the elevation, the architects of the Cathedral of Chartres succeeded in lightening the upper section of the walls, creating large spaces in which to insert the stained glass windows.

The Palace and Park of Fontainebleau

The Royal Palace of Fontainebleau, located inside the forest of the same name and first built at the turn of the twelfth century as a hunting lodge, was from the sixteenth century one of the most important and prestigious sites of the French Court. The construction of the royal palace began during the reign of François I, who in 1528 ordered an ambitious campaign of demolition and expansion of the old royal residence. Further modifications undertaken by his successors and carried on with varying degrees of intensity until the nineteenth century gave shape to the present-day complex, comprising clusters that vary by period and style, and whose element of primary interest is certainly the structures dating back to the sixteenth century. Here we find an original architectural synthesis of the French medieval tradition and the Italian Renaissance, which François I greatly admired. The refined decoration of the interiors constitutes the earliest and an exceptional document of the spread of Mannerism in northern Europe. This led to the creation of the current of painting known as the School of Fontainebleau, which made this residence an artistic centre with great international influence.

The Palace of Fontainebleau is presently composed of five courtyards, arranged irregularly and surrounded by wings of buildings and gardens. The earliest buildings were erected between 1528 and 1540 under the supervision of the master builder Gilles Le Breton, who was responsible for the Cour de l'Ovale, now located in the eastern section of the complex, and which stands on the ancient foundations. Construction developed from the Tower of Saint Louis, the only remnant of the medieval structures. The second storey of the courtyard presents an order of Corinthian pillars and is surmounted by a high roof with dormer windows topped by triangular pediments; the colonnade that surrounds much of the ground floor was added later (1541). The entrance to the palace, through what is known as the Porte Dorée (Golden Gate), was rebuilt in Renaissance style and was based on the model of the 'tower façade' of Urbino. It is a three-order loggia flanked by spaces framed by pillars. In each of these bays we find two vertically stacked windows, so that the pediment over the lower window serves as a base for the upper window, in keeping with a device that is entirely alien to the rigour of Italian classicism. The construction is completed by steep pitched roofs and, like all of the façades of the palace, it is devoid of decorations: the hard sandstone that was used, in fact, does not lend itself easily to carving. At the westernmost extremity of this first ring of buildings, then began the construction of a passage that was used to link the new buildings with the area occupied by the ancient Abbey of the Trinitarians, which stood near the medieval residence; the southern façade of the building, which contains the Gallery of François I, was redesigned on its exterior at the turn of the seventeenth century. The old church was demolished to make room for the courtyard, or Cour du Cheval Blanc, and only the north wing has been preserved intact; currently, the courtyard houses the main entrance to the palace, consisting of a magnificent seventeenth-century horseshoe staircase designed by Jean Androuet du Cerceau. On the eastern side of this courtyard stands the Pavillón des Armes (1535), with an entryway flanked by Egyptian caryatids which clearly reveals further references to Italian models. It is likely that in this case the Renaissance influences should be attributed to the presence at Fontainebleau of an Italian artist, Rosso Fiorentino who, in fact, came to France in 1530 at the behest of the king, and was soon appointed as general overseer of construction, paintings, and decoration

Panoramic view of the Palace and Gardens of Fontainebleau.

On the facing page
View of the Gallery of François I, designed entirely by Rosso Fiorentino from 1533.

The Ballroom, or Salle de Bal, built between 1552 and 1556. The walls of the Great Hall are frescoed with mythological scenes executed by Niccolò dell'Abate to drawings by Primaticcio.

View of the Cour du Cheval Blanc, characterized by a magnificent seventeenth-century horseshoe-shaped staircase, designed by Jean Androuet du Cerceau.

46

FRANÇOIS I

A cousin of Louis XII, François I (1494–1547) was named Duke of Valois by the monarch who was childless and therefore named him his successor. His reign began in 1515 and was distinguished by war with Spain and with Charles V for dominion over the Duchy of Milan: the French defeat at Pavia (1525) put an end to the rivalry and resulted in one long year of imprisonment for the French king. Later, François undertook a decisive policy of centralization which pushed the French monarchy in the direction of absolutism. François was a great patron of the arts, and he tried to turn his court into a cultural centre, rivalling in splendour and wealth the leading capitals of Europe. His admiration for Italian art can be seen in the choices made for his collection, the first of its kind in the history of the French monarchy. Assembled through acquisitions and gifts, it was housed at Fontainebleau and included the *Virgin of the Rocks* and *La Gioconda* (*Mona Lisa*) by Leonardo (who was a guest of the king from 1517), *La Bella Giardiniera* by Raphael, and works by other such Italian contemporaries of the king as Giulio Romano, Sebastiano del Piombo, and Savoldo. Among the sculptures, alongside a now-lost *Hercules* by Michelangelo, there were numerous casts of classical sculptures executed by Primaticcio and set in the palace gardens. In terms of architecture, the attention of the monarch was focused on his palaces (the Châteaux of Blois and Chambord), which marked the development of the French tradition from medieval forms towards modern typologies. Among the Italian artists summoned to his court we should mention the sculptor Benvenuto Cellini who executed for the king the sumptuous salt cellar now in the museum of Vienna.

Jean Clouet, Portrait of François I of France, *oil on panel, 1535. Paris, Musée du Louvre.*

On pages 48–49
View of the palace from the Carp Pond. On the right is the wing of the Belle Cheminée, designed by Primaticcio in 1568.

The architecture of Fontainebleau represents an original synthesis of the French medieval tradition and the Italian Renaissance.

On the facing page *View of the Cour de la Fontaine, with the wing that contains the Appartements des Reines-Mères, once occupied by the kitchens, but subsequently rebuilt by Primaticcio.*

Panoramic view of the royal complex of Fontainebleau, seen from the park.

View of the main entrance of the palace, with a wrought-iron gate.

of the new palace, alongside Gilles Le Breton. Then, in 1532, Francesco Primaticcio – a former collaborator of Giulio Romano's from Mantua – came to the French Court.

The work of the Italian masters radically altered the panorama of French decorative arts, giving origin to a style that was entirely new in its conception. Rosso Fiorentino, who was especially admired by the king, to the point that he became the leading artist of the French court, worked first of all on the Pavilion of Pomona (1532–35, in the Jardin des Pins), where Primaticcio worked alongside him. This was a small cube-shaped structure, open on two sides and set alongside the garden's enclosure wall, in the western area of the park. The pavilion, which was demolished in the eighteenth century, was adorned by composite pillars crowned by friezes and cornices, and contained two large frescoes with mythological subject matter, one of which was executed to an initial design by Primaticcio himself. Later, beginning in about 1533, Rosso Fiorentino oversaw the entire design of the Gallery of François I, which has survived almost com-

pletely intact and is located in the wing built by Gilles Le Breton to link the Cour de l'Ovale to the Cour du Cheval Blanc. The decoration, which was done by a small army of painters, stucco-artists, and carpenters, supervised by the master builder, breaks down into fourteen panels, framed by the windows that look out over the side walls; here, above a carved wooden socle done by Scibec de Carpi, large fresco panels devoted to a celebration of the deeds of François I are framed by elaborate cornices, composed of high-relief stuccoes and painted decorations. Around the main panels is arranged a vast repertoire of festoons and herms, curls and scrolls, botanical elements, mascarons and figures. The ornamentation, which plays a privileged role, underscores and integrates the theme of the main fresco; in the great variety of decorative motifs employed in the frescoes in the gallery, special popularity and diffusion fell to that which is nowadays described as strapwork, because it imitates the curls and scrollings of a strap of leather.

The work that Primaticcio did was carried on entirely independently of the work done by the Florentine master, and continued without interruption until 1570. Very little survives of the rooms that were decorated under his supervision: there are traces, however, of his exquisite and refined creations in numerous drawings and engravings, which had considerable influence on the tastes of the time. We have lost the decorations of the private apartments of the king and the queen, while those of the room of the Duchess d'Etampes (1541–44) still survive, converted into the vestibule of an eighteenth-century staircase, and deprived of its original ceiling. Here a series of frescoes devoted to Alexander the Great celebrate, symbolically, the love affair between the king and his favourite; the scenes are framed by high-relief stuccoes with elongated female figures and cherubs. Aside from a few paintings in the vestibule of the Porte Dorée, there also remain, although altered, the frescoes done by Niccolò dell'Abate to drawings by Primaticcio for the Salle de Bal (1552–56): the walls of this dance hall, covered by a wooden ceiling carved by Scibec de Carpi (since destroyed and painstakingly reconstructed), are adorned by mythological scenes. Entirely lost, unfortunately, are the decorations of two important rooms designed by Primaticcio: the Appartement des Bains, which stood on the ground floor of the Gallery of François I, and the Gallery of Ulysses. In the former, consisting of a series of seven rooms, was kept the king's art collection. In the Gallery of Ulysses, set in the southern wing of the Cour du Cheval Blanc, there were fifty-eight frescoed scenes with daringly foreshortened subjects inspired by Homer's epic poem, in keeping with the tradition that linked (through Francus, son of Hector) the French royal dynasty with the Trojan legend. Lastly, Primaticcio was probably responsible for the design of the Grotte des Pins, the only relic of the wing that housed the Gallery of Ulysses:

Detail of the decorations of the Chapel of the Trinity.

Francesco Primaticcio, detail of the decoration of the room of the Duchess d'Etampes (1541–44), later transformed into the vestibule of a staircase.

THE SCHOOL OF FONTAINEBLEAU

The phrase 'School of Fontainebleau' originated in the context of the studies of the history of engraving to describe a group of engravers, for the most part anonymous, whose activity was related to the construction of Fontainebleau. Generally considered as part of this critical category were etchings and engravings copied directly from the paintings of the palace (many of which were later lost), and possibly executed with the specific intention of handing down and spreading the inventions of the great Italian masters at work in the palace. Later the definition was extended to indicate a tendency found in the various types of art (painting, sculpture, decorative arts) characterized by a predilection for mythological and allegorical subjects, nude figures, scrolls and grotesques, elongated and sinuous forms. This trend, which developed at Fontainebleau in the wake of the decorative cycles done by the masters of Mannerism summoned by François I, later spread throughout France giving rise to a common style of Italian inspiration. When, under Henri IV, artistic activity at Fontainebleau flourished again, another generation of painters, educated on the examples of the first decorators of the castle, gave life to the so-called Second School. Some of them were of Flemish origin, and this led to a revival in both the selection of themes and in the style, with a predilection for a warmer colour with more contrast. Examples of this trend can be admired in the Cabinet Ovale (1606–09, now the Salon Louis XIII), decorated by Ambroise Dubois with the *Story of Theagenes and Chariclea*, arranged on broad canvases over a socle wainscoting adorned with exquisite landscapes, and in the Chapel of the Trinity (1608), whose long vault was painted by Martin Fréminet.

On the facing page
Interior of the Chapel of the Trinity (1608). The long vault was painted by Martin Fréminet, who supervised the decoration work done during the reign of Henri IV.

here a picturesque ashlar decoration framed
dramatic figures of telamons, probably inspired by Mantuan models well known to the
painter.

Among the Italian artists summoned by
François I to Fontainebleau we should also
mention Benvenuto Cellini (plans for the decoration of the Porte Dorée, with nymphs,
satyrs, and triumphs) and the architect Sebastiano Serlio, who in 1541 was named the director of royal buildings, substantially inau-
gurating a second phase of construction, with a
far more markedly classical imprint. The role
that Serlio actually played, however, is unclear:
it seems in fact that, although he produced numerous drawings and plans, little was actually
constructed. Traces remain in any case of his
activity at Fontainebleau in a few drawings,
linked with the initial design of the Salle de
Bal, a pavilion that was to be built in the gardens, and a building in the form of an amphitheatre that was meant to replace the Cour
de l'Ovale. His most important creation, the
Grand Ferrare of Ippolito d'Este, has since
been almost entirely lost.

Upon the death of François I in 1547,
therefore, the architectural complex extended
around two courtyards, which contained numerous other decorated rooms, completed
during the reigns of Henri II and Charles IX,
and now only partially preserved. The Cour
de la Fontaine, which stood on the south side
of the Gallery of François I, was not completed until 1568, when Catherine de Medici,
the wife of Henri II, commissioned Primaticcio to build the so-called 'Wing of the Belle
Cheminée'. Here the Italian artist created one
of the most exquisite façades in the entire
complex, overlapping the central structure,
with its classical style (round arches and niches), with an elegant two-ramp staircase. The
buildings set on the opposite wing, once occupied by the kitchens, were rebuilt by Pri-

maticcio as well, and were destined to contain the Appartements des Reines-Mères.

A new and important phase of construction came about during the reign of Henri IV (1589–1610), who created to the north a new courtyard around the Jardin de Diane, closed off to the east by a wing occupied by two stacked galleries, the Galerie des Cerfs and the Galerie de Diane. The entrance to the palace was moved to the easternmost end of the Cour de l'Ovale: once the existing buildings had been demolished, the Porte du Baptistère was erected, consisting of a triumphal arch designed by Primaticcio and topped by a dome. Facing the new gate was built the Cour des Offices (1606–09), designed by Rémy Collin. At the same time, the activity of decorating the interiors was carried forward by a new generation of French and Flemish artists known as the Second School of Fontainebleau.

It was during the reigns of Louis XV and Louis XVI that the complex underwent its most profound alterations: the Appartement des Bains was destroyed, as was the Gallery of Ulysses, to be replaced by a block of apartments for members of the court (Louis XV Wing). The Pavillon des Poêles, with its sixteenth-century interiors by Rosso Fiorentino, was transformed into the present-day Gros Pavillon while the wing of the Belle Cheminée was massively renovated, and the bedroom of the Duchess d'Etampes was reworked and incorporated into the Escalier du Roy. Among the various new Rococo rooms, there are a few that are especially noteworthy:

for example, the Council Hall (1751, with a ceiling by François Boucher), the Boudoir of Marie Antoinette and the Petits Appartements of Louis XVI (1785), later renovated during the Napoleonic period, with the insertion of Empire-style fabrics and furnishings. After the looting and destruction to which the palace was subjected during the French Revolution, Napoleon in fact began a series of enormous and expensive renovations in 1804, taking Fontainebleau as his new official residence.

Like the buildings, the gardens of Fontainebleau also underwent major transformations over the centuries. To the east, the Grand Jardin was originally composed of a series of square flower-beds and was criss-crossed by a canal; later, it was transformed into the Parterre du Tibre (with four fountains by Alessandro Francini), and then redesigned by Le Nôtre and gradually simplified until it attained its present-day configuration, with four grassy panels surrounded by flowering borders. On the western side were planted originally vines and maritime pines, hence the name Jardin des Pins; in the nineteenth century this part was transformed into an English-style garden, with exotic plants. The Jardin de Diane, located to the north, was originally an enclosed garden with ancient-style statues; redesigned by Le Nôtre, it was opened on its northern side and, likewise, given an English-style treatment. Facing the Gallery of François I is the Carp Pond, which already existed in the times of the medieval castle.

The Palace and Park of Versailles

In the little town of Versailles, just a few kilometres south-east of Paris, stands the renowned palace that was, from the time of Louis XIV until the French Revolution, the main residence of the French kings and of the government, becoming for more than a century the ideal model for every royal palace in Europe. Originally a hunting lodge, the castle was enlarged in two successive phases, both undertaken at the behest of the Sun King: the first phase was conducted under the supervision of Louis Le Vau, while the second phase was entrusted to Jules Hardouin Mansart. The decoration of the interior of the palace was designed by the painter Charles Le Brun, who also collaborated with André Le Nôtre on the planning and execution of the gardens. Some further modifications were done during the reigns of Louis XIV's successors; then in the revolutionary period, the castle fell into ruin and neglect, and was looted of its furnishings. It was restored to its original splendour at the behest of Louis Philippe, who wished to turn it into a museum dedicated 'to all the glories of France', and it was opened to the public in 1837. Nowadays, therefore, the palace houses in several of its rooms the Musée d'Histoire de France (Museum of French History), which was established by commissioning the most respected artists of the time to do some 3,000 paintings illustrating the military triumphs of the French state, from the Crusades to the Empire. Versailles was originally a small village in a wooded region that Louis XIII chose as his personal hunting preserve: the modest building that the king ordered built here in 1623 was two storeys tall and was surrounded by a moat. It soon became too small, and the little mansion was demolished in 1631 and replaced by a stone and brick castle, designed by Philibert de l'Orme in keeping with the forms of the French architectural tradition: the building, composed of three wings arranged in a horseshoe shape, developed around an interior courtyard, closed off by an arcaded portico. In this same period, lands were purchased for the construction of a garden.

The present-day layout of the palace was established, by and large, however, during the reign of Louis XIV, who had spent intermittent periods at his father's residence from his youth. In 1661, the young king entrusted Louis Le Vau with the task of undertaking a first expansion, which entailed, among other things, the addition of building structures meant to house kitchens and stables. In 1668, Le Vau undertook a second campaign of construction, which preserved the old castle but surrounded it by a curtain of buildings ('enveloppe'), leaving it visible only from the Court of Honour. The new building, made of blocks of white stone, featured a wing on the right reserved for the king and occupied by the Appartements des Bains on the ground floor and by the Grands Appartements on the upper floor. In the

View of the castle with the river gods of the parterre d'eau.

One of the river gods that lead towards the Fountain of Latona.

On the facing page
The Fountain of Latona, set along the main axis of the park. The fountain is formed of four circular marble steps arranged concentrically, and enlivened by statues and spraying jets of water.

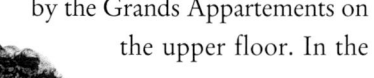

Pierre Denis Martin,
Perspectival View of the
Gardens of the Grand
Trianon, *eighteenth
century. Versailles, Musée
National du Château.*

opposite wing were the apartments of the queen and other members of the royal family; on the side overlooking the garden, the two wings were joined by a terrace, floored with marble and set on the first floor. The courtyard framed by the two new wings leads directly to the older courtyard, known as the Cour des Marbres, which is directly overlooked by the building of Louis XIII: the heavily renovated façade features a slightly jutting tripartite central forestructure, in which four pairs of columns on the ground floor support the elegant balcony on the main residential floor. Above that is an attic, surmounted by a Baroque pediment; the rich decorative effect of all this is enhanced by the presence of a balustrade with vases and statues that runs along the entire internal perimeter of the building.

The expansion of the castle was a constant concern with the king: between 1671 and 1679 two new wings were added, running perpendicular to the Court of Honour, so as to make it possible to accommodate the government ministers and their offices, which were transferred to Versailles in 1682. This helped to achieve fully Louis XIV's plans for centralization, which made the palace not only his own prestigious official residence but actually a symbol of his own absolute power.

With the addition of these last two structures by the architect Jules Hardouin Mansart, the palace attained its present-day dimensions, dominated by the long façade (580 metres): borrowing the motif that was used in the central structure of the Cour des Marbres, the elevations, flat and regular, are broken by colonnaded forestructures and feature two orders of windows, surmounted by an attic with a balustrade. The stable buildings were then built in front of the castle, for the deployment of the various service functions, while the creation of new reception areas reshaped in

LOUIS XIV, THE SUN KING

The son of Louis XIII and Ann of Austria, Louis XIV (1638–1715) succeeded his father in 1643, but remained under the regency of his mother, at first, and then later of Cardinal Jules Mazarin. The years of the king's youth were marked in France by the long civil rebellion known as the Fronde, which sorely tested the survival of monarchic power from 1648 to 1653. Upon the death of the cardinal, in 1661, Louis XIV took the governance of France into his own hands, undertaking a centralizing policy that earned him the nickname of Sun King by which he is generally remembered. He denied the Parliament all power by his de facto abolition of the *Etats Généraux*, and then surrounded himself with a bureaucracy made up of members of bourgeois extraction, and a state council with just three members, excluding ecclesiastics and princes of the blood. The political annihilation of the nobility, reduced to the rank of an elegant courtly aristocracy and distracted by a dizzying round of continual fêtes and spectacles, occurred primarily in the palace of Versailles. Among the king's achievements, we should mention the expansion of the Louvre, for which a plan by Gian Lorenzo Bernini was initially chosen; Bernini also did a bust-portrait and an equestrian monument of the king.

On pages 58–59
Aerial view of the Palace of Versailles.

Anonymous French artist,
Portrait of Louis XIV
Pointing to the Plans for
the Royal House of Saint
Louis at Saint Gyr, *oil on
canvas. Versailles, Musée
National du Château.*

The Théâtre de l'Opéra, designed by Jacques-Ange Gabriel, was inaugurated in 1770.

Bedroom of Louis XIV. The especially lavish decorations include gilt boiseries and brocades.

On the facing page One of the monumental reception halls in the palace; the decorations were supervised by Charles Le Brun.

part the structure of the central body of the palace itself: in the two side wings built by Le Vau, the Salon de la Paix and the Salon de la Guerre were built, while the linking terrace in the rear of the palace was enclosed and converted into the gallery better known as the Hall of Mirrors. The Grands Appartements were transformed into State Suites, and the private rooms of the king were moved to the old palace, directly overlooking the Cour des Marbres. In this private apartment were the king's bedroom and a series of halls and small galleries in which Louis XIV kept his collection of paintings and *objets d'art*.

The decoration and layout of the interior of the renovated palace were begun as early as the 1670s, while the construction work continued. The supervision of the immense construction project was entrusted to Charles Le Brun (1619–90), Chief Painter to the King and director of His Majesty's Cabinet of Drawings and Paintings. Supervising teams of painters, decorators and craftsmen, Le Brun created in the halls of the palace a remarkable complex of frescoes, marbles, stuccoes, gilded bronzes, fabrics, furniture and accessories, becoming the mastermind of the refined style commonly known as the 'Louis XIV' style. His great compositional skill and his predilection for a sumptuous palette show Le Brun's debt to Nicolas Poussin, his teacher, and to the Italian classicism he had studied in Rome.

The exceptional array of seventeenth-century interiors was partially compromised both by renovations done in the following century as well as by, above all, the plundering and destruction of the French Revolution. Among the most spectacular setting from the period of Louis XIV, we should mention, in addition to the Hall of Mirrors, the Grands Appartements. This array of public halls, also known as the 'Apartment of the Planets', contains important ceiling frescoes with mythological sub-

Overall view of the vault of the Royal Chapel, dedicated to Saint Louis.

The magnificent Hall of Mirrors was built between 1678 and 1684.

jects: the identification of the titular divinities of the various halls (Mercury, Mars, Venus, Apollo, and Diana) with the principal planets makes an allusive reference to the celebration of the Sun King. In 1710 the Hall of Hercules was added to the apartment, created to house the monumental canvas by Paolo Veronese, *The Dinner in the House of Simon the Pharisee* (c. 1570), donated to the king in 1664 by the Venetian Republic. The ceiling of the hall, which stands out for the richness of the marble decorations and for the quality of the chased bronzes on the fireplace, is covered by the vast creation of François Lemoyne, depicting the *Apotheosis of Hercules* (1733–36, 480 square metres).

An absolute masterpiece of French Baroque architecture is the Royal Chapel (1699–1710), designed by Mansart for the right wing of the palace. Consecrated to Saint Louis, patron saint of the French monarchy, the chapel rose over two levels: the lower level was reserved for the court, while the upper level, composed of a tribune and a lofty loggia overlooking the central nave, was reserved for the king, who could enter it directly from his

private apartments. The church, which reveals odd affinities with the French Gothic tradition (especially in its extraordinary soaring verticality, and in the configuration of the exterior), is dominated by the white colour of its columns and pillars, finely chased with trophies of liturgical objects. A contrast is provided by the flooring of coloured marble, the gilded bas-reliefs of the altar, and the paintings of the vault, focusing on the theme of the Holy Trinity, and executed by Jean Jouvenet, a pupil of Le Brun. Above the royal tribune is a spectacular painting of *Descent of the Holy Ghost*, symbolically placed to harken to the divine nature of the French monarchy.

The successors to the Sun King showed a profound respect for the physiognomy of the castle, leaving virtually intact its exterior elevations, and for the most part limiting their modifications to the private apartments. Louis XV redesigned a section, creating a suite of small rooms, richly decorated and furnished, all overlooking an interior courtyard known as the Cour des Cerfs (1738). At his behest, as well, the venerable Appartements des Bains were replaced by a series of rooms reserved

THE HALL OF MIRRORS

Between 1678 and 1684, Le Brun oversaw the decoration of the gallery, created by Mansart on the site of the terrace that had previously been designed by Le Vau at the back of the central building.
The great hall, over 70 metres in length, features on the side wall an arcade composed of seventeen mirrors, framed by arches and interrupted by pilaster strips. The mirrors correspond to the windows overlooking the gardens, from which they receive direct daylight. The charming array of decorations was made even more impressive by the profusion of exquisite materials such as the red marble of the columns and the gilt bronze of the capitals; the capitals inaugurated the so-called 'French order', established by the symbolic combination of lilies and roosters. On the ceiling, a series of allegorical paintings celebrated the deed of the king. This gallery, which owes its allure to the light effects and the indeterminate extension of space in a suggestive continuum between the exterior and the interior, was considered in the past a genuine wonder precisely because of the profusion of mirrors, at the time exceedingly rare and precious objects. The mirrored slabs, over 350 in number, were made in Paris at a manufactory established by Colbert with the intention of rivalling Venice for leadership in the production of glass.

*Detail with the entrance
to the Hall of Mirrors.*

THE TWO DÉPENDANCES:
THE GRAND TRIANON AND THE PETIT TRIANON

In 1668 Louis XIV acquired the area of Trianon, near the estate of Versailles, with the intention of building there a private retreat, designed by Louis Le Vau. The building, covered with tiles which earned it the name of 'Trianon de Porcelain', was surrounded by gardens. In 1687, this construction was replaced by a new residence, made of white stone and pink marble, designed by Mansart. The palace consists of two one-storey wings, joined by a central peristyle and adorned with pillars; the low roof is surrounded by a parapet with vases, trophies, and statues. Among the various interior rooms there is a gallery, decorated with paintings illustrating views of the palace gardens. The Park of the Grand Trianon, on which Le Nôtre and Mansart also worked, is criss-crossed by avenues and broad paths and embellished with statues, fountains, parterres, and *bosquets* (groves); a small bridge links it with the area of the Petit Trianon, acquired by Louis XV in 1749 to establish a farm and botanical gardens. In 1761, at the advice of Madame de Pompadour, Jacques-Ange Gabriel built there a small mansion with two-storey façades punctuated by Corinthian columns. The Petit Trianon was given by Louis XVI to Marie Antoinette (1774) who made a number of interior modifications, but also had a new park laid out there. The garden, English and Chinese in style, is dotted with man-made hillocks and grottoes, streams and little lakes, and houses the Hameau (1783–85), a small hamlet of peasant cottages built for courtly pastimes.

The façade of the Petit Trianon was built by Jacques-Ange Gabriel in 1761.

Aerial view of the complex of the Grand Trianon, with the gardens.

On the facing page Reception hall with the boiseries and other decorations from the era of Louis XIV.

for the royal family. In 1770, on the occasion of the marriage of the Dauphin, the Théâtre de l'Opéra was inaugurated at the far end of the right wing; it was designed by Jacques-Ange Gabriel and it seated over 700 guests. The opera house is surrounded by two orders of boxes, surmounted by a high loggia whose vertical extension is enhanced by the cunning use of mirrors; the overall decorative effect is provided by the profusion of gold, alternating with expanses of pink and green *faux-marbres*. The structure, built entirely of wood, was equipped with a mechanism that made it possible to raise the flooring of the orchestra seating until it was level with the stage, transforming the entire opera house into a vast ballroom. A design by Gabriel for the restructuring of the façades facing the city remained practically unused, with the exception of the elevation of the right wing, which was equipped with a colonnade in neo-classical style, later reproduced on the left wing as well.

The execution of the gardens which serve to complete the palace proceeded along with the general construction; the design was entrusted to André Le Nôtre , who had already designed the royal gardens of Vaux-le-Vicomte. It is generally agreed that he was responsible for the creation of the typology of the 'French-style' garden, an open system of axial paths extending as far as the eye can see, punctuat-

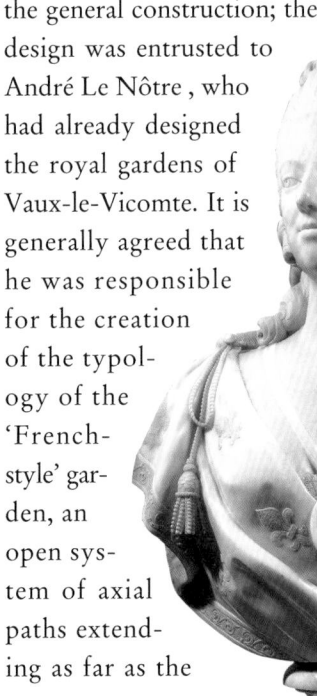

ed geometrically by parterres of flowers and low hedges, little streams, large ponds and fountains. At Versailles this layout is articulated around a main east-west axis, along which are arranged the elements of the iconographic programme of the garden. The starting point for this path is set precisely behind the palace, in the *parterre d'eau*, comprising two parallel ponds in which the palace building is mirrored. From these two basins, you proceed along a staircase and a broad pathway until you reach the Fountain of Latona, formed by four circular marble risers arranged concentrically, and enlivened with statues and sprays of water. Across a gently sloping lawn, the path leads to the immense Fountain of Apollo (1663), built to plans by Charles Le Brun and adorned with a spectacular statue of Apollo on a partially submerged chariot pulled by horses and accompanied by Tritons and dolphins. From here the path extends along the Grand Canal, which runs through the park for more than 1 kilometre, and which was dotted with a small fleet of pleasure boats available for the guests during courtly fêtes.

In the grid created by this principal axis, its parallels and the avenues that intersect it, Le Nôtre and his successor Mansart placed other fountains, sculptural groups, *bosquets*, and small buildings. Here we find the renowned marble sculpture by François Girardon and Thomas Regnaudin depicting *Apollo Served by the Nymphs* (1666–72).

On the facing page
This imposing sécretaire from the reign of Louis XV is one of the most significant pieces of furniture in the Rococo style, typical of Versailles.

Marble bust of Queen Marie Antoinette. Versailles, Musée National du Château.

François Girardon, Thomas Regnaudin, Apollo Served by the Nymphs, 1666–72. Versailles, Fountain of the Baths of Apollo.

The Church of Sainte Madeleine at Vézelay

The Abbey Church of Sainte Madeleine, in the Burgundian village of Vézelay, constitutes a priceless document of Romanesque sculpture and architecture in Burgundy in its phase of maximum splendour. Founded in the ninth century as a convent, it became a possession of the Abbey of Cluny in 1058. Its importance over the course of the eleventh and twelfth centuries was linked to its possession of the relics of Saint Mary Magdalene (their authenticity was recognized by Pope Leo III in 1050), which made this church one of the leading destinations for pilgrims throughout Europe.

The building was constructed in the forms of Burgundian Romanesque, between 1120 and 1140, on the site of an earlier building that had been damaged in a fire. Its vast and well-lit interior, 63 metres in length, is divided into a nave and two side aisles and is interrupted by a short but ample transept. Vertically, the walls of the nave are articulated on two levels (as in the Church of Anzy-le-Duc and in contrast to the more common tripartite elevation, modelled upon Cluny): the lower level is punctuated by round arches, supported by cross-shaped pillars to which are attached half-columns which rise to support the ribbed cross vaults of the roof. The upper level, instead, is occupied by a simple clerestory, in each bay of which there is a sober centred window. The interior of the church is characterized by the two-tone effect created by the limestone blocks quarried in the region, whose dark and light colours alternate, punctuating the volumes of the pillars and the curves of the longitudinal and transverse arches. Later, between 1171 and 1198, the area of the apse took on Gothic forms: in particular, on the model of the Abbey of Saint-Denis, the choir was arranged on three levels, inserting a deambulatory, punctuated by ogival arches and by five radial chapels, and surmounted by the twin-light triforium and the exceedingly luminous clerestory.

A vast porticoed atrium (or narthex) was added to the façade of the building around 1140. The narthex, like the church, is divided into three aisles by pillars that support ribbed cross vaults; at the end of those vaults are the three splendid entrance portals, adorned with reliefs done around 1225.

If the depictions of the portals have a solemn style that is reminiscent of the Ottonian and Byzantine culture, the tone in the capitals of the aisles and the narthex becomes more realistic and narrative. The latter space, however, was the one most affected by the nineteenth-century restoration done at Vézelay by Eugène-Emmanuel Viollet-Le-Duc. The only original capital now visible is the one that depicts the *Story of Tobias*.

The capitals of the nave, more than 100 in number, depict with effective naturalism and considerable plastic emphasis scenes from the Old and New Testaments, episodes from the lives of the saints (including Saint Benedict, Saint Paul and Saint Anthony), but also episodes drawn from classical mythology (the abduction of Ganymede and the education of Achilles) and allegorical motifs: the signs of the Zodiac, the Seasons, the animals of medieval bestiaries (the basilisk, the locust, the pelican), the scene of the Mystical Mill, interpreted as an allusion to the links between the Old and New Testaments, or the depiction customarily interpreted as the 'gathering of honey', but actually an allegory of the Four Winds.

The large interior of the Romanesque Church of Vézelay.

The scene of the Mystical Mill, *carved on a capital in the church.*

On the facing page
The façade of the Church of Sainte Madeleine, heavily rebuilt around 1140, when the narthex was added.

THE PILGRIMAGE CHURCHES
IN THE ROMANESQUE ERA

In the eleventh century, the practice of pilgrimages to the sanctuaries that housed precious relics was so common that it was transformed into a wide-ranging social phenomenon. This form of devotion was encouraged by the growing safety of the roads and by the development, after the year 1000, of urban centres (which it, in turn, encouraged). For people of the Middle Ages, the pilgrimage represented not only an act of penitence, often linked to the fulfilment of a vow, but also the most effective instrument – for the lower strata of society, often the only instrument – of ensuring the benevolence of God and saints. Especially in the case of voyages to distant regions, it took on the value of an experience of regeneration, fundamental in the course of the lives of those who performed them. In Europe, there were many destinations for pilgrimages: the most prestigious were the tomb of Christ in Jerusalem, the tombs of the Apostles Peter and Paul in Rome and the tomb of Saint James, the pilgrim Apostle *par excellence*, at Santiago de Compostela, in Galicia. The pilgrimage to Compostela, already practised in the tenth century but reserved to aristocrats and knights, began to become an immense mass phenomenon in the eleventh century. Affecting masses of the faithful, not only from France, but also from Flanders, England, Germany, and Italy, it gave rise to a network of roads along which sprang up gathering places and hospices for the pilgrims. Among these roads, a fundamental importance resided in the four main French *chémins*, running out radially to accommodate the voyagers coming from every part of Europe, and meeting in Navarre, at Puente la Reina, from which began the only road that ran through northern Spain and finally reached Santiago.

The Sanctuary of Sainte Madeleine in Vézelay marked the beginning of one of the four French *chémins*, the one that ran to Navarre after running through Limousin (with fundamental stops at Limoges, with the Sanctuary of Saint-Martial, and at Périgueux): and so it was that this church, because of its precious relics, became one of the most important stages in the pilgrimage. The very structure of the church, with the exceptional width of the transept and the deambulatory, and with the importance attributed to its side entrances, was functional to the liturgical requirements and the need to accommodate the great numbers of pilgrims who arrived there.

Detail of a capital in the nave, with Moses Killing the Egyptians.

Capital in the nave, with Saint Eustace Hunting.

On the facing page *Exterior of the apse area of the cathedral, seen from the cloister, with the southern transept and the Tower of Saint Antoine.*

*The sculptures
of the tympanum of
the central portal depict,
through a complex
system of symbols, Christ
as the Master of Time,
in the act of entrusting
the Apostles with the
mission of evangelizing
the Earth.*

*The three Romanesque
portals of the Church
of Vézelay are visible
from the narthex which,
around 1140, was added
to the building
on the western side.*

*On the facing page
The narthex, which
offers access to
the church, is divided
into three aisles by
the pillars that support
the cross vault.*

THE PORTALS OF VÉZELAY

In the main façade of the Church of Sainte Madeleine, after the narthex which was added around 1140, there are three carved portals that constitute one of the masterpieces of Burgundian sculpture. The reliefs on the central portal, whose figures constitute a wonderful synthesis of the medieval conception of history and religion, demonstrate the singular skill of the Burgundian stone – carvers of the Romanesque era at varying their tones, from hieratic mysticism to dramatic realism. In the lower section of the portal, the figures of John the Baptist, carved into the dividing pillar (*trumeau*) in the act of holding up a medallion (upon which was originally carved the *Agnus Dei*), and of the Apostles, on the sides of the *trumeau* and in the splays, prepare one for the theophany of the tympanum, which depicts Christ in the act of entrusting the Apostles with the task of evangelizing the Earth: He is seated in a throne in the middle, surrounded by the mandorla, and He wears an outfit that envelops his body with folds and drapings fluttering dramatically in the wind. From the arms of Christ, extending outwards, shoot luminous rays which enlighten the heads of the Apostles, divided into two groups of six, in an image dominated by the violent interplay of tensions engendered by the close-knit rhythmic correspondences between the figures. In the architrave and in the radial compartments are, instead, depicted with lively naturalism the peoples destined to receive the good message before the end of time. In the archivolt, set within small medallions, are depicted the signs of the Zodiac and the Labours of the Months; their sequence is interrupted in the centre of the lunette, on a line with the slab that, set among the various radial compartments, frames the head of Christ. At this point, in fact, three medallions enclose the figures of a man, an animal, and a mermaid, folded in upon themselves to form a ring, a symbol of the perfection of celestial time, motionless and imperturbable. This intricate image was meant to show Christ as the 'chronocrator', that is, the master of time, meant both in terms of the terrestrial time and the 'sacred' and circular time of eternity. The themes of the side portals harken back to those of the central space, developing to the south the theme of Jesus' infancy and childhood (with the *Adoration of the Magi* in the tympanum and the *Annunciation*, the *Visitation*, the *Annunciation to the Shepherds*, and the *Nativity* in the architrave), and to the north His apparition to the Apostles after the Resurrection (with the scene of the *Apparition* in the tympanum and the *Voyage to Emmaus*, the *Supper at Emmaus*, and the return of the Apostles to Jerusalem in the architrave).

The Cathedral of Aachen

Aachen (Aix-la-Chapelle in French, Aquisgrana in Italian) was a thermal bath site already known to the ancient Romans with the name of *Aquae Grani*, 'reddish water', for the colour of the water, which contained a high percentage of iron. The presence of the hot springs and the woods rich in game led Charlemagne to select this location to build the pre-eminent capital of his empire, his 'new Rome'. The Franco-Carolingian Dynasty, of which he was the most illustrious representative, had no fixed court, but moved from city to city depending on political conditions and the personal preferences of the monarch. Generally speaking, the royal palaces were not located in the major urban centres, but in relatively out-of-the-way places, where the king could relax and devote himself to his favourite pastimes, foremost among them hunting. Charlemagne (742–814), the son of Pippin the Short, crowned King in A.D. 768 and Holy Roman Emperor in 800, after a long and victorious war against the Saxons had managed to dominate most of the lands of the Eastern Roman Empire, with the exception of the British Isles and the Iberian Peninsula. In order the prove the greatness, the power, and the wealth of his empire, he undertook, and for the most part completed, immense structures of unprecedented size, at least since the decline and fall of the ancient world: 232 monasteries, seven cathedrals, and seventy-five palaces, including the Palaces of Nijmegen and Lorsch. In the most magnificent of them all, the one at Aachen, Charlemagne established his home, making it the heart of the Holy Roman Empire. Two parts of the original imperial complex have survived: the Coronation Hall (or Aula Regia), which is currently located in the Town Hall, built in the fourteenth century, and the Palatine Chapel, around which the cathedral would later be built.

The Palatine Chapel, the most noteworthy example of Carolingian architecture, was built between A.D. 796 and 803. It formed part of a much larger religious complex, which seems to have included two smaller churches, one to the north and one to the south. An atrium on the western side led, through a portico, to the imperial apartments. It was apparently built under the supervision of Einhard, Charlemagne's biographer, or else of his trusted associates – perhaps Gerhard, the palace librarian. The design was probably by Otto of Metz, to whom the design of the imperial palace is also attributed.

The entrance, with a portal, is preceded, as is the case in Constantinian basilicas, by a jutting quadriporticus, clamped between two staircase towers and carved out by a large external niche that frames, above the portal, a tribune. Above it, the emperor would appear to his subjects to receive their acclaim.

The majestic interior is punctuated on the lower storey by round arches set upon eight stout cruciform pillars, and on the upper storey by the matroneum, a gallery for women, with more soaring arches. The lower section of the ground floor features two columns with classical Corinthian capitals supporting three small arches, which in turn serve as the base for the upper section, composed of two new columns that appear to support directly the arches of the second floor. The upper arches on both floors are formed with an alternating array of light and dark items, constituting a particularly original decorative element. The populace was admitted in the lower part of the chapel; the emperor sat up high, facing the altar, on the stone throne upon which, for centuries, the kings of Germany would be crowned. The exquisite Gothic choir, which in the fourteenth century replaced the original and much smaller rectangular choir, and the series of chapels that were added

The high dome that for four centuries made the Cathedral of Aachen the tallest building north of the Alps.

On the facing page
The Gothic choir of the cathedral which replaced, in the fourteenth century, the original, smaller rectangular choir from the Carolingian era.

Among the precious
furnishings preserved
in the Cathedral
of Aachen is the ambo
from which liturgical
texts were read, evidence
of the skill of medieval
goldsmiths.

Interior of the Palatine
Chapel, adorned
with exquisite marble
decorations acquired
in Rome, as were
the monolithic columns
adorned with Corinthian
capitals.

THE MODELS FOR THE PALACE OF AACHEN

The Imperial Palace of Aachen, which contemporaries often called the Lateran, was meant to evoke the Roman residence of the Pope Saint John Lateran, which the legendary donation of Constantine defined as the palace of the emperor, handed over by him to the pontiff as a symbol of the sovereign authority of the Pope over the city of Rome. The combination of palace and church, the great apsed hall adorned with mosaics, similar to the Lateran triclinium, the equestrian statue of Theodoric transported from Ravenna (which corresponds to the Marcus Aurelius, then thought to be a portrayal of Constantine, placed alongside the Roman basilica), all indicate a relentless reference to the Roman model with its specific ideological significance: all of these elements connote, in fact, the building of Aachen as the residence of a latter-day Constantine. The structure of the Palatine Chapel is derived, instead, from Eastern models and models dating back to late Antiquity, such as the Church of San Lorenzo in Milan and especially San Vitale, the church in Ravenna that was built in A.D. 530 by the Roman Emperor Justinian and considered, along with Hagia Sophia, a masterpiece of Byzantine architecture. It should come as no surprise that Charlemagne turned his attention to Ravenna, which had been in the fifth century the residence of Roman emperors and, subsequently, part of the Byzantine realm in Italy, since he himself aspired to build a Christian empire that would be a direct descendant of the Roman political heritage, and which would play in Western Europe the same role as the Byzantine Empire in the East. In imitation of San Vitale, the courtly church took on the shape of an octagon covered by a dome, surrounded by two storeys of galleries, and from Ravenna itself were brought ancient columns and marble for the palace.

Eighteenth-century portrait depicting Charlemagne, holding up a model of the Cathedral of Aachen.

The Coffer of the Virgin Mary *preserved in the Cathedral of Aachen demonstrates the high level of accomplishment attained by Carolingian craftsmen.*

The reliquary-bust
of Charlemagne *is made
entirely of silver
and gold, and is studded
with gems and cameos.
Aachen, Cathedral.*

THE CAROLINGIAN RENAISSANCE

The term Carolingian Renaissance is used to describe the artistic flowering that took place in central Europe between the middle of the eighth century and the end of the tenth century. Its basic presupposition was political and social unification in the cultural world that, directly under the leadership of the emperor, emphasized a conscious return to classical culture. Charlemagne had in fact proposed the only form of *renovatio* acceptable to the medieval mind, one based on authority instilled by God, a model established by the Christianized Roman Empire conceived by Constantine. So it was that Charlemagne became the promotor of a major cultural movement directed towards a recovery of the ancient heritage, the first of the 'renaissances' that flourished throughout the rest of the Middle Ages, forerunners of the great season of fifteenth-century Humanism. Suffice it to mention the Capitularies emanated by Charlemagne in 789 and in 807, establishing schools and *scriptoria* near every bishopric and monastery, encouraging the education of clerics and laymen and the restoration and construction of churches. The centre of this intense cultural activity was the Palatine Academy, presided over by Charlemagne, into which were conveyed all the enlightened spirits of the period – the Englishman Alcuin of York, the Irishman Gall, the Spaniard Theodulf, the Lombard Paulus Diaconus, the Tuscan Peter of Pisa – and the anonymous artists who, harkening back to traditions that were, variously, Roman or Byzantine, Lombard or Armenian, Irish or Syrian and Egyptian, created throughout Europe buildings with similar structures and methods of construction, painted similar miniatures and frescoes, executed ivory and goldsmithery that are almost impossible to tell apart, no matter where they came from, which were all however characterized by a new attention to the examples of classical art.

*On the facing page
In the Palatine Chapel,
facing the altar, stands
the massive stone throne
upon which the emperor
sat during celebrations.
For centuries the
monarchs of Germany
would be crowned
on this throne.*

throughout the Middle Ages created the composite array of features that today characterizes the cathedral.

The high dome, an architectural miracle which for 400 years made the chapel the tallest building north of the Alps, gathers light from eight open-arched windows above the tambour; originally, it was entirely sheathed with a great mosaic depicting Christ Enthroned, in purple robes and surrounded by the Elders of the Apocalypse. The present-day mosaics date back to the years 1870–73. In the tribune, facing the altar, is located the stone imperial throne.

In the contrast of the masses of the walls and the stout pillars – elements that reappear and are developed in later Romanesque architecture – there is an evident influence of Roman architecture of late Antiquity. Also inspired by the ancient style are the bronze doors and screens. The interior of the chapel is then further embellished by coloured marbles that, according to the sources, Charlemagne ordered be conveyed there from Rome and from Ravenna. The Palatine Chapel currently constitutes a perfectly unitary nucleus, despite the subsequent additions of more modern elements, including a finely carved and intarsiated Gothic choir, consecrated in the year 1414 on the occasion of the 600th anniversary of Charlemagne's death.

The crypt of the cathedral contains some of the most important artistic treasures of the European Middle Ages, such as the Cross of Lothar (990), made of solid gold and intarsiated with precious stones, and at its centre an ancient Roman cameo originally belonging to the Emperor Augustus; the dark blue velvet chasuble with embroidered pearls, donated by Saint Bernard of Clairvaux in 1147; a reliquary-bust of Charlemagne made of silver and gold; and the marble sarcophagus decorated with a relief of the Abduction of Proserpine, which contains the body of Charlemagne.

The Cathedral of Saint Mary and the Church of Saint Michael at Hildesheim

View of the southern side of the Cathedral of Saint Mary.

On the facing page
Interior of the Church of Saint Michael, founded as early as A.D. 996.

Legend has it that Louis the Pius (778-840), the son of Charlemagne and his successor in 814 on the throne of the Holy Roman Empire, decided to order the construction of a chapel dedicated to the Mother of God on the precise site in which he had hung his weapons and armour and Christian insignia upon a rose-bush during one of the long marches of the army. The year was A.D. 815, but the final plan of the building only dates back to 872, when it became the Cathedral of the Bishopric of Hildesheim, then an extremely important centre of power, as was required for the territorial articulation of the empire built by the Frankish king. If Saint Mary's Cathedral mirrors the style of Carolingian art in its volumes and in the architectural articulation borrowed from Roman building techniques, the bronzes that form part of its treasure, instead, are closely linked to Ottonian art, related to palaeo-Christian iconography and encouraged by the Saxon House of the Ottonians, who attempted to re-establish the unity of the Roman Empire under the Christian religion.

The treasure consists of the bronze doors, and the so-called Column and Cross of Bernward, also in bronze, initially intended for the Church of Saint Michael. The work of the Bishop Bernward (*c.* 960–20 November 1022), tutor of Otto III (980–1002) until 993, they show the astounding toreutic skill of the German crafts workshops. These doors, standing 5 metres tall and created between 1008 and 1015, were each cast in a single piece with the ancient lost-wax technique, and decorated with scenes from the Old Testament and the New Testament. In this masterpiece, the protagonist is the human figure – on the one hand Adam, on the other Jesus Christ – who draws his dramatic stature from greater relief in comparison with the scarcely emphasized backgrounds, with plants and simple architectural structures. The same artistic approach is seen in the bronze

triumphal column (1020–30), clearly based on Trajan's Column; the frieze, in fact, follows a spiral, like a papyrus being unscrolled, and tells the story of the Life and Passion of Jesus Christ. Another piece in the treasure is the magnificent copper candelabrum dating back to the mid-eleventh century.

The towers linked by walls with a 6-metre diameter are the depiction of the earthly city of Jerusalem which, when lit by candles, is symbolically transformed into the celestial Jerusalem, dispenser of light, the light of the Truth of God. Fortunately, these treasures were preserved during the Second World War, which nonetheless gravely damaged the cathedral, entirely rebuilt in the 1950s. Another survivor of the war was the rose-bush that adorned the ancient chapel and cloister and, it is said, was first discovered by the emperor.

Bishop Bernward was also a skilled architect and planned the construction, which took place between 996 and 1033, of the Romanesque Church of Saint Michael, rebuilt after the Second World War. A work of great proportional rigour, the building spans three aisles created by two rows of columns alternating with pillars. Its remarkable feature lies in the presence of two transepts on both sides, with the same dimensions as the nave and the side aisles, opened on the western side by a large apse above the crypt furnished with a Gothic altar and a wooden choir around which runs a deambulatory, and on the eastern side by a three-apsed choir.

The exterior is rendered lively by the different heights of the aisles, the great tower that marks the intersection of the nave with the transepts, the curves of the apses and the lantern-towers, polygonal at the base and cylindrical in the upper section, enclosing the four sides of the transepts and containing the staircase that leads up to the towers.

UNESCO added the two ecclesiastical structures to the World Heritage List in 1985.

Detail of the bronze column with The Dance of Salome, *preserved in the Cathedral of Saint Mary.*

Detail of the doors built at the behest of Bishop Bernward, dating back to 1008–15, with The Three Magi.

On the facing page *Scene depicting* Adam and Eve, *painted on the ceiling of the Church of Saint Michael.*

The Palace and Park of Potsdam

Mentioned for the first time in a donation made in A.D. 993 by Otto III as a locality by the name of *Poztupimi*, Potsdam took on the status of city in the thirteenth century, and from 1660 on it became increasingly well known as the seat of the Princely Electors of Brandenburg. From here, in 1685, emanated the edict that allowed the French Huguenots to obtain political asylum in the territories of Brandenburg. In 1744 Frederick II, known as Frederick the Great (1712–86) chose Potsdam as his personal residence and ordered the construction there of the Castle of Sans-Souci; the name, of French origin, means 'carefree', and it well expresses the character of light-hearted leisure that the sovereign attributed to the place. Frederick supervised the design, intervening personally with a number of sketches, on the basis of which the architect Georg Wenzeslaus von Knobelsdorff built between 1745 and 1747 a palace in the Rococo style, making use of a myriad of artisans and artists who laboured away at the decoration of the building.

The palace stands atop a hill upon which the king decided to create terraced greenhouses for the planting of vines, the northernmost example in Europe, alongside the great staircase that leads into the castle. At the base of the hill a great fountain was installed, with sculptures of Venus and Mercury by Jean-Baptiste Pigalle which were donated by Louis XV of France himself to Frederick II.

The single-storey façade is surmounted by an architrave and a balustrade and is punctuated by large French windows framed by caryatids; the central structure of the building juts out and is covered by a dome; in the rear two build-ings with extended wings embrace a portion of the garden. The interiors are characterized by an ostentatious pomp, featuring the widespread use of Carrara marble, fine woods, gilding, and stuccoes, with design by Knobelsdorff himself and Johann August Nahl. Among the twelve halls that make up the castle, we should mention the Marmorsaal (Hall of Marble) and the library, which houses thousands of volumes (principally translations of French literary works and writings by Voltaire) in a setting of richly decorated boiserie. To the main structure of Sans-Souci was added from 1840, as an area for the use of the court, the wing known as the Damenflügel, designed by the architect Ludwig Persius, which still contains a collection of works by Karl Wilhelm Wach.

Frederick II wished to place his private residence within a magnificent park, following the model of all suburban palaces that were being built during the course of the eighteenth century. Extending over a surface area of 290 hectares, the park was designed with the model of the gardens of Versailles in mind, and the sovereign adorned it with numerous classical sculptures, in part ancient Roman originals, in part contemporary copies. The present-day state of the park dates back to the turn of the nineteenth century, and was the work of Peter Joseph Lenné.

Frederick wanted to have near him as well the collection of paintings that he loved best; and with this objective he ordered the construction between 1755 and 1764 of the Bildgalerie, the first building in Germany specially constructed to house a collection of paint-

The Orangerie, built between 1851 and 1860, was created in order to house the emperor's sister, widow of Czar Nicholas I of Russia.

Detail of one of the columns, shaped like a palm, from the portico of the Chinese Teahouse.

On the facing page *View of the central structure of the magnificent building of the Neues Palais, built for Frederick II between 1763 and 1770.*

The single-storey building of the castle bears on its architrave the carved legend SANS SOUCI, French for 'carefree', a name that was selected by Frederick II for his personal residence.

The sumptuous interior of the Bildgalerie, created as a collection of the artworks of Frederick II, still contains masterpieces by Titian, Rubens and Caravaggio.

On the facing page
The private library of Frederick II in Sans-Souci is housed in a circular room covered with boiseries made with exotic and rare woods.

The room known as the Marmorsaal, entirely faced with Carrara marble, is the hub of the Castle of Sans-Souci. This is where the concerts held by Frederick II took place.

The Chinesisches Teehaus was built between 1754 and 1757, in keeping with the taste for chinoiseries and the exotic that had spread throughout the courts of Europe.

ings. The project was assigned to the architect Johann Gottfried Büring, who built a single-storey elongated pavilion with a rotunda in the centre, crowned with a dome; the walls and the floors were sheathed in marble and the vault of the ceiling was decorated with ornamental stuccoes. The façade of the picture gallery is reminiscent in form and decoration of the neighbouring Castle of Sans-Souci, with a series of large windows to light the paintings hanging on the facing walls. In the autumn of 1755, the monarch had already collected 100 canvases, but because of the Seven Years' War, the installation of the Bildgalerie was delayed until 1764. It was not until 1770 that the first catalogue of the gallery was published, with a collection including 172 paint-

ings by such artists as Rubens, Titian, Caravaggio and Van Dyck.

Between 1763 and 1770, in order to send a more magnificent message of Prussian power following the war, Frederick ordered the construction of the Neues Palais, located at the far end of the park, linking it to the main entrance – the Obelisk Portal, erected in 1747 – by an avenue stretching for two and one-half kilometres. The palace, begun by Johann Gottfried Büring and Heinrich Ludewich Manger, and completed by Karl Philipp Christian von Gontard, combines in its grandiose structure the forms of French Baroque with a precocious neo-classical austerity. The two-storey façade is punctuated by giant-order pilaster strips that frame the double order of windows;

FREDERICK II THE GREAT

Frederick II of Prussia, known as Frederick the Great (1712–86), was one of the first of the enlightened despots: under the influence of the French philosopher Voltaire, he abolished torture and limited the use of the death penalty. He also conceded freedom of religion and political opinion, though still within the unchangeable system of absolute monarchy. Thanks to his military conquests, Prussia doubled the size of its territory over the course of the eighteenth century, making inroads into the power of the Habsburgs, anchored to the weakening Holy Roman Empire, and establishing itself as the hegemonic state of the German Confederation. From 1756 to 1763 Frederick II was one of the leading protagonists of the Seven Years' War against Austria, Saxony, France, and Russia, and in 1772 he took part in the first annexation of Poland. He was himself a painter and a musician, as well as being a major client and patron of the arts.

On the following pages
Interior of the Römischen Bäder, built at the behest of Frederick William III and constructed between 1829 and 1844.

The Neues Palais contains the renowned Grottensaal, where the elements of nature were reinterpreted in keeping with the Rococo tastes of the artists working at the Court of Frederick II.

Johann Christoph Frish,
Frederick II the Great
with the Marquess
d'Agens As They
Supervise the
Construction of
the Castle of Sans-Souci,
*oil on canvas. Potsdam,
Schloss Sans-Souci.*

the top of the palace is crowned by a balustrade decorated with 428 statues and by a central dome surmounted by the Three Graces, holding up the Prussian crown. On either side, two lowered, single-storey wings extend out as the servants' quarters. The interior, composed of more than 200 rooms, is entirely furnished and decorated with the grace and lightness typical of French Rococo. On the ground floor is the renowned Grottensaal, its walls entirely decorated with sea shells, minerals, and semi-precious stones, suggesting the illusion of a natural grotto; on the upper storey is the vast Marmorsaal, with its floors and walls decorated with slabs of polychrome marble, arranged according to geometric motifs. Facing the main entrance of the palace, the architect von Gontard built, between 1766 and 1769, two large buildings adorned with colonnades in the neo-classical style, to be considered as a theatrical backcloth for the Neues Palais, and built to house the court offices. During the reign of Frederick II the Park of Sans-Souci was increasingly enriched with numerous constructions, for the most part small in size, and characterized by exotic names; among them were the Drachenhaus (House of Dragons) and the Chinesisches Teehaus (Chinese Teahouse) designed by Johann Gottfried Büring between 1754 and 1757. The teahouse has a circular plan opened by pronaoi, with gilded palm-tree columns, at the bases of which are seated life-sized exotic characters; the roof is decorated with oriental motifs and is surmounted by the statue of a mandarin holding a parasol. Nowadays it houses a collection of eighteenth-century porcelains. Other constructions present in the park illustrate the revival of classical architecture, such as the Neptungrotte, completed in 1757, and the Antiketempel, a structure in the form of a small classical temple, intended to house the king's art collections.

Following the death of Frederick the Great, the interest of the kings of Prussia for Potsdam did not waver. Frederick William III, in fact, gave the hereditary prince a new portion of the park, designed by Peter Joseph Lenné, Karl Friedrich Schinkel and Ludwig Persius, upon which was built the Schloss Charlottenhof. Designed and constructed by Schinkel in 1826, the castle has the form of a Roman villa from the imperial period, decorated with grotesques, and it features at the centre of the vestibule a large bronze fountain of clear classical inspiration. Between 1829 and 1844, to plans by Schinkel and Persius, the Römischen Bäder were built, imitations of Roman baths, with a large pool of hot water set in a room decorated in the purest neo-classical style.

The last great construction in the Park of Sans-Souci was the Orangerie. Inspired by the Renaissance buildings of the Villa Medici in Rome and the Uffizi of Florence, it was built between 1851 and 1860 to plans by Ludwig Persius as a residence for the sister of Frederick William IV, widow of Czar Nicholas I. A series of terraces with curving retaining walls embellished by zoomorphic fountains lead to the construction, which has a façade extending 33 metres in length, flanked by belvedere towers; upon the façade are lines of allegorical statues set within niches. The western wing of the building is still used as a greenhouse, while the central hall, the Raffaelsaal, contains forty-seven copies of the best-known works by Raphael.

The second half of the nineteenth century was a period of decline for the city of Potsdam, which became a summer residence. Under the Weimar Republic (1919–33) the entire park, with all its buildings, was nationalized. In April of 1945, RAF bombing destroyed the city, and the complex of Sans-Souci survived by a miracle. In 1990 it was added to the UNESCO World Heritage List.

The Bildgalerie, and behind it, the large mill, rebuilt at the orders of Frederick II, as a testimonial to the country life that the emperor wished to lead at Potsdam.

View of one of the interiors of the Römischen Bäder.

On the facing page
In the Marmorsaal every decorative element, from floors to walls, is made of polychrome marble.

The Sanctuary in der Wies

The little Sanctuary 'in der Wies' (in German, literally, 'in the meadow') takes its name from its location, isolated in the centre of a clearing surrounded by woods. A symbol of Bavarian Rococo, it was added to the UNESCO World Heritage List in 1983. The late Baroque typologies were very well suited to the task of reaffirming the validity of Catholicism and exalting the Church of Rome; Bavaria, in fact, is a Catholic state in a large, Protestant nation, and these sanctuaries that were being built all over its territory were meant to constitute a sort of bulwark of the faith against the spread of the doctrines of the Reformation, relying upon miraculous occurrences that took immediate hold upon the minds of the faithful. The choice of the site for the construction of the sanctuary was said to be, according to legend, linked to a miraculous event: a local peasant woman found in the Abbey of Steingaden a statue of the *Ecce Homo*, executed for the procession of Good Friday in 1730, but soon set aside because of its crude realism, considered excessively traumatic for the faithful onlookers; she took it to her farm. On 14 June 1738, the statue began to shed tears, and so great were the repercussions of this miracle that devotional pilgrims began to converge on the site from every corner of Europe; the dimensions of the crowds persuaded the Abbot of Steingaden to order the construction of the sanctuary. The project was assigned to Dominikus Zimmermann (1685–1766), who supervised construction from 1745 to 1757, with the help of his brother Johann Baptist (1680–1758) for the decoration; he also built a house for himself right behind the church, and lived there until his death.

The building, with simple spare lines, presents a façade with a convex shape, with three entrances punctuated by semi-columns that support the high, polylobate pediment. Along the walls, which are covered with a simple plaster facing, there are numerous tall windows; behind the apse rises the bell tower. The composition of the volumes of the sanctuary is the highest expression of Zimmermann's artistry, merging the scheme of the Gothic *Hallenkirche* (a church hall in which the nave and the side aisles are the same height, so as to create a unified and luminous space) with the elliptical plan so dear to the poetics of the late Baroque period. The simplicity of the exterior stands in contrast to the richness of decoration on the interior. The space is especially luminous because of the predominance of the white walls, upon which the gilded stuccoes and the frescoes are lightened by the windows over the aisles. The dominant theme in the sanctuary's iconographic array is the adoration of Christ flagellated: the statue thus becomes a fulcrum of the church's interior space, located on a main altar surrounded by an apse dominated by the colours red, linked to the symbolism of the Passion, and dark blue, with reference to Grace. The rich sculptural decoration with the depiction of prophets and evangelists is the work of the German sculptor Egidius Verhelst the Elder; the vault of the presbytery is adorned with the grandiose fresco by Johann Baptist Zimmermann *The Angels Present the Instruments of the Passion to God*. The sanctuary, as a destination for pilgrimages, is filled with votive offerings gathered in the side passages of the church; in one of these Dominikus Zimmermann actually portrayed himself, in 1757, partly as an offering of thanksgiving for the completion of the building. In the nave, between the twinned columns, stand the monumental statues of the Fathers of the Church, the work of the sculptor Anton Sturm. The vault is decorated with a complex theatrical portrayal that involves both paint and decoration in stucco, so as to accentuate the relief of the ceiling, which in reality is almost flat. The fresco, which is also the work of

The little Sanctuary of Wies was built between 1745 and 1757 by Dominikus Zimmermann.

On the facing page *The rich Baroque decoration of the main altar encloses at the centre a sculpture of the* Flagellation of Christ.

Johann Baptist Zimmermann, depicts Christ risen in glory, placed at the summit of a rainbow, surrounded by the heavenly host, the Virgin Mary, and the Apostles; in the highest part of the fresco is set the throne of the Last Judgement, while on the opposite side a scroll emphasizes the need for a life of rectitude with the words: 'THERE WILL BE NO MORE TIME'.

Fitting in with the concept of total decoration is the wooden pulpit, with a rich stucco decoration which features the symbolic depictions of the Holy Ghost, with the dove set in the centre of the baldachin above the lectern, Faith represented by the heart and the cross, and Hope, incarnated by the anchor.

On the facing page
Panoramic view
of the nave, punctuated
by twinned columns.

Detail of one of the putti
in the vault; the refined
execution of the flesh
and the draperies show
the high levels of skill
of the German masters
in the technique
of working stucco.

The pulpit of the
Sanctuary of Wies is
the product of a complex
development of subjects
and themes linked to the
symbols of Redemption,
Hope, and Faith.

The Castle of Würzburg

The city of Würzburg, in Franconia, a region of upper Bavaria, dates back to early times: it is mentioned in the sources for the first time in 704 with the name of *Castellum Virteburch*, in connection with the martyrdom of Saints Kilian, Kolonat and Totnan, who had come from Ireland to evangelize Franconia. From 742 on, the city was an episcopal see, thus increasing its prestige in the assembly of other German cities. It became so well known that in 1156 the Holy Roman Emperor, Frederick I Barbarossa, was married there to Beatrice of Burgundy, and he elevated it in 1168 to the status of independent duchy. Ruled always by bishop-princes, it enjoyed moments of great splendour following the Thirty Years' War (1618–48) and the installation of the dynasty of the bishop-princes of Schönborn (1642), who had the opportunity, following the destruction of the city by Swedish troops, to transform the medieval *borgo* into a modern Baroque city. In the context of this great reconstruction came the building of the Residenz, which began in 1720. The Bishop-Prince Johann Philipp Franz von Schönborn entrusted the role of superintendent over the new residence to the Bohemian architect Johann Balthasar Neumann, already involved in the urbanistic renovation of the city. For the design and execution of the project the architects Robert de Cotte and Germain Boffrand were also consulted; from Vienna, Hildebrandt was summoned, and Johann Dientzenhofer also intervened.

In his conception of the new spaces, the architect Neumann took on all the architectural themes typical of the period: the elliptical central plan, the system of the uncovered pillars, and the fusion of various rooms into single spaces. The result was a magnificent castle with two jutting wings that created the great square that extended out before the principal entrance. The façade is subdivided into two storeys by a large floor-marking cornice and punctuated by pilaster strips within which were located the large windows topped by triangular pediments adorned with statues; atop the entire building runs a continuous balustrade with sculptural decorations.

The interior arrangement consists of over 300 rooms, with the octagonal Kaisersaal as the centre; it is reached from the low and dark atrium – which is overlooked by the Gartensaal, richly decorated with the stuccoes by the Lugano maestro Antonio Bossi – via the grandiose staircase of honour, which in Neumann's conception was featured as the most representative space in the castle. Its construction, after the abandonment and modification of a variety of designs, took place in 1737: the solution that was adopted was to insert into the large rectangular space a single-flight staircase, with no walls, that would separate and turn 180 degrees once it reached the main landing, thus transforming into two parallel flights of stairs and generating a highly articulated space, capable of offering a continuous series of points of view and perspectival foreshortenings. At the same time, work was progressing on the upper floors, where, thanks to the skill of the decorator Antonio Bossi, the reception rooms of the palace were taking shape. Dating from 1745 is the sumptuous antechamber to the Kaisersaal where Bossi's mastery expressed itself at its best in the limited use of colour and in the fantasy attained in the creations in the purest rocaille style.

In order to decorate a number of the rooms of the castle with frescoes, Giambattista Tiepolo was summoned from Venice, probably at the suggestion of Bossi. In December 1750 the painter, accompanied by his sons Giandomenico and Lorenzo, reached Würzburg with the assignment, entrusted to him by the Bishop-

The central structure of the Residenz, seen from the gardens.

On the facing page *The magnificent double-flight staircase, created by Johann Balthasar Neumann, leads to the spectacular reception suites of the palace.*

GIAMBATTISTA TIEPOLO

At the beginning of his career, Tiepolo was trained in the workshop of the Venetian painter Gregorio Lazzarini. His youthful paintings, such as the *Sacrifice of Isaac* (Venice, Church of the Ospedaletto), the *Martyrdom of Saint Bartholomew* (Venice, San Stae), and the *Madonna del Carmelo*, or *Our Lady of Mount Carmel* (Milan, Brera Art Gallery) are marked by an intense array of colours and powerful chiaroscuro effects which Tiepolo was to abandon in his later works. As early as the frescoes in the Archbishopric of Udine, considered the masterpiece of his younger years, we can see that the artist has acquired a greater freedom and looseness in his spatial construction, and has lightened his colours into delicate and more luminous shades.

In 1731 Tiepolo went to Milan where he completed a number of excellent works with mythological subjects (the ceilings of the Palazzo Archinto, destroyed during the Second World War; *Allegory of Magnanimity*, Palazzo Dugnani). In 1739 the congregation of the Carmine in Venice entrusted him with the commission of decorating the ceilings of their *scuola*. The execution of this project occupied Tiepolo until 1743 and fired him with great enthusiasm. Before he finished it, he returned to Milan where he decorated the ceiling of the Palazzo Clerici with *The Course of the Chariot of the Sun*. In this work what prevailed was the intense luminosity of the sky, which filters through the clouds and envelops groups and figures in a magical light. During these same years, he did the frescoes of the *Stories of Antony and Cleopatra* for the Palazzo Labia in Venice. In 1750 the artist moved to Würzburg with his sons Giandomenico and Lorenzo, who assisted their father in the execution of his massive works. He returned to Italy, where he executed numerous other frescoes, including those at the Villa Valmarana and the *Apotheosis of the Pisani Family* in the Villa Nazionale in Stra. In 1762, again accompanied by his two sons, Tiepolo left for Madrid where he entered the service of King Charles III of Bourbon, who commissioned the painter to decorate three halls of the Royal Palace. The artist, by this point, was sixty-six years old, but he took on the colossal project with his usual dash and vigour. Thus were created the *Glory of Spain*, the *Apotheosis of the Spanish Monarchy* and the *Apotheosis of Aeneas* which, despite their solemnity, are totally pervaded by that atmosphere of lightness, verging on enchantment, that has always characterized Tiepolo's paintings.

In the vault of the staircase, Tiepolo depicted himself with his son Giandomenico, as a fitting conclusion to the impressive series of frescoes that featured as protagonists the gods of Olympus and the Four Continents, all paying homage to the bishop-prince.

On the facing page
Rising from the square overlooking the city is the monumental façade of the Palace of the Bishop-Princes of Schönborn, begun in 1720.

The Gartensaal, located on the ground floor, richly decorated with stuccoes by the Lugano master, Antonio Bossi, is the first of the castle's reception halls.

The Kaisersaal represents the high point of the synthesis of stucco decoration and fresco technique. In the background, a fresco with Frederick Barbarossa with Beatrice of Burgundy.

On the facing page The Court Chapel, *built to plans by Neumann between 1733 and 1735.*

Prince Karl Philipp von Greiffenklau, of decorating the great dining room, later known as the Kaisersaal. Within the context of the elaborate decorations in white and gold stucco done by Bossi, Tiepolo depicted in the centre of the ceiling the large scene of *Apollo Leading Beatrice of Burgundy to the Genius of the German Nation*; the other two scenes depict *The Wedding of Frederick I Barbarossa with Beatrice of Burgundy* and *The Investiture of the Bishop Harold as Duke of Franconia*. The decoration of the hall was completed in 1752 to the complete satisfaction of the client. The conception of the decorative cycle, with the *Wedding* and the *Investiture*, formed part of the overall programme drawn up, at the bishop's request, by the Jesuit Fathers Seyfried and Gilbert in 1735 for the glorification of the bishop-prince. Tiepolo's art attained its fullest consummation in the oval at the centre of the vault, with the chariot of Apollo appearing suddenly from among the clouds in a composition in which painted figures and stucco creations overlap to create extraordinary illusionistic effects. The fresco with *The Wedding of Barbarossa* is enclosed within a miraculously executed stucco curtain, which opens to reveal the scene of the wedding to the public in an interplay of luminous colours.

Tiepolo's inimitable creative imagination manifested itself to an even greater degree in the decoration of the immense vault of the staircase, a surface covering over 600 square metres and almost entirely unsupported, which discharges its own immense weight into the load-bearing walls. The fresco was completed in some 218 days, and it depicts *Apollo and the Four Continents*. At the centre of the vault, surrounded by the Olympian deities in a transparent sky, Apollo, radiating golden light, emerges from the Temple of the Sun, its cornice just within sight, and readies himself for his daily voyage through the heavens. In a

*The antechamber
of the Kaisersaal, built
in 1745 by Antonio Bossi,
remains one of the finest
representations
of the rocaille style.*

*On the facing page
The fresco by Rudolf
Byss with the Glory
of the Virgin Mary
decorates the ceiling
of the Court Chapel.*

The oval ceiling of the Kaisersaal contains a fresco of Beatrice of Burgundy, accompanied by Apollo, who leads her towards her husband-to-be, Frederick Barbarossa.

The central flight of steps of the staircase of honour designed by Balthasar Neumann.

On the facing page Detail of the fresco of The Investiture of the Bishop Harold as Duke of Franconia, *signed and dated by Tiepolo in 1752.*

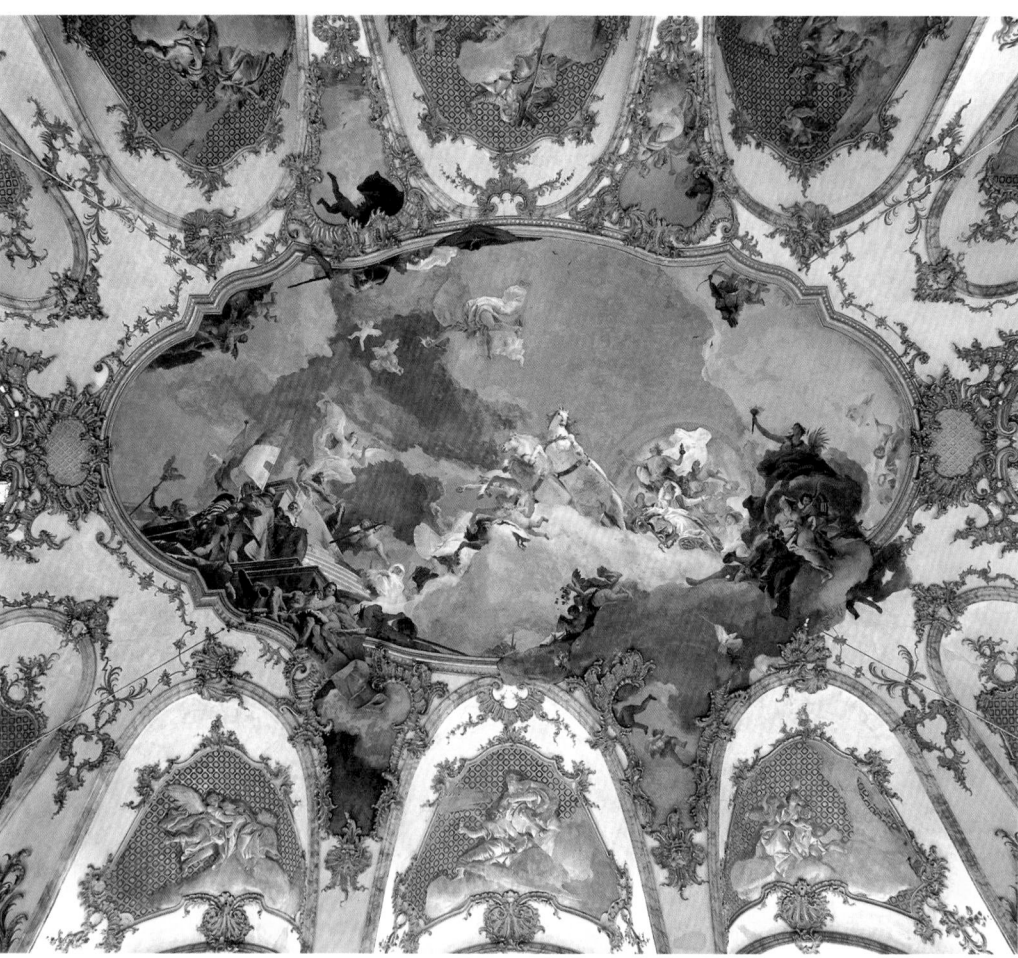

pose derived from the *Belvedere Apollo*, he holds a statue of Fortune (Fortuna) in his left hand. The Hours (Horae), with butterfly wings, bring him his horses, while putti push his chariot into place. On the cornice Tiepolo inserted the symbolic depictions of the continents, taken in part from the celebrated *Iconology* by Cesare Ripa. America is represented by an American Indian woman, adorned with feathers and seated on a crocodile; Asia is represented by an Indian woman on an elephant; Africa is depicted as a black princess riding a camel; and Europe, represented by Europa, surmounts the entrance to the first-floor salons, seated near a bull and surrounded by the Liberal Arts. In this portion of the fresco, Tiepolo introduces the portraits of the protagonists of the creation of the castle: Balthasar

Neumann portrayed as an artillery colonel, Antonio Bossi identifiable as the person standing, wearing a mantle, and finally Tiepolo himself with his son Giandomenico, visible at the far left. All the artists are overwhelmed by the portrait of the bishop-prince supported by Fame and crowned by Virtue.

Completing the construction of the Residenz was the Hofkirche (Court Chapel), located in the castle's southern wing. Built by Neumann between 1733 and 1735, it is sumptuously adorned with stuccoes and decorations by Antonio Bossi and frescoes by Johann Rudolf Byss. The two side altars are surmounted by two altar pieces by Giambattista Tiepolo: *Our Lady of the Assumption* on the right-hand altar piece and *The Fall of the Rebellious Angels* on the left-hand altar piece.

The Tower of London

The complex of fortifications generally known as the Tower of London constitutes a fundamental document of the military architecture of the Middle Ages, preserving the traces of various phases of construction that succeeded each other in the centuries following the Norman era. The setting for countless and renowned historic episodes, it is traditionally considered one of the symbols of the British monarchy and contains, among other things, the precious Crown Jewels.

The Tower of London was founded in 1066 by William I the Conqueror, who that same year had invaded England with the support of a vast European coalition, having himself crowned at Westminster and thus becoming the founder of the Norman Dynasty beyond the English Channel. The fortress stood on the banks of the Thames, in a strategic position downstream from the ancient bridge and at the south-east corner of the ancient Roman walls around London; from here it was possible to defend the city from any external invasions, but it was also possible to ensure that within the city no revolts erupted against the new rulers. At first, the structure was nothing more than a small square enclosure, consisting on two sides of ancient walls and, on the northern and eastern sides, of wooden palisades guarded by moats. In 1077, just a little over one decade after its foundation, the first major construction projects were undertaken under the supervision of Gundulf, the Bishop of Rochester, and were completed in 1100; this resulted in the creation of the building that even now constitutes the centre of the Tower of London, the stronghold-palace commonly known as the White Tower. This is a massive donjon made of local white stone, with an almost perfectly square base, standing more than 27 metres tall. The building, with its buttresses and its four corner tow-

ers, has three storeys, with a double-height middle floor; the apse, located at the far end of the eastern side, contains the Saint John Chapel; this room, bare and stern, has a nave surrounded by massive columns and a triforium gallery.

William II, who succeeded the founder on the throne, endowed the castle with masonry fortifications on the north and west sides, to join with the Roman walls. The Tower became a model of reference for the Norman castles of the feudal period, and in the century following its foundation it underwent modifications and additions until, at the end of the thirteenth century, it attained a size roughly equivalent to its present size, about 7 hectares; its perimeter, enclosed by high walls, is punctuated by the presence of twelve towers, and was once bordered on the eastern side by a moat that was later filled in and transformed into a field. Massive campaigns to enlarge the walls (subsequent to those undertaken by Richard I and King John, of which only the Bell Tower survives) took place first under Henry III (1207–72), and then under his successor, Edward I (1239–1307). In the middle of the thirteenth century, the enclosure wall of the Tower was extended beyond the Roman ring and endowed with perimeter towers, still preserved; the parish Church of Saint Peter ad Vincula was thus enclosed in the interior of the fortress, and was transformed into a chapel. Henry III also ordered the construction of a sumptuously furnished rich palace, of which only the Wakefield Tower now survives, to the south of the ring of walls. This construction, placed so as to survey the gate that allowed access from the river, features an upper hall with a vaulted ceiling and a small oratory decorated with wall paintings. Edward I had the ring of walls built by Henry III enclosed within a larger ring of walls, thus transforming the Tower of London into an

View, from above, of the fortified complex of the Tower of London.

On the facing page *The White Tower, a fortified palace equipped with counterforts and four corner towers, set in the centre of the fortified area.*

Silhouette of the White Tower, which constitutes an exceptional example of medieval English architecture.

Illuminated manuscript showing the duke in the White Tower after the battle of Agincourt, from a book of poems by Charles, Duke of Orléans, c. 1487. London, British Museum, Ms. Royal 16 f. 73.

invincible concentric fortress, increasing its defences with the construction of a moat on the eastern side. The main entrance from land, which was located at the centre of the eastern bastion, was moved to the south-east corner and replaced by the Beauchamp Tower. Before the new gate were placed, as defensive structures, a semi-circular barbican (Lion Tower) and two fortified entrances guarded by towers. On the side overlooking the river, a new water-gate was opened, the imposing Saint Thomas Tower, inspired perhaps by a similar one built in Paris for the Louvre; here were housed, on the upper floor, the apartments for official receptions, linked by a bridge to the palace.

Once the physiognomy of the external perimeter had been defined under Edward I, the Tower of London was the object of further campaigns of construction focusing for the most part on individual buildings founded to correspond to the varied functions that the castle served over the course of the centuries: fortress, royal palace, seraglio (which housed, among other things, lions and leopards), arsenal, mint, and prison. Successive demolitions cancelled almost all traces of these uses, although they profoundly marked the history of the building, often remembered especially for the famous people that have been imprisoned there. John II of France, taken prisoner at the battle of Poitiers (1356), and Charles, the Duke of Orléans, captured in 1415 at Agincourt, were both held captive in this fortress, which was also the prison of Anne Boleyn and Catherine Howard, wives of Henry VIII. Also sequestered here were numerous victims of the Anglican schism as well as the future Queen Elizabeth I, accused of conspiracy by her sister Mary. The episode that, more than

THE CROWN JEWELS

The collection of precious objects and ceremonial garb belonging to the British monarchs and known as the 'Crown Jewels' has been housed in the Tower of London since 1303, when the original location in Westminster Abbey (chosen by Edward III at the turn of the eleventh century) proved none too secure. The collection contains objects traditionally used in the coronation ceremonies and in other official solemnities: crowns, royal maces, sceptres, swords adorned with precious stones, the decorations and insignia of the knightly orders, outfits studded with gold and gems, ritual objects. The Crown Jewels were pawned many times over the centuries to finance expensive military campaigns, and they were scattered during the republican era, when Oliver Cromwell (who was also responsible for the destruction of the royal apartments in the Tower of London) ordered in 1649 that they be eliminated inasmuch as they were symbols of the hated power of the monarchy. Of the ancient garb and jewels, in any case, a thorough documentation did survive, making it possible to recreate some of the pieces for the coronation of Charles II in 1661; from then on, with additions and modifications, the present-day collection began to grow.

The oldest item is a ceremonial spoon dating back to the twelfth century, which survived the destruction of the republican revolution. Some of the pieces of jewellery contain precious stones of astounding value, such as the renowned 109-carat Kohinoor diamond, acquired in 1849 and set in the Queen Mother's Crown. The Imperial State Crown, made in 1838, contains more than 3,000 precious stones.

Queen Elizabeth I, on the day of her coronation with the 'Crown Jewels', painted by an anonymous English artist of the sixteenth century.

any other however, gave the Tower of London a sinister reputation, was the murder of the two young sons of Edward IV (1483), which is traditionally said to have occurred in the building known as the Bloody Tower.

The residential function, for which the castle had originally been built, declined from the time of Henry VIII (1491–1547). There are some traces of this period in the Chapel of Saint Peter ad Vincula, rebuilt in 1519 by James Nedeham after a fire, and consisting of a longitudinal structure with a presbytery and a broad nave to the north. The same architect reconstructed in 1540 the Queen's House, once known as the Lieutenant's Lodging, consisting of a complex structure of wooden pointed arches and subsequently modified with the creation of an ample upper hall (1607). From the second half of the seventeenth century and through until the nineteenth century, the principal function of the Tower of London was that of a military stronghold, the reason why numerous buildings for the manufacture and storage of artillery were built there. Most of these buildings were demolished during the campaign of restorations undertaken in 1853 by Anthony Salvin, with the intent of restoring the Tower of London to its medieval appearance.

Detail of the pointed-arch vaults of the cell in which Thomas More was imprisoned.

114

Traitor's Gate directly overlooks the Thames, and was therefore also known as the Water-Gate.

The Saint Thomas Tower housed, in its upper storey, the reception suites, linked by a bridge to the Wakefield Tower and the palace.

Westminster Abbey in London

The monumental complex that comprises the Abbey and the Palace of Westminster is an important political symbol in the English tradition: the two buildings are in fact the historical settings for, respectively, royal coronations and assemblies of Parliament, which still take place there. Both buildings boast long-ago medieval origins, which are however best documented by the church, a remarkable example of the English Gothic style. The palace, in fact, which originally housed only the royal residence, was rebuilt for the first time from 1512 and then (after the fire of 1834 that spared only Westminster Hall, the Crypt Chapel, and the Jewel Tower) was newly rebuilt during the Victorian period, in keeping with the neo-Gothic taste then so popular. The abbey, which preserves intact its splendid thirteenth-century structures, is also well known for its function as a national pantheon: it contains, in fact, an immense number of illustrious tombs, including those of kings and members of the royal family, nobles and dignitaries, but also artists, writers, and scientists. The exceptional array of these funerary monuments makes Westminster a genuine museum of English and British sculpture from the thirteenth to the twentieth centuries.

The foundation of the abbey probably dates back to the late seventh century, but its architectural history is entirely lost up until the moment, around 1042, when Edward the Confessor decided to rebuild it and dedicate it to Saint Peter, placing his own palace nearby. In 1066, the king was buried in Westminster and the abbey served as the setting for the coronation of his two immediate successors, Harold and William the Conqueror, thus originating an age-old tradition. The church, few traces of which survive in the foundations of the present-day structure, was probably based upon contemporary French models and included, among other things, an apsed and vaulted chapter hall. A few ruins survive of the structure of the old monastery, probably dating to periods later than the construction of the church itself: the most important is the ruined Romanesque Chapel of Saint Catherine, which dates back to 1160.

In 1220 Henry III began to take a certain interest in the buildings of the abbey, which he finally ordered entirely rebuilt, commencing in 1246. At first, his patronage was limited to the foundation of the Lady Chapel, located to the east of the apse, in the area where the Chapel of Henry VII now stands. This piece of construction can hardly be considered as a first phase in the reconstruction of the church, but it is possible that it may have suggested to the monarch the idea of the much larger undertaking that resulted in the present-day structure of the church. Underlying the origin of this project we can mention a number of different factors, first and foremost the devotion of the king towards the original founder of Westminster, Saint Edward the Confessor, whom Henry perhaps wished to emulate. It is moreover possible that Henry III wished to imitate the French monarchy, who had in the Cathedral of Reims (an evident model for Westminster) the solemn setting for their royal coronations. The king, for that matter, was driven by sincere religious fervour, and that may have been the most important factor that led him to construct the most sumptuous and impressive church of his time.

The abbey, similar in form and size to a cathedral, has a Latin cross plan with three aisles and a transept, also tripartite. The space is subdivided into rectangular bays, singled out by very high pointed arches and covered by cross vaults, richly marked by sculpted ribbings. On the side walls, beneath an order of windows, runs a tribune, lit from the exterior, which overlooks the nave with a series of

The façade is one of the most recently built sections of the building, and was completed in the eighteenth century.

On the facing page
Rose window and stained glass windows of the thirteenth-century north end of the transept.

trilobate twin-light windows set in large arches, and a tympanum marked by a large rose window. The emphatic plastic effect of the whole is ensured by the articulation of the pillars and the deployment of the windows, recessed with respect to the longitudinal arches. The plan culminates with a narrow, soaring choir, composed of three bays of decreasing depth; the eastern structure terminates in a polygonal apse surrounded by a deambulatory and by five radial chapels (the central one, the Lady Chapel, was replaced in the sixteenth century by the present-day Chapel of Henry VII). The walls of the choir, articulated like those of the nave, have high windows and are punctuated by vertical supports that rise to the vaults, extending the columns set in the pillars.

The rich surviving documentation concerning the financial conditions underlying the construction of the building provides us with the names of the three architects who succeeded in the supervision of the project: Henry of Reins, John of Gloucester (who followed the plans of Henry of Reins), and Robert of Beverley, who made some minor changes to the original project. The figure of Henry has been much discussed by scholars, in an effort to determine whether he was an architect of French origin (as his surname would suggest, coming as it does from an old form of the toponym for Reims), or, more likely, an Englishman who had travelled in France. In fact, his architecture shows an original blend of French elements with distinctly island-based characteristics. In particular, the influence of French models is evident in the proportions and rhythm of the elevation and, above all, the structure of the choir, which breaks with the English tradition of the single axial chapel apse, harkening back directly to the example of Reims. Also French is the shape of the terminal windows, composed of

THE CHAPEL OF HENRY VII

A substantial modification to the thirteenth-century plan of Westminster was made in 1503, when the Lady Chapel (built at the behest of Henry III and placed at the centre of the radial system of the apse) was demolished and replaced with a new and much larger chapel, intended to house the remains of King Henry VII, his wife Elizabeth of York, and his mother, Margaret Beaufort, as well as the remains of Henry VI and Catherine of Valois. Inspired by the eastern wing of Westminster and the Saint George Chapel in Windsor Castle, the construction consisted of a broader nave, flanked by two smaller side aisles and placed so as to extend the main axis of the church, which culminates in a polygonal apse articulated by radial chapels. The roofs, worked with fine tracery, constitute the exceptional culmination of the English tradition of the fan vaults, typical of the style known as 'perpendicular'; on the walls, the windows have elegant cornices and complex structures. The identity of the artist who oversaw this refined project is unknown, and attributions vary between Robert Vertur I and Robert Janyns.

The chapel is decorated by a rich array of sculptures that originally consisted of 107 statues, 95 of which are still standing. Executed by a variety of artists (some of them Dutch) and with varied success, the statues have different dimensions: those set in the niches of the triforium measure roughly 1 metre, while those arranged in the side aisles and the lateral chapels are larger.

View of the so-called Poet's Corner, in the southern arm of the transept: in this space we find the funerary monuments of many English writers, beginning with Geoffrey Chaucer.

Detail of the niches in the triforium of the Chapel of Henry VII.

On the facing page
The sixteenth-century funerary Chapel of Henry VII appears from the exterior as an elaborate array of late Gothic motifs, such as spires, pinnacles, and finely decorated arches.

twin lights and a rose window, forming a single aperture in the corner areas and running down well below the beginning of the arches of the vaults. All the same, numerous and major details distinguish this church from its continental counterparts.

An extraordinary document of the creation of a national Gothic style, deeply influenced by French models, is the Chapter House, completed in 1253 and placed, as is customary, on the exterior of the perimeter of the church, connecting with the cloisters through a corridor. In the main hall, with its octagonal plan, central pillar, and fan vault, in keeping with the traditional typology, the Gothic ideal of the 'glass cage' was attained, similar to the model of the upper chapel of the Sainte-Chapelle in Paris: the elevation is entirely resolved in the large windows, divided into two twin-light windows contained within pointed arches, with quadrifoil tracery and surmounted by a six-lobe rose window.

Over the course of the thirteenth century, the construction of the main aisle of the church extended to the first four bays of the transept; the successive seven bays were built from 1376, completely following the thirteenth-century model and therefore giving rise to a uniform whole. The second architect responsible for the continuation of the nave, Henry Yevele, probably also designed the western façade, upon which work was interrupted in 1534. The façade of Westminster is characterized by the presence of four buttresses, sheathed in semi-columns and little arches; the two powerful lateral towers were added in 1734–45 by Nicholas Hawksmoor. On the exterior, the items of greatest interest are certainly the Chapel of Henry VII (an elaborate array of late Gothic motifs) and the thirteenth-century north façade of the transept, with deeply splayed portals, a large rose window, and flying buttresses in the French style.

Mount Athos

Mount Athos (Holy Mountain, from the Greek *agion oros*) is located at the very tip of the Athos Peninsula, the easternmost of the three spits of land of the Chalcidice Peninsula, thrusting like a trident into the Aegean Sea. The narrow strip of land is dominated by the rocky pyramid of the mountain, which rises in an almost sheer wall 2,033 metres above the sea. Its shape and its location attracted the attention of sailors from the earliest times, giving rise to numerous legends. According to Greek mythology, this land formation was the setting of the battle between Poseidon, god of the sea, and the giant Athos, who supposedly ripped a mountain off of the mainland and hurled it into the sea in an attempt to crush his adversary. Described by Homer and Sophocles, cited by Herodotus as a theatre for military operations during the Persian Wars, and by Pliny as a place inhabited by men who lived well past the age of one hundred years and who lived upon snake meat, Mount Athos is still famous today. This is in fact the one location where Byzantine monasticism still survives in its original form, governed for one thousand years now with laws and customs that have been faithfully preserved from all modifications or contaminations.

In fact, Mount Athos houses a sort of little independent republic, isolated from the world and run according to its own regulations, beginning with a law that strictly prohibits women from entering; women are not even allowed to land in the port of Daphne. This prohibition dates back to 1046, when the Byzantine Emperor Constantine Monomachus, in the same document whereby the territory of Athos was awarded administrative independence from the empire, forbade women, girls, and 'beardless' boys to enter there. Today, the monastic population of Mount Athos is distributed throughout its twenty monasteries, called *moni* (the oldest and most important monastery is the Great Lavra, *Megisti Lavra*), each of which owns a portion of the territory on the peninsula. Each of these monasteries has the structure of a full-fledged citadel, surrounded by defensive walls and guarded by a tower, and has a number of satellite communities, the *skite*, monastic centres without walls, dependent upon a neighbouring monastery to which they pay a tribute or by which they are in turn represented on the Central Council. The *moni* are points of reference for other smaller foundations: the *kellia*, monastic settlements with a few houses scattered around a church; the *kalive* (from *kalybe*, hut), also known as *kathismata* (places in which one sits), austere and isolated buildings inhabited by a few monks, with a shared prayer chapel; and the *isychastiria*, places of quiet, or *askitiria*, that is, places of asceticism, residences of the hermits who live there in absolute solitude, assisted by the monasteries only in case of need.

The earliest religious settlements arose in this region in the eighth and ninth centuries, in conjunction with the persecution conducted by the iconoclastic emperors of Byzantium against those who supported the cult of images (*ikònes*), especially the monks. The 'image-worshippers' sought refuge from the persecution in the remote and virtually uninhabited land of Mount Athos, and there they lived their ascetic lives in isolation. The best known of these early hermits, about whom we have only the scantiest of information, were Saint Peter the Athonite and Saint Euthymius the Younger; they are often portrayed in the frescoes of Mount Athos. It was at the end of the tenth century that, with the foundation of the Lavra by Saint Athanasius, Mount Athos acquired the monastic organization that it still preserves, sanctioned in the year 972 by the autonomous status awarded it by the Emperor John I Tzimisces.

Mount Athos occupies the easternmost spit of land of the Chalcidice Peninsula, which extends into the Aegean Sea.

On the facing page *Surrounded by massive walls, the monasteries of Mount Athos are still closed to women, and still respect laws and customs that have been preserved unchanged for 1,000 years.*

SAINT ATHANASIUS
AND THE FIRST MONASTERIES

The first monastery of Mount Athos, the Great Lavra, and the overall organization of the Holy Mountain, still in effect, were the work of Saint Athanasius (*c.* 920–1003). Born in Turkey at Trebizond (present-day Trabzon), he had originally withdrawn to lead the monastic life in the Monastery of Kyminas in Bithynia, where he had made friends with the future Emperor Nicephorus Phocas. To avoid succeeding as the father superior of the monastery, Athanasius withdrew into anonymity, under the name of Barnabas, on Mount Athos. Here he lived as a hermit for a number of years, but in 960 Nicephorus tracked him down and asked him to come with him as he went to wage war against the Saracens who had occupied Crete. The military expedition culminated in victory and Nicephorus II Phocas, now that he had been made emperor (963–69), offered his friend Athanasius a sum of money with which to build a monastery dedicated to the Virgin Mary. And so, with the help of the hermits who already lived on Mount Athos, he built the Great Lavra. Athanasius became the father superior of the new monastery. He wrote the rules of the community (or *typikòn*), with the goal of organizing its internal operation, but also to govern the behaviour of the hermits who lived in cells or huts outside of the monastery. In A.D. 969, Nicephorus, who had hoped to spend the last remaining years of his life as a monk alongside his friend Athanasius, was murdered in his sleep by his own nephew John I Tzimisces, with the complicity of Nicephorus's wife, Theophano. The new emperor (969–78) publicly professed his repentance, shut his accomplice up in a monastery, and then succeeded his murdered uncle on the throne. Even before the death of Athanasius, other monasteries had been founded: the Monastery of Vatopedi (972), founded by three leading citizens of Adrianople; the Monastery of Dochiariu (976), fouded by a disciple of Saint Athanasius; the Monastery of Iviron, that is 'the monastery of the Iberians', a name that was used to indicate the Georgians who founded it around A.D. 979; and the Monastery of the Amalfitans, founded around 990 by the monk Leo of Amalfi, and meant to house monks from the cities of southern Italy that were under the Byzantine protectorate. Saint Athanasius died in 1003, crushed by a beam that fell during the construction of the church; great veneration is still lavished upon the saint's tomb, the grotto in which he liked to pray, and a spring that supposedly spurted out following an apparition of the Virgin to the saint.

On the facing page
*View of the Monastery
of Megisti Lavra,
the largest one
on Mount Athos.*

*The saints of Mount
Athos, frescoed
on the exterior wall
of the Protaton at Karies.*

*The scene depicting
Christ enthroned among
the Saints is one of
the numerous figurative
themes traditionally
used on Mount Athos.*

In the centuries that followed, the imperial power of Byzantium, with the Dynasty of the Macedonians first, and the Dynasties of the Comneni and the Paleologi later, continued to protect the privileges and the autonomy of the monasteries of Mount Athos. Even when the Eastern Empire fell to the armies of the Ottoman Turks (1453), the monks obtained a confirmation of their autonomous status, although they were obliged to pay a yearly tribute to the coffers of the sultan. A dark period began in 1821, when the monks openly showed their sympathy for the Greek independence movement; in that year, a military detachment occupied Mount Athos, bringing violence and physical destruction and remaining an occupying force until 1829. When, in 1912, Greece took its northern provinces back from the Turks, it also took over stewardship of the Holy Mountain, and in 1924 promulgated a statutory charter to regulate the rights of its monasteries, largely confirming the privileges enjoyed for many centuries.

The monasteries are all surrounded by massive walls, and guarded by a tower, which gives them the appearance of invincible fortresses. These structures served the defensive needs of the helpless monastic population in an area that was both isolated and exposed to the attacks and plundering of pirates. Once you pass through the entrance, invariably guarded by massive nail-studded portals, each monastery presents an irregularly shaped courtyard at the centre of which stands the central church, the *katholikon*, devoid of a monumental façade and extending around a central dome with a high tambour. Around the church are scattered various structures with specific functions: the military structures of the arsenal and of the defensive walls, the sacred fountain or water cistern (*fiali*), the refectory (*trapeza*), the libraries, the hospitals, and the residences of the monks. The residences are arranged on several floors, rendered accessible by stacked porticoes and loggias, enlivened by long balconies supported by large wooden consoles or brackets, and by lovely little domes that crop up above the roofs of the prayer chapels.

The monasteries of Mount Athos can follow either the coenobitic or the idiorrhythmic organization. In the coenobitic monasteries, nobody possesses either money or private property, while everything (home, work, prayer, food) is done in common. A council of elders elects the monk who will hold power for the rest of his life, assisted by two or three advisers who alternate on an annual basis. In the idiorrhythmic monasteries, house and prayer are shared, but food and work are left to one's private initiative; the organization of the community is governed by an assembly with lifelong terms, which choose two or three monks a year to assign executive power. In reality, each monastery possesses its own history and its own peculiarities which are reflected in the various structures and architectural forms: the massive size of the Great Lavra, with its *katholikon* dominated by a vast dome, its exceedingly rich library, and the refectory decorated by frescoes by Frangos Castellanos; the lively colour palette of Panteleimonos, with green onion domes in the Russian Orthodox style; the austerity of the monasteries of Stavronikita, with its silhouette, so reminiscent of a military fortress, and of Karakalu, with its imposing defensive tower. The value of the monasteries of Mount Athos is also bound up with the hoard of Byzantine icons, frescoes, and mosaics contained in its buildings, as well as the exquisite patrimony of illuminated codices preserved in the libraries and the cast and chased fine metalwork (reliquaries, censers, and Gospel covers) assembled in the treasure chamber (*skevofylakion*) of each monastery.

View from the sea of the Monastery of Diocheiarion on Mount Athos.

View of the Panaghia Portaitissa Chapel in the Megisti Lavra.

On the facing page
The rocky pyramid of Mount Athos, standing more than 2,000 metres tall, has attracted the curiosity of mariners since ancient times, both because of its shape and because of its position looming sheer over the sea.

THE FRESCOES

The monasteries of Mount Athos contain a great number of frescoes, executed between the thirteenth and the eighteenth centuries by artists who, faithful to a tradition that developed over several hundred years, perpetuated a fixed scheme for the placement of the subjects in the churches and refectories. Thus, the interior of the church is always dominated by the half-length portrayal of *Christ Pantocrator* (the Omnipotent), depicted in the dome in the act of benediction, with a book in His left hand and the inscription *Ho On* ('He who is') in His halo, surrounded by prophets or Apostles. On the triumphal arch is located the image of the *etimasia* (preparation), that is, the empty throne of Christ, guarded by angels awaiting the Last Judgement. In the apse is the portrayal of the Virgin Mary and beneath that, to symbolize the eucharistic celebration, the communion of the Apostles. A place of great emphasis is reserved for the *desis* (supplication), that is, the depiction of Christ on His throne flanked by the Virgin Mary and Saint John the Baptist in the act of interceding on behalf of the Christian people: this scene, in fact, is located above the iconostasis, the carved and gilded wooden screen, covered with sacred images, which in all churches that follow the Byzantine rite separates the *vima* (that is, the area where the altar and apse are located, corresponding to the presbytery of a Latin church) from the rest of the sacred space.

Frescoes also adorn the narthex and the refectory of the monasteries, with scenes that could not be inserted into the triumphal and celestial decoration of the churches: the Last Judgement and other scenes taken from the Revelation, with demons and the damned, or the 'stairs of heaven', which portrays monks in the act of climbing up to heaven on a steep staircase. The frescoes of Mount Athos can be traced back to two schools: the so-called 'Macedonian' School, because it was driven by artists from Thessalonica, sinks its roots in the need for realism that developed in the first Byzantine 'renaissance' (thirteenth and fourteenth centuries), and is characterized by the strong need for dramatic effect and graphic power; it left its finest fruit on Mount Athos in the Monasteries of Vatopedi and Chilandari. The second school, called the 'Cretan' School after its leading exponent, Theophanes of Crete, affirmed itself following the fall of Constantinople and is distinguished by its tendency to idealize its subjects and by its refinement; Theophanes executed frescoes in the Great Lavra (1535), at Stavronikita (1546), and in the Chapel of Saint George in the Monastery of Aghiu Pavlu (1555).

On the facing page
The image of Christ
Pantocrator *issuing
a blessing, surrounded
by the symbols of
evangelists, dominates
the domes of the churches
in the monasteries
on Mount Athos.*

*The dome of the apse
always houses the image
of the* Virgin Mary
with the Christ *Child
and, beneath it,
the* Communion of the
Apostles, *symbolizing
the Eucharistic
celebration.*

*Detail of the frescoes
in the Monastery
of Koutloumousion.*

*One of the magnificent
scenes decorating
the churches of Mount
Athos depicts the funeral
of one of the saint monks.*

The Basilica
of San Francesco in Assisi

The Basilica of San Francesco, the mother basilica of the order of Minorite friars, is not only one of the most important Christian sites on earth, but is also a priceless artistic complex, noteworthy for its architectural structure, as well as the frescoed masterpieces on its walls.

Construction of the church began in 1228, in response to a wave of popular religious fervour prompted by the death of Saint Francis, two years earlier, which had immediately attracted crowds of pilgrims to his birthplace and the site of his tomb. This groundswell of devotion had, moreover, been encouraged by Pope Gregory IX (Pope from 1227 to 1241), who laid the cornerstone of the basilica. The basilica was destined to house the body of the future saint; Francis's canonization had been proclaimed in Assisi that same year, 1228. On 25 May 1230, construction of the lower basilica was already sufficiently under way that Francis's body was able to be moved there. In 1239 the bell tower was completed. In 1253, both churches – lower and upper – were consecrated by Pope Innocent IV (1243–54), who ordered that the substantial sums of money contributed in Assisi over the course of the next twenty-five years should all be spent on the decoration of the two buildings.

The church was conceived as the burial place of one of the most important saints in the history of Christianity, and so it was clearly destined to become the object of popular worship and a destination for great numbers of religious pilgrims. At Assisi, as had been the practice for many centuries in Christian sanctuaries, it was decided to place the tomb of the saint in the crypt. But because the designers of the church wished the space to be much larger and more impressive than crypts traditionally were, it was decided to build two stacked basilicas, linked by a staircase located in the left transept: the lower crypt and church were

intended for the veneration of Saint Francis, while the upper church, more spacious and brightly lit, was intended as a space for preaching, an activity of central importance by the doctrine of the mendicant orders. These strictly spiritual objectives were accompanied by a more concrete purpose: the determination on the part of the Popes to encourage the growth of the Franciscan order, which – following the first phase of suspicion and hostility towards Francis in the first part of his life – was viewed by Rome as a powerful religious and political ally, capable of strengthening ties between the Church and the lower classes of the cities.

Precisely because it was founded as a papal chapel, the basilica of Assisi harkened back to the models of the papal and episcopal chapels from the pre-Romanesque and the Romanesque periods, revealing the influence as well of Sainte-Chapelle in Paris, all distinguished by the stacking of two single-hall churches. Each of the two Assisi basilicas has a single aisle, a jutting transept, and a single apse pointing east. Outside they are supported by flying buttresses in the lower section and by soaring cylindrical counterforts on the upper section. This simple layout was, however, elaborated in the lower basilica, whose original plan was modified with the addition of side chapels and a second transept in the western section, making it capable of accommodating the growing number of pilgrims arriving from all over Europe.

The lower basilica has a cross-vault roof, laid down on round arches (only in the first bay is there a hint at a pointed, or ogive, arch) standing on short, massive pillars. Its flattened structure clearly conveys the idea that it serves as a basement for the upper church, supporting its weight and unloading its thrusts through massive counterforts and, especially, the solid flying buttresses on the exterior.

The Basilica of San Francesco, flanked by its campanile, belongs to a vast convent complex, consecrated by Pope Innocent IV in 1253.

On the facing page
The two stacked basilicas culminate in the east with a single apse, flanked by two massive cylindrical buttresses.

On pages 132–33
*Overall view
of the basilica.*

Above
*Crypt with the tomb
of Saint Francis.*

Below
*Giotto, detail of the face
of the demon in the scene
with* Saint Francis
Driving the Devils from
Arezzo, *upper basilica.*

On the facing page
*The large hall
of the upper basilica,
punctuated by square
bays covered by cross
vaults, combines
an attention to light
that is typical of Gothic
architecture, with the
solidity and 'murality'
of Romanesque
architecture, useful
in the execution of
the vast series of frescoes.*

These flying buttresses, set very low, have a very vague resemblance to the slender soaring shapes of the flying buttresses used in the same years on French construction sites.

The upper church appears as a vast, luminous space that perfectly fulfils the requirements of a place in which to preach to the huge crowds that gathered there. The broad aisle is punctuated by square bays, covered by pointed cross vaults. These vaults, marked by massive square-section ribbings, are supported by high pilaster strips lining the walls. The ogival arches, arranged transversely along the aisle, run at right angles to the large longitudinal arches, which cut into the upper section of the perimeter walls, framing the windows. The lower section of the walls, on the other hand, features a high continuous wall socle, broken only by jutting pillars and perfectly suited to housing the vast pictorial decoration, which is enhanced and rendered easily observable by the good lighting provided by the two-light windows in the upper section of the walls. These tall and narrow windows are actually thrust a little outward with respect to the socle

by a continuous walkway located just below them, and running all the way around the aisle. This layout of the walls, which has led many scholars to draw a link between the Basilica of San Francesco and the contemporary French cathedral of Angers, actually finds its first fully consistent and harmonious formulation in Assisi, as is documented by the masterly equilibrium between the soaring verticality of the arches and the horizontal qualities of the walls and the walkway. In fact, the Assisi basilica does present strong similarities to the Gothic architecture practised north of the Alps, especially in England and in north-west France, both geographic areas with which, we may presume, artistic exchanges were especially intense when the Minister General of the Franciscan order was an Englishman named Haymo of Faversham (1240–44).

The Basilica of San Francesco represents a prototype of what was imparted by Gothic architecture in Italy, a region where the traditions of building linked to classical and early Christian models were especially powerful. In Assisi, in fact, the achievements of Gothic ar-

chitecture did not culminate – as they did in northern Europe – in a series of technical experiments that aimed to empty and lighten the walls; rather they merged with the Romanesque heritage, characterized by a volumetric solidity and a tendency towards 'mural structure' that was the necessary basis for the pictorial decoration of the fresco form. The Basilica of San Francesco, therefore, became a model of the peculiar Gothic style of Italy, destined to great popularity especially in the Franciscan foundations.

Because of these structural decisions, the two basilicas were able to house a singularly extensive complex of frescoes of capital importance to the history of Italian painting, executed by the great artistic schools of the thirteenth and fourteenth centuries: from Cimabue to Giotto to Giotto's followers, from Simone Martini to the Roman masters, from Pietro Lorenzetti to the 'Master of Isaac'.

In the lower basilica, on the walls of the central nave, we find the earliest cycle of frescoes, done in the years 1250–60. Even though they are fragmentary, the series develops with exemplary symmetry the parallel between Saint Francis and Christ, a religious motif that was to be developed in other frescoes in the same church. In compliance with this iconographic programme, unified even though it was actually executed by different schools over considerable spans of time, in the great painted spaces of the cross vault and the transepts of the lower church, the *Poverello*, or 'poor little saint', is presented as a perfect imitator of Christ: from the *Maestà* by Cimabue (1277–80) to the fourteenth-century works by Giotto and his school, by Pietro Lorenzetti, and by Simone Martini. In the four webs, or ribbed vaults, that soar over the main altar, the splendid frescoes painted either by Giotto himself or else by an artist from his school (the 'Maestro delle Vele', or the so-called 'Par-

THE FRESCOES BY PIETRO LORENZETTI IN THE LOWER BASILICA

The left transept of the lower basilica houses a series of frescoes painted around 1319 by Pietro Lorenzetti, dedicated to the Passion, Death, and Resurrection of Jesus Christ. Realistic and dramatic details enliven *The Last Supper*, rendered more human by the depiction, on the left-hand side, of the kitchen and the fire, the servants, the plates and the domestic animals, or the episode of *Judas' Betrayal and Kiss*, set under a very modern night sky. The Passion, narrated with an extraordinary visual and didactic power, culminates with the *Crucifixion*, where the crosses of Christ and the two thieves loom above an excited crowd that is entirely indifferent to the event, with the exception of the Virgin Mary, the women, Saint John, and the Roman centurion. The importance attributed to this scene in the iconographic programme is documented by the fact that the *Crucifixion* by Lorenzetti is placed in an asymmetrical location with respect to the scene frescoed by Giotto in the other arm of the same transept, while both of the other scenes correspond in their locations to the large *Crucifixions* painted by Cimabue in the upper basilica.

At the foot of this great painting, Lorenzetti placed his triptych of the *Virgin of the Sunsets*, which refers to the scene on the facing wall in which we see *Saint Francis Receiving the Stigmata*. The three-part work takes its theme from a homily pronounced in Assisi in 1235, in which Pope Gregory IX, on the occasion of a solemn celebration in the square before the basilica, compared the saintliness of John the Evangelist, Jesus' favourite disciple, with that of Francis, and named the latter as the most perfect imitator of Christ: indeed we see a depiction of the Christ Child who, turning to His mother, seems to question Her about the saintliness of John and Francis; the Virgin Mary, with a gesture of Her right hand, answers Him by indicating Francis, worthy of being considered particularly saintly because he had received the stigmata.

A symbolic meaning appears in the macabre scene of *Judas Hanged*, which Lorenzetti placed at the end of the cycle of the Passion, in the corner of the staircase, almost as a warning to the pilgrims who were climbing to the upper basilica. The significance of this image is clarified by the content of the symmetrical fresco in the right transept, where Giotto depicted Death with the appearance of a skeleton: Francis approaches Death and calls it 'sister', stripping it of the royal crown on its head. The pilgrim who was leaving the basilica, then, received the clear message that traitors of Christ were inexorably subjected to death, while His followers, like Francis, were immune to death's power.

The left transept of the lower basilica houses the frescoes by Pietro Lorenzetti devoted to the Passion of Christ, *as well as the staircase that leads up to the upper church.*

Stained glass window in the apse, with the Stories of the Old Testament *and the* Stories from the Life of Jesus, *upper basilica.*

On the facing page
Pietro Lorenzetti,
The Last Supper *(detail),*
fresco, c. 1319, lower
basilica, left transept.

ente di Giotto' – Relative of Giotto – who may be identified as Stefano Fiorentino) are marked by a refined taste for allegory: the figure of *Saint Francis Enthroned* is associated with the personifications of the virtues that the Assisi-born saint managed to achieve through a long and ascending struggle – *Chastity*, *Obedience*, and *Poverty* – all depicted on the peaks of three high mountains. Chastity is portrayed as a woman protected in a tower, defended by two handmaidens (Purity and Strength) and by angels armed against the attacks of temptation. On the right, Francis invites three people to follow him: a nun, a monk with a tonsure, and a layman. The latter has been identified as Dante Alighieri, a Franciscan tertiary and a friend of Giotto's. The web of Chastity, in a reference to the innocence of childhood, introduces the frescoes of the right transept, devoted to the childhood of Christ. Obedience, assisted by Humility and Prudence and portrayed in the left-hand web, refers instead to the frescoes of the left

transept, devoted to the *Passion of Jesus Christ*. The allegory of Poverty, in turn, depicts Francis, at Christ's side, in the act of slipping a ring on to the finger of Lady Poverty, flanked by Hope and Charity. In the lower right-hand section we see one of the faithful in the act of offering a poor man his red cape embroidered with gold thread; in the upper section he is shown being carried up to heaven by an angel. On the left-hand side, in contrast, the appeal issued by an angel to forsake earthly pleasures is rejected by three people: the first of the three holds a hawk in his hand (a symbol of hunting and amusement), the second holds a purse (money), and the third holds a book (science and learning).

Also attributed to Giotto or to his school were the frescoes in the right transept that depict the *Incarnation* and the *Childhood of Jesus*. This cycle culminates with the scene of the Nativity, in which the painter, in order to illustrate the mystery of the two-fold nature of Christ, divine and human, depicts him

THE STORIES OF SAINT FRANCIS

When he painted the *Stories of Saint Francis* on the walls of the main aisle of the upper basilica at Assisi, Giotto was already the master of an exceedingly modern and mature language. A number of scholars, however, have suggested attributing the murals of Assisi not to Giotto, but instead to one or more anonymous artists (who are therefore termed, in accordance with the works attributed to them, the Master of the Legend of Saint Francis, the Master of the Funeral of Saint Francis, and the Master of Saint Cecilia), of various provenance but all linked by their training to the Roman milieu and the painting of Pietro Cavallini. Rome under Pope Nicholas III, who had shown a renewed interest in early Christian art by encouraging the restoration and reconstruction of ancient basilicas, in any case represents a major point of reference and a fertile starting ground for the artist of Assisi, whoever he may have been; if we accept Giotto as the artist of the *Stories* of the saint, considered quite likely according to the generally accepted view among art critics, then we must imagine that, in order to have been appointed to take part in the prestigious project under way in Assisi, the young painter must already have succeeded in attracting some attention in that city. Attribution is also an open question as far as the *Stories of Isaac* are concerned. These are frescoed on the northern wall of the main aisle, and are generally attributed to a Master of Isaac, likewise identified by most scholars as the young Giotto because of his masterful depiction of spatial volume and his modulation of light in a plastic function. The *Stories of Saint Francis*, which run along the entire right-hand wall of the church and continue in the counterfaçade and along the opposite wall (in reverse, back towards the altar), are set within a false loggia, punctuated by columns set on a slightly jutting base and supported by consoles. The twenty-eight panels describe the episodes of the life of the saint from his youth to his death, alternating historic episodes with the legends spread in popular hagiography, concluding with his posthumous miracles. Abandoning the hieratic and symbolic Byzantine-style images, with these frescoes Giotto brought the reality of everyday life – for centuries excluded from the figurative arts – into the world of painting.

The haloed head of Saint Francis, from the panel by Giotto depicting the Gift of the Mantle.

On the facing page Giotto in his Renunciation of Worldly Goods *succeeded in depicting with great realism both the half-naked body of Francis and the wrathful expression of his father.*

On page 140 Detail of the face of the Bishop of Assisi in the Renunciation of Worldly Goods.

On page 141 The roofs of the city of Arezzo, in the scene of Saint Francis Driving the Devils from Arezzo.

twice: a Jesus God-child, in Mary's arms and adored by the angels, and lower down, a Jesus human-child, washed and cared for by the women, watched over by Joseph, and visited by the shepherds. The Giottesque frescoes of the right transept are broken off in order to make room for the fresco executed earlier by Cimabue, which depicts the *Madonna in Throne Adored by Francis.*

The frescoes of the upper basilica are probably linked to a commission from Pope Nicholas IV (1288–92). Around 1288 he entrusted Cimabue and his school with the frescoes of the walls and the vaults of the transepts and of the choir, to tell the *Stories of Saints Peter and Paul*, the *Stories of Mary* and the *Apocalypse*. Today the frescoes are practically incomprehensible because of the fading and alteration of the colours, but the *Crucifixion* in the left transept shows how the master was capable of staging powerfully dramatic and engaging representations.

In the same years, artists from Rome, Florence, and from north of the Alps did the paintings in the nave, contrasting the archaic style of Cimabue with a new kind of painting, capable of suggesting with the techniques of illusionism a sense of spatial depth.

This lesson would be grasped and developed fully only by Giotto with his series of twenty-eight *Stories of Saint Francis*, which he frescoed in the years 1290–95, a work that was as revolutionary in stylistic terms as it was perfectly integrated in iconographic terms. With the S*cenes from the Old and New Testament* painted in the upper register of the nave, the Franciscan *Stories* in fact play upon the customary parallelism between biblical and evangelical episodes and Franciscan episodes.

After the earthquake that hit Umbria on 26 September 1997, the most severely damaged frescoes were subjected to a careful and thorough restoration.

The Palace and the park of Caserta

The massive structure of the Reggia di Caserta, or Palace of Caserta, and its park, were placed on the UNESCO World Heritage List in 2001.

The construction of the palace was undertaken at the behest of Charles III of Bourbon, King of Naples from 1734 to 1759, who played a decisive role, according at least to the tradition of official royal praise, in the design of the 'gran palazzo', whose main outlines he supposedly supplied to the architect, in collaboration with his consort Marie Amalie of Saxony. The choice of the site upon which to build a place for leisure for the Neapolitan court was determined by criteria that involved climate and other political and economic considerations for the proper use of lands that had hitherto been overlooked.

The monarch, who was born in Madrid and had certainly had opportunities to visit both Versailles and Schönbrunn, wished to construct a palace that combine the magnificence of those foreign constructions with the sober style of classical architecture. The palace was meant to be a place that was perfectly suited to house the court with all its spectacular luxury, but at the same time act as headquarters of the kingdom's political and administrative government. At first, the commission to design the palace was assigned to Mario Gioffredo, a renowned Neapolitan architect, who proposed a fortress-palace that was much more old-fashioned than what the monarch had in mind. Charles of Bourbon therefore thought of Nicola Salvi, the architect of, among other things, the Trevi Fountain in Rome; but Salvi was too old so turned down the job. Therefore, at the advice of Cardinal Gonzaga, the king chose Luigi Vanvitelli (1700–73), the architect who had supervised the construction of Saint Peter's Cathedral and the son of the renowned Dutch landscape painter Gaspard van Wittel.

The design phase of the Palace of Caserta is documented, nowadays, by only four surviving sketches. After a stay in Naples and long meetings with the king, Luigi Vanvitelli presented the final plan to the court on 22 November 1751. Here too there is very little graphic documentation: the project is based upon the great octagon of the vestibule with the royal staircase, from which two perpendicular axes extend. The plan of the building shows a rectangular shape, with the interior area subdivided by a cross into four courtyards. The front of the building extends over 252 metres while the sides are 202 metres in length; the height of the pediment over the main entrance is 41 metres. For the façade, Vanvitelli planned a plinth with smooth ashlars to the height of the mezzanine, upon which are giant-order Corinthian pilaster strips which frame the pedimented windows on the first and the second storeys; the palace is crowned by a continuous frieze out of which open the small windows of the upper floors, with a balustrade broken by triangular pediments corresponding with the entrances, both towards the city and towards the park.

Construction began in January 1752. Work proceeded quickly and in the summer of 1753 the foundations of the building were completed. In 1759, when Charles of Bourbon left for Spain, where he became king under the title of Charles III, the building was completed up to

View of the waterway, or via d'acqua, of the Palace of Caserta.

Detail of one of the marine deities in the Fontana di Eolo.

On the facing page
View of the monumental Staircase of Honour designed by Luigi Vanvitelli as a celebration of royal power.

View of the façade overlooking the park, extending 252 metres in length and 41 metres in height.

the main floor on the southern side. The monarch's departure undermined the progress of the great project, and work slowed down significantly, in part due to the prickly relationship between Vanvitelli and the regent Bernardo Tanucci, who disagreed with the grandiose ideas proposed by the architect and worked to scale down sharply the original plans, eliminating the corner towers and immense dome that was to arch over the vestibule. Nevertheless during the 1760s the vestibules, the great staircase, the Palatine Chapel, and the court theatre were all completed. The theatre was finished in 1768 and reproduces the layout of the Teatro San Carlo in Naples, with a horseshoe plan and an orchestra lowered beneath the entrance level so as to provide a better view for the occupants of the royal box. The theatre's rear portal, set behind the stage, can be opened so as to show, during performances, the setting offered by the park in the background.

The palace has its central structure in the upper and lower vestibules, the intersection point for the two axes and the ideal point of confluence of the four rectangular courtyards and the rooms on both floors. From the main entrance, you walk down the 'great portico', a gallery laid out along the north-south axis, linking the city with the park and creating a remarkable line of sight, of great visual and symbolic impact. The royal staircase, consisting of a monumental central flight of stairs and two long lateral ramps, is the architect's true masterpiece, a complex structure to celebrate the monarchic power of the House of Bourbon. On the first ramp, one is greeted by two marble lions, symbols of royal power, set at the first landing; on the wall of the pediment we find the depictions, set in niches, of the *Royal Majesty* at the centre, the work of the sculptor Tommaso Solari, the *Merit* by Andrea Violani on the left, and the *Truth* by Gaetano Salomone on the right. Beneath the

In the so-called 'Appartamento del Settecento', or Eighteenth-Century Apartment, is the renowned Sala dell'Autunno, or Hall of Autumn. The vault is decorated with a fresco by Antonio Dominici of The Meeting of Bacchus and Ariadne.

central niche is a door that led to the upper gallery, where musicians could remain out of sight while they performed during the entrance of the most important guests. The vault of the staircase is frescoed with a depiction of the *Palace of Apollo* and, in the tondoes, we find the allegorical depictions of the *Seasons* by the painter Gerolamo Starace Franchis. From the upper vestibule, octagonal in shape, with a deambulatory, extend the palace's reception halls, as well as the Palatine Chapel. The latter, built at the behest of Charles of Bourbon on the model of its counterpart at Versailles, was entirely incorporated into the building. The interior features a single nave and a gallery that stops at the apse, and then continues in the royal tribune; the entire space is decorated with gilded stuccoes and polychrome marble.

Luigi Vanvitelli designed the immense park behind the palace, built after his death by his son Carlo, according to Vanvitelli's sketches and landscape descriptions, laying out broad and sweeping views and perspectival vanishing points designed in conformity with the lay of the land. From the palace, one enters the vast and grassy parterre that culminates in a fountain, the Fontana della Margherita, with its simple, French-style form, consisting of a circular recessed basin with a central spray of water.

From here the slight slope of the hill, or Colle di Briano, begins, and down it runs the magnificent waterway, or 'via d'acqua', which draws the eyes of spectators towards the last fountain and, behind it, the waterfall. The Fontana dei Delfini, and the successive Fontana di Eolo, where the water plunges down from atop a semi-circular portico, with the god unleashing the winds depicted with puffed-out cheeks, captures the imagination of the visitor with its monumental and lavish sculptural decoration. Once you make your way past these fountains, the waterway runs up again, flanked by balustrades topped by

The huge Throne Room was not finished until 1847, with the execution of the fresco in the ceiling with The Laying of the Cornerstone of the Palace, *by the Neapolitan painter Gennaro Maldarelli.*

Portrait of Luigi Vanvitelli in a drawing by Francesco Solimena.

The royal box in the court theatre. It was the only part of the project of the palace to be completed under the supervision of Luigi Vanvitelli, and was inaugurated in 1769.

On the facing page The long gallery that runs the length of the central axis of the construction constitutes a 'telescopic' perspectival axis along the avenue leading up to the palace and the park.

LUIGI VANVITELLI

The architect Luigi Vanvitelli was born on 12 May 1700 in Naples, where his father, the great Dutch landscape painter Gaspard van Wittel, had moved in 1699 to decorate the apartments of the palace of the viceroy Luigi de la Cerda, the Duke of Medinacoeli. Trained as a painter from the teachings of his own father, he is mentioned with that title in the documents of the construction of Saint Peter's Cathedral up to 1736. Again, through his father, he entered into contact with the members of the Accademia di San Luca, where he had the opportunity to make the acquaintance of Filippo Juvarra. His first commission as an architect came from the Reverenda Camerata Apostolica, for the construction of the aqueduct of Vermicino. This project was then followed by a succession of assignments and projects that were not always completed, such as the project of the façade of the Basilica of Saint John Lateran and for the Trevi Fountain. In 1733 he was given by Cardinal Neri Corsini, nephew of Pope Clement XII, the commission to build a leper hospital in Ancona and to modernize the port of that city in the Marches. From the 1740s, Vanvitelli began a long series of projects in Rome and surrounding areas, including in 1749 the installation of Michelangelo's *Pietà* in the first chapel of Saint Peter's Cathedral and the stucco decoration of the tribune. In 1751 he was in Loreto to complete Bramante's loggia in the Palazzo Apostolico and to build a new bell tower. That same year, he received from the Pope permission to work for Charles of Bourbon on the design of the Palace of Caserta. At the end of the 1760s, he was summoned to Milan by Count Carlo Firmian, the plenipotentiary of Maria Theresa, for the renovation of the ducal/royal palace. He travelled there with Giuseppe Piermarini, who actually went on to build the palace after Vanvitelli's plan was rejected by the court in Vienna, because it was considered excessively ambitious. In the last years of his career, Vanvitelli went back to designing theatrical sets and spectacular party amusements. He died in 1773 at Caserta and was buried in the Church of San Francesco di Paola.

148

pairs of slaves bearing sea shells and goblets. Once you pass the Fontana di Cerere and the Fontana di Venere e Adone, you will stop before a monumental fountain, the Fontana di Diana e Atteone, with two sculptural groups: on the right, Diana surprised in her bath, and on the left Acteon, already partially transformed into a stag, being attacked by his own hunting dogs. On the right extends the English garden built at the behest of Queen Marie Caroline of Habsburg from 1786, marked by a naturalistic and picturesque layout, in sharp contrast with the layout of the French garden. On the interior are located such typical architectural features of the period as the Bagno di Venere (Bath of Venus), the fake ruin of a Roman temple, and a cryptoporticus.

The grandiose conception of the park required a considerable flow of water to feed the fountains and the waterfalls, as well as to meet the requirements of the palace itself. To this end, Vanvitelli designed and built the magnificent Acquedotto Carolino, inaugurated on 7 May 1762, which linked the springs of the Fizzo, through valleys and canals all the way to the Colle Briano, to feed the park's waterfall. One distinctive feature of the aqueduct is the bridge with its three levels of arcades spanning the distance between the Monte Longano and the Monte Garzano: when it was built, in 1759, it constituted the longest bridge in Europe, extending to 529 metres.

Inside the palace, which was never inhabited by Charles of Bourbon, the first rooms to be used were those now called the 'Appartamento del Settecento' (Eighteenth-Century Apartment), built at the behest of Ferdinand IV and by his consort Marie Caroline. The reception halls of this suite of rooms are called the Stanze delle Stagioni (Rooms of the Seasons) because of the allegorical depictions that decorate the ceilings of the various halls. Included in the eighteenth-century rooms are

On pages 148–49
Mariano Rossi, Marriage of Alexander the Great and Roxanne, *fresco, 1787, Sala di Alessandro.*

The second room in the Apartment of Queen Marie Caroline is called Gabinetto degli Stucchi (Cabinet of Stuccoes), and it features mirrored walls and stucco decorations with white and gilt festoons.

Fontana di Diana e Atteone. At the centre is the waterfall on the hill of Briano, which serves to operate the complex theatrical machinery of the fountains.

On the facing page
The sculptural group of Diana depicts the goddess, surrounded by nymphs, surprised in her bath, covering herself in a pose of modesty.

four small rooms that formed the apartment of Marie Caroline, marked by decoration in the rocaille style executed by Neapolitan crafts-men: the Stanza da Lavoro (Work Room), the Sala degli Specchi (Hall of Mirrors), the Gabi-netto degli Stucchi (Cabinet of Stuccoes), and the Gabinetto per Uso del Bagno (Cabinet of the Bath). The Palatine Library was also com-pleted during the reign of Ferdinand IV and Marie Caroline; the frescoes were done by the painter Heinrich Friedrich Fugger, summoned from Vienna, and are marked by the neo-clas-sical style, in sharp contrast to the Neapolitan culture, still tied to Baroque style.

The great reception rooms of the palace, designed by Luigi Vanvitelli, were completed only after his death by his son Carlo. After the Sala degli Alabardieri (Hall of the Hal-berdiers), the first of the antechambers of the royal apartments, come the Sala delle Guardie del Corpo (Hall of the Bodyguards), also known as the Sala dei Ricami (Hall of the Embroideries) for the richness of the stuc-coes adorning it and the Sala di Alessandro (Hall of Alexander), named after the ceiling fresco depicting the *Marriage of Alexander the Great and Roxanne,* painted by Mariano Rossi in 1787.

The work in this second section of the structure was begun during the years of the French rule of Joaquin Murat and continued after the return to the throne of Ferdinand I

of Bourbon and his successors, Francis I and Ferdinand II, the last ruler of the Kingdom of the Two Sicilies, overthrown by Giuseppe Garibaldi's army in 1859. The design was assigned to Antonio Di Simone, who had already been named the architect 'for the Palace of Naples and the structures located in Caserta, Belvedere, and Carditello and all related sites'. The series of rooms opens with the Sala di Marte (Hall of Mars), its ceiling adorned with a fresco of *The Death of Hector and the Triumph of Achilles* by Antonio Galliano, dating from 1815; next comes the Sala di Astrea (named after Astraea, a Titaness and the goddess of justice) and the Sala del Trono (Throne Room). The last hall, the largest in the palace, remained undecorated until the reign of Ferdinand I, who commissioned the Ticinese architect Pietro Bianchi, who was already working at Naples, to do the job. Work began in 1827, and underwent various halts due to technical problems, and then again upon the death of the king, in 1830. It was not until 1839 that the architect Gaetano Genovese, already working on the royal palace of Naples, was able to resume construction, completing it in 1847, and finally concluding work upon the palace itself.

On the facing page
In the English Gardens, built at the behest of Queen Marie Caroline, we find the Swan Lake with, in the centre, the fake ruins of the Roman Temple.

The imposing hulk of the aqueduct, or Acquedotto Carolino, inaugurated on 7 May 1762, brought the waters from the springs of the Fizzo.

Castel del Monte

Castel del Monte, one of the most solemn and magnificent monuments of the Middle Ages, is the largest and most important of the castles built at the behest of Frederick II of Swabia, King of Naples from 1208 to 1250 (and Holy Roman Emperor from 1220). The castle takes its name from the fact that it stands on an isolated highland in the Murge, and it enjoys splendid panoramic views of part of Apulia, Basilicata, and the Adriatic coast.

In 1240, its construction must have been close to completion because, as we read in a surviving document, Frederick ordered material needed to construct the roof. The castle was used as a residence by the imperial family (wedding celebrations were held there in 1249 for the emperor's illegitimate daughter Violante) and as a prison. After 1268, with the fall of the Swabians, Charles I of Anjou imprisoned there the three sons of Manfredi, Frederick's illegitimate son; even later the castle was mostly used as a prison. It then fell into the hands of the Spanish and, after 1552, it was passed to the Counts Carafa of Ruvo, whereupon it became the retreat of several aristocratic families of Andria during the pestilence of 1656. It was then abandoned, and from the eighteenth century it became a hideout for brigands, shepherds, and political outlaws until, in 1876, it was purchased by the Italian state which undertook the most urgent restorations. More careful restoration work was begun in 1928 and more recently in the 1980s.

Castel del Monte represents a successful eclectic synthesis of the architectural models of Graeco-Latin antiquity, the medieval models of Cistercian and Norman architecture, and the models of the desert fortresses and the fortified monasteries of the Near East and Northern Africa. It appears as a monumental block with an octagonal shape, at the eight corners of which stand eight towers with the same shape. A floor-marking cornice surrounds the entire structure, indicating the division of the building into two storeys. Each wall, framed by two towers, presents two windows towards the exterior: a single-light, round-arch window on the lower floor (except for the eastern and western sides, the former being occupied by the main portal and the latter being occupied by the service entrance), and a twin-light window on the upper floor (with the exception of the northern side, which features a three-light window). Dotting the towers are numerous loopholes which provide light to the interior spiral staircases, the service facilities, and the interior rooms.

On the main façade of the castle, two symmetrical flights of stairs, rebuilt in 1928, lead up to the majestic portal made of coralline breccia, clearly inspired by classical models. It is in fact composed of slender fluted pillars with Corinthian capitals, surmounted by an architrave, silhouetted at the bottom, which in turn supports a cuspidated tympanum.

The courtyard that opens up in the centre of the castle repeats in its octagonal shape the structure of the building. Each of the eight walls has, high up, a round blind arch, set on corner pilasters; the compactness of the walls is broken by three unadorned portals that link the open space with the rooms on the ground

Castel del Monte takes its name from its location, set on an isolated highland in the Murge region.

Figured capital located in the seventh hall.

On the facing page
A crystalline geometric rigour dominates the structure of Castel del Monte, a monumental block with an octagonal form, with eight ctagonal towers on each of its eight corners.

The courtyard that opens up in the centre of the castle repeats in its octagonal shape the rigorous mathematical structure of the building.

FREDERICK II AND CASTEL DEL MONTE

The Emperor Frederick not only spoke various languages, but was also interested in astronomy, mathematics, and the natural sciences. He ordered the translation into Latin of the works of Aristotle, Ptolemy, and Averroe, he founded the University of Naples, and he gave new vigour to the medical school of Salerno. He was passionately interested in literature and the arts; he protected the poets of the Sicilian School and he surrounded himself with the finest artists of his time, from his own kingdom, but with Arabs and Greeks as well. His complex personality has been interpreted in various ways and some have sought possible symbolic meanings of his actions and the buildings that are associated with him. While most historians consider Castel del Monte to be a building erected by the sovereign for specific, concrete reasons (to reproduce the ancient art and architecture he so loved, to create a headquarters, safe from attack, for the government of his realm, to devote himself to his favourite pursuits, hunting, loving, and fine cooking), some scholars consider this building to be a product of the most refined medieval symbolism, influenced by the esoteric culture of the Knights Templar and the mystery-based sects of the East. In their view, the absence of kitchens, cellars, stables, moats, drawbridge, or any other defensive elements typical of medieval castles rules out the possibility that Castel del Monte served any civil or military functions and leads them to believe that it was instead a sort of secular temple, designed and built with a view, for instance, to the shadows of the sun cast on certain days of the year, as well as according to principles of numerology and astrology. Although the octagonal shape that echoes the shape of the imperial crown has triggered all sorts of intriguing symbolic interpretations (and there can be no doubt that Frederick did mean to allude to the allegorical significances bound up in the number eight), it should be emphasized that Castel del Monte, *castrum* as Frederick himself described it in one document, was certainly built as a castle, that is, a fortified structure set within the intricate network involved in the control of a territory, with residential, representative, and secondary symbolic functions as well as a prison, a typical function of castles, which the building served during the emperor's lifetime.

The octagonal shape of Castel del Monte seems to mimic the shape of the imperial crown.

A fundamental role is played at Castel del Monte by the colours of the materials utilized: the pinkish white of the limestone used for the architectural structure, the white of the marble around the windows on the first floor and the warm shades of the coralline breccia which characterizes the main portal and the exterior doors and windows.

floor, and by the three door/windows of the upper floor, which were probably once linked by a suspended wooden structure.

The materials used in the construction of the castle play a very important role: the pinkish white of the limestone that characterized the architectural structures and a number of decorative details goes with the white of the marble in the windows on the first floor and the warm nuances of the coralline breccia, a conglomerate of red earth and limestone, used in the main portal and in the cornices of the outer doors and windows. The interior rooms of the building were, in the past, sheathed in red breccia on the ground floor and in marble on the upper floor, while the fireplaces, the door jambs and the frames of doors and windows were also made of breccia. The lovely interplay of colours was further enriched by the mosaics that covered floors and vaults, and by the paintings that may have decorated the walls on the first floor.

The interior extends over two storeys, each of which has eight trapezoidal rooms, all of them similar in size but serving different functions, determined by the presence of fireplaces, service structures and corridors placed in the towers. The ceilings of these rooms are built, in the square central section, with a ribbed cross vault, and, in the two lateral triangles, with two pointed-arch half-barrel vaults. The ribbing served a purely decorative function, underscored by the presence of a figurative keystone in the vault, different in each room (on the ground floor, in the seventh hall, the head of a faun framed by grapes and vine leaves; on the first floor, in the seventh and the eighth rooms, four little human heads and four hybrid heads, intertwined, and in the 'throne room', the bearded face of a faun, or else of an astrologer or philosopher). On the ground floor, the central square room of the roof is emphasized by four lateral semi-columns

The six-part vault on the seventh hall of the upper floor of the castle features telamons, supporting the ribbing, portrayed in unusual poses and attitudes.

The Bust of an Emperor *in the Museo Civico of Barletta, dating from later than 1230, mirrors the typology and schema of an ancient imperial portrait. If the face of the statue, as is believed, shows the features of Frederick II, this would be the first individual portrait of post-classical art.*

On the facing page
The main portal of the castle, made of coralline breccia, reveals its classical inspiration in the fluted pillars surmounted by Corinthian capitals, in the shaped architrave and in the cusped crowning tympanum.

made of coralline breccia, as are the capitals adorned with carved leaves and the cornices of the windows and the doors. Nothing remains of the original breccia wall facing, while in the eighth hall fragments survive of the geometric intarsias in white marble and slate.

You reach the upper storey via the spiral staircase of two towers: the third – accessible from the fourth room – known as the Torre del Falconiere (Falconer's Tower), with a tripartite vault supported by two consoles depicting the head of a faun and the head of a woman; and the seventh tower – accessible from the eighth room – with a six-part vault supported by telamons depicted in poses and stances of great originality. The fifth tower contains the only staircase that leads without interruption to the terrace, from which one can enjoy a magnificent panoramic view.

The upper storey displays a great devotion to detail in its decoration. With the exception of the second hall, which has a three-light window, there is a twin-light window of clear Gothic inspiration in each hall, while the light ribbings on the vault run up from slender bundled columns surmounted by plant-motif capitals. Along the walls run a marble bench and a floor-marking cornice at the base of the vaults. It is customary to imagine that Frederick must have met with the wise men of his court in what is traditionally described as the 'throne room', situated on the eastern side.

The Church of Santa Maria delle Grazie and the refectory in Milan

The wealth of fifteenth-century Milan, along with the city's new political and cultural importance, was continually increased by exchanges with areas across the Alps, encouraging the acceptance of numerous 'outsider' architects (German and French for the construction of the Duomo; Florentines like Filarete, Ferrini, and Leonardo; Umbrians such as Bramante), though never to the point of falling into the passive adoption of imported styles; these artists influenced the Milanese architecture of those years in a radical way, powerfully affecting the development of the craftsmen and artists led by Giovanni and Guiniforte Solari.

The last two decades of the fifteenth century were entirely innovative, oriented towards the new forms of the Renaissance, and dominated by the figure of Lodovico the Moor, client of Bramante and Leonardo. The architecture became distinctly classical, based explicitly upon the observation of antiquity and the study of the monuments of late antiquity and early Christianity in Milan.

The Church of Santa Maria delle Grazie was built at the behest of the Dominicans in 1463 by Guiniforte Solari, in keeping with a traditional layout that called for a double width of the central nave with respect to the narrower side aisles, side chapels and a cross vault set on pointed arches; the exterior is conceived as a shell dominated by the two tones of the terracotta and the white plaster. On 29 March of 1492, at the express behest of Lodovico the Moor, the first stone was laid in the rebuilding of the tribune; the duke in fact wished to use the church as the mausoleum of the Sforza family and he assigned the project to Donato Bramante, who probably also worked on the façade, adding the porch. On the simple façade, punctuated by buttresses, there are oculi and single-light windows. Jutting out from the centre is the marble portal thought to have been designed and built by Bramante (1488–90), with a lunette decorated with an eighteenth-century fresco. The tribune built by Bramante consisted of a cubic base supported by corner counterforts with two side exedrae which function as apses, while on the third side the parallelepiped of the presbytery is attached to the structure. The decoration reproduces the white-and-red two-tone motif, establishing continuity with the previously existing building; it is however organized in strictly geometric forms, even if the array of adornment clearly resembles the Lombard tradition. Running along the exterior moulding are marble tondoes depicting the heraldic crests of the House of Sforza, while above it runs a series of rectangular bays set within terracotta cornices. On a line with the apses, the facing of the walls is punctuated by pilaster strips and candelabra, set upon a socle with *clipei* depicting saints. The highest order is broken up into panels featuring oculi at the centre of each; set upon this fascia is the tambour, by Amadeo, with sixteen sides, subdivided into two orders. On the first is a series of architraved twin-light windows, while on the upper we find a loggia set on slender twin arches made of polychrome windows, upon which rests directly the domed roof.

The fresco decoration that adorns the vaults over the aisles re-emerged following the late nineteenth-century restorations. The large lunettes over the nave contain thirteen tondoes painted in foreshortened perspective, depicting busts of Dominican saints. On the pillars of the side aisles, generally attributed to Bernardino Butinone, Bernardino Zenale, and Donato Montorfano, we can also admire Dominican saints.

Along the right-hand side aisle, the fourth chapel is decorated with transferred frescoes by Gaudenzio Ferrari and his workshop por-

Aerial view of the urban area with the complex of Santa Maria delle Grazie.

On the facing page
The magnificent tribune designed by Donato Bramante and constructed from 1492.

traying the *Flagellation* and the *Ecce Homo*; on the right-hand wall is the *Crucifixion*. Proceeding towards the main altar, one enters the tribune, square in plan with four large arches that, merging with the pendentives, support the dome, set on a low tambour, punctuated by sixteen pilaster strips, with false twin-light windows. The graffito decoration of the entire tribune, rediscovered by Piero Portaluppi in the course of his restoration during the 1930s, and partly restored, is thought to be by the hand of Bramante himself. At the far end of the tribune extends the presbytery, also square in plan and covered with an umbrella vault. In the trabeation and in the pendentives, Amadeo executed, in stucco, busts of the Evangelists and the Doctors of the Church. The choir dates back to the first decade of the sixteenth century.

At the end of the left aisle is the Chapel of Santa Maria delle Grazie, the original core of the complex, built at the behest of Gaspare Vimercati. Passing through the chapel and the adjoining new sacristy, a small portal leads to the little cloister, attributed to Bramante himself and built immediately after the tribune. It is square and features five bays per side, punctuated by arches decorated with terracotta lintels. From this cloister, one enters the old sacristy, completed in 1499, which preserves on its interior intarsiated armoires and paintings; it is one of the finest pieces of cabinet work commissioned by the Sforza family at the end of the fifteenth century, and it is thought that Bramante may have designed it. Between 1553 and 1778, the convent was the headquarters of the Tribunal of the Inquisition; later, with the suppression of religious orders by the Habsburg Emperor Joseph II, the building was converted into a military barracks. At the end of the nineteenth century, Luca Beltrami completed the restoration work that had been begun a few decades before, with the isolation of the monumental sections, the church and the convent, from the constructions that had grown up around them over the course of the centuries. In the years 1934–37, Piero Portaluppi undertook a restoration project to eliminate the neo-classical decorations in the apse. In 1943, the monumental complex was hit during the bombing of Milan, and the main cloister and the chapter hall were destroyed. The church also lost part of its main body, though it was later reconstructed.

Leaving the church, we emerge on to the Piazza Santa Maria delle Grazie, overlooked by a series of buildings that housed the offices of the Inquisition, through which we reach the convent's refectory where, between 1494 and 1498, Leonardo da Vinci painted *The Last Supper*; on the far walls, Montorfano painted in the same years a monumental *Crucifixion*. The complex of Santa Maria delle Grazie was added to UNESCO's World Heritage List in 1980.

Façade of the Church of Santa Maria delle Grazie, built by Guiniforte Solari for the Dominican Order in 1463.

On the facing page
View of the tribune and the lantern designed by Bramante, as seen from the old cloister.

The luminous interior of Bramante's square-plan tribune, featuring the graffito decoration.

THE LAST SUPPER

All that survives of the original painting by Leonardo da Vinci, brought back to light through a lengthy and recent restoration, adorns the northern wall of the refectory. Here, between 1494 and 1498, the artist illustrated, in an unprecedented level of physiognomic research and luministic rendering, one of the moments of the greatest emotional tension in the narrative of the Gospel. Although it is in fact typical to portray *The Last Supper* in the decoration of refectories, in part because of the allusion to the Eucharistic theme of sacrifice and therefore to the institution of the Mass, Leonardo chose to represent the instant that followed Christ's announcement that one of His Apostles would betray Him, when the twelve Apostles, looking at one another in a moment of wild surmise, stand in bewilderment. Generally, the iconography called for the depiction of the successive moment, when Jesus identified the traitor, offering Judas bread dipped in wine. The scene, set in a hall with a coffered ceiling, adorned with false tapestries on the walls, opened at the far end by three windows and lit, principally, from the left, as it must have been in reality, allowed Leonardo to reproduce many phenomena that he had observed in nature, such as the propagation of concentric waves when a stone is dropped in the water, similar in mechanism to the effect of Christ's words on the Apostles. The result, even if it has been blurred by centuries of tortuous restorations, still strikes the viewer with its great emotional power.

On pages 164–65
Leonardo da Vinci,
The Last Supper, *wall painting, 1494–98, Milan, Refectory of the Monastery of Santa Maria delle Grazie.*

On the facing page
Detail of The Last Supper, *with Saints Bartholomew, James the Less, Andrew, Judas, Peter and John.*

The Apostles Thomas, James the Great, Philip and Matthew occupy the right-hand side of the table.

Villa d'Este at Tivoli

View of the main avenue of the park with a view of the palace in the background.

On the facing page *Fontana di Nettuno. The basin is enlivened by high sprays of water and by little waterfalls. On the balcony that overlooks the basin stands a monumental architectural elevation, designed by Pirro Ligorio and occupied by a hydraulic organ.*

Celebrated for its splendid gardens and the fountains in its park, the villa that was built at the behest of Cardinal Ippolito II d'Este (1509–72) stands at the westernmost point of the little town of Tivoli, which contains important classical relics and sites. To the north of the town, in fact, stand the Temple of the Sibyl and the Temple of Vesta, overlooking the charming waterfalls of the River Aniene, and a few kilometres from the settlement are the monumental ruins of Hadrian's Villa. The ruins of the Temple of Hercules Victorious, from the second half of the first century B.C., are instead located in the general area selected by the cardinal for his own magnificent residence. This is where the thirteenth-century Palazzo del Governo, or town hall, once stood, built in the structure of a Benedictine monastery linked to the Romanesque Church of Santa Maria Maggiore; in 1550 the building was assigned to Cardinal d'Este, who that year had been named Governor of Tivoli.

The son of Lucretia Borgia and Duke Alfonso I d'Este, Ippolito boasted close blood ties to the King of France, François I, who supported him at length in his ecclesiastical career, even hosting him at his own court for a certain period as an adviser. A refined patron of the arts and collector, the cardinal assembled a spectacular court around him, a court that was at the same time also an academy and an artistic coterie. A lover of Roman antiquities, of music, and of architecture, Ippolito had another residence at Fontainebleau and a villa in Rome, where he assembled a noteworthy collection of sculptures and where he ordered the construction of splendid gardens. When he took possession of the see at Tivoli, the cardinal undertook a campaign of expansion and renovation of the ancient palace, entrusting its design to the Neapolitan architect Pirro Ligorio, who created for the patron of

the arts a villa surrounded by exquisite gardens. Construction was interrupted in 1555 when the cardinal, accused of simony, was stripped of the see of Tivoli; work resumed in 1559, after Ippolito had been rehabilitated by the new Pope, Pius IV.

The palace has a fairly simple structure: the central structure overlooks the garden and is embellished by a central element with a loggia within which two flights of stairs converge, in keeping with a scheme inspired by the designs of Michelangelo for the Senatorial Palace of the Campidoglio. At either end of this ceremonial reception wing are located the private apartments, which constitute the sides arms of the porticoed internal courtyard. The rooms, small in size, were all decorated with stuccoes and frescoes in the Mannerist style, executed by, among others, Federico Zuccari and Girolamo Muziano, and displaying an elegant alternation between mythological themes, landscapes, and grotesque subjects.

The most substantial portions of the work carried out by Pirro Ligorio were certainly devoted to the park, which should be considered an integral part of the house; massive hydraulic projects were undertaken as well as earthmoving and terracing. Over the years the existing formal garden gradually took shape, consisting of a flat lower area and two other terraced areas that climbed up towards the villa. The space, constructed perspectively, is punctuated by the insertion of fountains, complex architectural and sculptural arrays that characterize the entire complex. Once enough land had been bought to constitute the square lot of some five hectares occupied by the garden, work began in 1560 to provide the water needed for the fountains of the park: an aqueduct was built to take advantage of the neighbouring springs on Mount Sant'Angelo and in 1564–65 an underground conduit was run under the city to convey water from the River Aniene. The ground

*Fontana dei Dragoni.
Set in the centre
of the garden as a scenic
element dominating
the main axis of the park,
this fountain is enclosed
within a horseshoe-
shaped staircase.*

*Fontana della Rometta.
The fountain, a
miniature reconstruction
of ancient Rome,
enlivened by sprays
and jets of water, is
a remarkable invention
by Pirro Ligorio.*

of the garden was entirely remodelled, creating a steep slope at the foot of the ancient monastery and another, shallower slope on the left-hand side of the area. With the landfill that had been excavated, a large terrace was built on the right-hand side, making use of the city walls as retaining walls. Work on the construction of fountains and grottoes continued until 1572, when the garden was visited by Pope Gregory XIII. An etching done in 1573 by Étienne Dupérac presumably illustrates the original design of the villa and the garden, documenting the elements that were modified at later dates or even left unbuilt.

Originally, the entrance to the park was meant to be located in an uphill portal; the transverse east-west axis established by the portal was underscored by the presence of fishponds and by exedrae adorned with allegorical statues overlooking a belvedere above the neighbouring valley. A wooden pergola in the form of a cross subdivided the level downhill area into four square flower–beds, equipped with little pavilions in which to halt and linger;

at the intersection of the two arms of the pergola was set a large pavilion, later replaced by a rotunda of cypresses which now constitutes the chief botanical jewel of the garden.

Nowadays, you pass through the garden from south to north, that is descending from the villa along the principal axis, criss-crossed by secondary axes at the ends of which are the most important fountains of the complex. A first important avenue is the Viale delle Cento Fontane, nearly 150 metres in length: the route is skirted by a line of fountains featuring jets of water that spurt from obelisks, eagles, little ships, and French lilies. The water pours into a single canal shaped like a trough from which, through spouts shaped like chimaera heads, it flows into a second canal located beneath it. The charming overall setting was completed by decorated panels with subjects taken from the *Metamorphosis* by Ovid. Upstream, the avenue leads to the so-called Fontana dell'Ovato, named for the oval shape of its basin, surmounted by artificial grottoes and fed by a huge waterfall. The fountain is a

The Fontana delle Aquile features the symbols of the Este family, the eagles (hence the name), and lilies.

Detail of the Fontana della Madre Natura (Fountain of Mother Nature) with a depiction of the Diana of Ephesus.

PIRRO LIGORIO

The Neapolitan architect, painter and antiquarian Pirro Ligorio (*c.* 1513–83) worked in Rome as well as at Tivoli and Ferrara; his body of work reflects his distinct interest in the classical world, expressed both through excavations, studies and research, and with his effort to reproduce in his buildings the splendour of ancient Rome. After entering the service of Pope Paul IV in 1555, he built in the Vatican Gardens the Casino of Pope Pius IV, with a façade richly encrusted with stuccoes inspired by the decorative motifs of ancient sarcophagi, and he supervised the completion of the monumental courtyard of the Belvedere. During his work at Tivoli, he oversaw on behalf of Cardinal Ippolito the excavations of the Hadrian's Villa, extracting from it, among other things, numerous ancient marble reutilized for the fountains of the d'Este gardens. At the end of 1568, he was named the court antiquarian of Alfonso II d'Este, and he moved to Ferrara, where he spent most of his time overseeing the organization of the ducal collections of antiquities. A substantial body of manuscripts document his studies; the most significant core of that collection, some thirty volumes, is housed in Turin. His notes range widely over various subjects: epigraphs, coins, topographic reconstructions, mythology, music, customs and ways of antiquity.

Detail of the frescoed ceiling of the Stanza delle fatiche d'Ercole (Room of the Labours of Hercules), executed by Girolamo Muziano and assistants. The decoration of the little salon, in the Mannerist style, includes little scenes with mythological themes, alternating with landscapes, allegorical figures, and grotesques.

Pirro Ligorio probably also laid out the iconographic programme of the frescoes of Tivoli, focusing on themes closely linked to those developed in the sculptural groups and in the paths through the garden.

THE INTERIOR DECORATION OF THE PALACE

The themes of the paintings and the decorations that adorn the interior of the villa correspond to the complex iconographic programme, possibly developed by Ligorio himself and strictly linked to the themes that had been developed in the sculptural groups and in the paths through the garden. The most prestigious room is the great reception hall on the lower floor, where the frescoes depict an illusionistic colonnade looking out over a landscape; the views illustrate the possessions of the cardinal, including the villa at Tivoli itself. On the ceiling, above a powerfully foreshortened fake loggia, is the scene of the *Wedding of Amor and Psyche*; the elegant decorative effect is obtained with the insertion of a dense network of grotesques, studded with aedicules and ovals framed by ribbons. In the four corners of the ceiling a broad vertical fascia adorned with figures is emblazoned with two heraldic crests of the House of Este in stucco. The hall was decorated in a first phase (1565–66) by Girolamo Muziano and subsequently (1567), for the execution of the ceiling, by Federico Zuccari and assistants. In the great hall, there is a rustic fountain flanked by caryatids and adorned with multicoloured mosaics dated from 1568; the landscape painted in the panels reproduces a view of the Tiburtine Temple of Vesta.

In the great central hall: the rustic fountain. Flanked by caryatids and adorned by multicoloured mosaics and encrustations, the fountain contains a frescoed view of the Tiburtine Temple of Vesta.

One of the frescoed views in the great central hall, decorated by Girolamo Muziano and Federico Zuccari. The pictorial decoration depicts an illusionistic colonnade looking out over the possessions of the cardinal.

A sphinx set alongside the Viale delle Cento Fontane. In a striking overall view, a series of obelisks, eagles, chimaerae, ships, and French lilies produce the sprays of water that fill the long fountain.

The She-Wolf Suckling Romulus and Remus, detail of the Fontana della Rometta. In the complex system of symbols of the garden, the Fontana della Rometta constitutes a clear tribute to the glory of ancient Rome, the object of the antiquarian passions of the Cardinal Ippolito and of Pirro Ligorio.

On the facing page Fontana di Tivoli, also known as the Fontana dell'Ovato. The basin is surmounted by man-made grottoes and is fed by a large waterfall, at the summit of which is a statue of the Tiburtine Sibyl.

homage to the city of Tivoli, evoked by the presence of mountains and allegorical statues that personify the Rivers Anio, Albuneo, and Erculaneo, represented by the Tiburtine Sibyl; in the niches of the exedra-shaped nymphaeum that surrounds the basin, we see statues of nymphs carved by Giovanni Battista della Porta, to designs by Pirro Ligorio. At the far end of the Viale delle Cento Fontane is the Fontana della Rometta, clearly the product of the fanciful antiquarian taste of the designer of Villa d'Este: this miniature reconstruction of ancient Rome, which occupies a large semi-circular space, is enlivened by sprays and jets of water.

Another transverse axis, occupied by three large fish-ponds, culminates upstream with the Fontana di Nettuno, whose broad basin is enlivened by high jets of water and little waterfalls; on the balcony that overlooks the basin is set a monumental architectural elevation, designed by Ligorio, decorated with caryatids and telamons and surmounted by an eagle, the symbol of the House of Este. At

the centre of the spectacular array, in the Baroque style, a hydraulic organ is set within a niche, and many years ago music would be produced naturally by the blast of air that was pushed out by the violent rush of water into a round cavity; associated with the organ were a number of statues of automata, which were also put into movement mechanically by the rushing water. Similar devices enlivened the Fontana della Civetta, where the hydraulic mechanism put an owl and a group of birds into motion, with birdsong produced by small metal pipes located in the nymphaeum behind it. At the centre of the garden, along the main axis, is set, as a dominant piece of theatrical scenery, the Fontana dei Dragoni, enclosed by a horseshoe-shaped staircase; on the interior of the circular basin is set a sculptural group composed of four dragons, which echoes the theme of the heraldic crest of Pope Gregory XIII, and which were built just before his visit to the garden.

The present-day physiognomy of the park is due, to a minor degree, to the subsequent in-

terventions of Gian Lorenzo Bernini who, in the seventeenth century, added the Fontana del Bicchierone (*c.* 1660), situated along the main avenue at the base of the palace's terrace: here the sprays of water overflow from a vast chalice, pouring down into a sea shell-shaped basin. The Baroque sculptor and architect also designed and built the naturalistic waterfall that was added beneath the hydraulic organ, which pours into the basin of the Fontana di Nettuno, in imitation of the renowned Tiburtine waterfall of the River Aniene.

The complex of Villa d'Este has been over the years the object of numerous studies and interpretations, with special reference to the garden, which have revealed in some cases the architectural and landscaping models in question, and in other cases the complex celebratory and symbolic significances. It is in fact quite evident, in the light of the tradition of the Mannerist garden, that the design of the park reflects an elaborate synthesis of allegorical and philosophical elements, legible on different levels and entirely in keeping with the cultural climate of which Pirro Ligorio and his client were authoritative exponents. One example of the complexity of the possible interpretations is offered by the writings in which Ligorio, while reflecting on the nature of fountains, identified various symbolic values of water, based on interpretative approaches that were quite close to those dictated by scholastic philosophy: according to the secular interpretation offered by Ligorio, the element of water is in its physical corporeality the physical and vital lymph of the garden, but it is also a symbol of human life and the passage of time, and, in its infinite characterizations arrayed throughout the park of the villa, it mirrors the variety of nature and of human destiny. And in effect the water of the numerous minor and major fountains is presented in countless aspects: soaring jets, burbling springs, wreaths, cascades, and broad veils of water spraying in fan-like sheets. In the ancient world, the sense of marvel and wonder prompted by the presence of water was increased by the surprise of the *scherzi*, sudden jets of water that would leap forth upon the passage of visitors.

As for the reference to learned models in the definition of the layout and landscaping of the garden, scholars have especially pointed out the presence of motifs of classical origin, due to the archaeological and antiquarian interests of the architect and the client. It can be noted, however, that the garden appears as a full-fledged *castrum*, organized in accordance with a rigid gridwork of roads at the top of which is the aristocratic palace, corresponding to the ancient *praetorium*; the layout of the park, for that matter, seems to provide a continuation of the Roman layout of ancient Tibur. Another model that has been mentioned more than once in connection with the theatrical succession of spaces and the monumental dimensions is that of the Roman baths, which were also a site of *otium* and leisurely thought. Lastly, it should be taken into account that many of the iconographic and compositional characteristics of the Tivoli gardens have their immediate predecessors in the parks of the so-called *delizie estensi*, villas built on the outskirts of Ferrara as early as the fifteenth century.

On the facing page
View of the main avenue through the garden. The design of the park reflects an elaborate assembly of allegorical and philosophical elements, which can be read on different levels, and entirely in keeping with the cultural climate of Italian Mannerism.

View of the park of Villa d'Este; detail of the frescoes in the great central hall, with a view of the Viale delle Peschiere, with the Fontana di Nettuno and the hydraulic organ in the background.

The Convent of Christ in Tomar

The monumental complex of the Convent of Tomar, founded in the twelfth century, constitutes an important document of the developments of Portuguese architecture from the Middle Ages to the sixteenth century, from the *manuelino* style to the Italian-influenced trends of the full Renaissance. The oldest core of this abbey also boasts special features of interest, inasmuch as it is an example of elevated formal perfection of ecclesiastical architecture.

The birth of the convent dates back to 1159, when King Alfonso I of Portugal donated the site to Gualdim Pais, Grand Master of the Order of the Knights Templar in Portugal. In keeping with their vocation, both religious and military, the Knights Templar undertook the construction in 1160 of a fortified abbey, dominated by a castle shaped like an irregular pentagon, with an isolated central donjon. In the course of the Turkish invasions, the fortress of the Knights Templar withstood the siege of the Almohads (1190), becoming a defensive bulwark for the little city that had grown up around it.

Adjoining one of the walls of the castle was built in 1160 a church as well, whose construction stretched out until the middle of the thirteenth century. Inspired, according to the tradition of the Knights Templar, by the model of the Holy Sepulchre of Jerusalem, the church has a central plan and appears, from the outside, as a massive building with sixteen equal sides, equipped with battlements and narrow pointed-arch windows; the original pyramidal roof was destroyed by a fire in 1506. In the interior, a circular deambulatory with barrel-vault roofs encloses a central octagonal room, bounded by pointed arches: the capitals are carved with fantastic animals, human figures, and biblical scenes.

In 1319, following the suppression of the order of the Knights Templar, King Dinis entrusted the convent to the Order of Christ, which he had founded himself as the heirs to the traditions and the possessions of the Portuguese Knights Templar. The new monks undertook a massive campaign of expansion of the convent in the fifteenth century, which led to the construction, under the supervision of Fernão Gonçalves, of the Palace of the Knights, the Cloister of the Lavabo, and the Cloister of the Cemetery. During the reign of Manuel I, who became king in 1495, the monastery was further enriched, thanks to the growing power of the order and the prestige acquired by hosting in 1503 an important General Chapter. The new phase of construction began with the building of a rectangular choir with a sacristy, adjoining the western side of the rotunda and designed by the architect Diogo de Arruda. The original building constitutes a significant example of the *manuelino* style, named after the sovereign under whose rule it flourished. Developing in conjunction with the expansion of the great geographic discoveries and the growth in trade, this artistic lexicon can be considered substantially as an extreme development of Gothic architecture, with the exclusion however of that style's original formal rigour. As can be noted from the example of Tomar, the *manuelino* style is characterized by a profusion of plastic decorations that, in contrast with the great empty wall surfaces, are clustered on portals, windows, and columns, sheathing them with flamboyant masses of motifs, such as sea shells and plants. Underlying the development of this decorative language, which has a counterpart in the *plateresco* style in neighbouring Spain, we should mention, among other things, the Hindu architecture that the Portuguese Conquistadors were exposed to in Asia. In the apse of the rotunda of Tomar, there is a remarkable repertory of sculptures, composed with motifs

Panoramic view of the complex at Tomar.

On the facing page
The Cloister of John III, the work of Diogo de Torralva, constitutes an original reinterpretation of models of Italian classicism.

Detail of a cornice in the manuelino *style.*

View of the church from one of the cloisters. The rectangular choir added to the west side of the old rotunda by Diogo de Arruda constitutes a significant example of the manuelino *style.*

THE KNIGHTS TEMPLAR

The religious and military order of the Knights Templar was founded in 1119 by the Frenchman Hughes de Payns to defend the Holy Sepulchre and the Holy Land. The rule of the order, which derived from the rule of the Augustinian order, but was adapted for the military purposes of the new order, called for the members to be divided into lay knights with religious orders and priestly chaplains. Heading the order was a Grand Master. The main headquarters was located in the ancient Temple of Jerusalem, and the uniform consisted of a white mantle with a red cross on the chest. Quite soon, the military activities of the Knights Templar expanded to include hospital duties, which won for the order the favour of the populace at large. The Knights Templar became, over the course of the thirteenth century, one of the influential political, military, and financial powers in all European Christendom, winning them the suspicion and dislike of, among others, Philip IV of France who, with the assistance of Pope Clement IV, had them condemned as immoral heretics. With a Papal Bull in 1312, the Pope declared the suppression of the order; in France, many of the members, denying their guilt, were burned alive.

The manuelino *style, which is characterized by the profusion of decorations, emphasizes plant or fanciful motifs, inspired by ropes and other maritime elements, as well as coral and seaweed, as shown in this detail of a frieze.*

copied from sailor's knots, placed as cornices over the windows, with mouldings in the shape of buoys tied to cables, and decorations shaped like coral and seaweed on the buttresses. In the composition of the eastern window of the apse, instead, there appear themes linked to the iconography of royalty: in a complex combination of heraldic and biblical elements, the history of Portugal and the life of the king are set within the context of an eschatological vision, focusing on the prophecy of Isaiah concerning Emanuel.

In the second decade of the sixteenth century, another important *manuelino* architect was active in Tomar, João de Castilho, who added to the rotunda an entrance, located to the south and crowned with statues, and a large arch at the juncture with the new choir. The interior decorations of the church were also executed in these years, with gilded stuccoes and wooden statues of saints and prophets. There remain few traces of the old wooden choir stalls, largely destroyed in 1809–10, though what does survive are six of the ten painted panels that decorated the deambulatory. In the vaults are spectacular monochrome frescoes with *trompe-l'œil* compositions.

In 1530 João de Castilho was commissioned to carry out major work, marking the introduction to Tomar of a new architectural language developed out of the combination of the late Gothic tradition with a familiarity with Italian classicism. In this phase, the convent was given a monumental two-storey chapter hall (unfinished), a refectory, and six cloisters, one of which was later destroyed. In the Cloister of Saint Barbara, Castilho completed a daring experimentation with hybrid solutions, while the four remaining cloisters, more classical in style, are surrounded by two stacked orders of arcades on Tuscan-style columns, alternating however with a trabeation. The cloisters are connected to the

Cruzeiro, a construction with a Latin-cross plan inspired by contemporary buildings with similar service functions, such as the Ospedale Maggiore by Antonio Filarete in Milan and the Real de Todos-os-Santos Hospital in Lisbon. In the chapel on the eastern wing, the coffered ceiling is richly decorated with reliefs illustrating sacred and profane subjects. In 1551 Castilho designed for the novitiates' quarters, finally, two halls with a regular plan, with a wooden ceiling rising from non-canonical Ionic columns. A third and larger hall, destined for use as an oratory, is surrounded by sixteen Corinthian columns, possibly inspired by the illustration of the tetrastyle hall contained in the edition of Vitruvius's treatise done by Cesare Cesariano (Como, 1521).

The last important project undertaken at Tomar was the construction of the new main cloister, the Cloister of John III, by Diogo de Torralva, the most important architect of the Portuguese Renaissance. The cloister, which was completed by the Italian architect Filippo Terzi (1587), presents two orders: Doric on the lower floor and Ionic on the upper floor, which is punctuated by Serlian-motif windows; at the corners are set little cylindrical turrets which contain spiral staircases, visible from outside through the large windows. Later, a new sacristy was added to the convent (1593) along with the Portaria Nova, a monumental seventeenth-century entrance.

On the facing page
*Main entrance
to the church. Beneath
a large archway, the
broad surface of the wall
is covered with a mass of
sculptures, among which
stand out the statues of
the* Prophets *and a statue
of the* Virgin Mary
with the Christ Child.

*View of the Cemetery
Cloister.*

*Panoramic view
of the church adjoining
one of the bastions
of the castle.*

The Castle of Kroměříž

As early as the ninth century A.D., there was a castle in the Bohemian city of Kroměříž, whose strategic function was bound up with its proximity to the River Morava and the intersection of the ancient Salt Road, running from Austria to Moravia in the north, and the Amber Road, which linked the Baltic Sea with the Adriatic Sea. Around 1260, Bishop Bruno von Schaumburg built a castle there to establish his personal residence, making it the centre of the feudal organization of the entire region. This first nucleus of construction was the object in the sixteenth century of a major restoration in Renaissance style, at the behest of the Bishop Stanislav Thurzo (1497–1560), but when in 1643, towards the end of the Thirty Years' War, Kroměříž was occupied and plundered by Swedish troops, it suffered terrible damage.

Its reconstruction was due to the patronage of the arts of the enlightened Bishop Charles II of Liechtenstein (1664–95), who gave princely form not only to the castle, but to the entire city. This campaign of construction, supervised first by the imperial architect Filiberto Lucchese and, after 1666, by Giovanni Pietro Tencalla, was responsible for the general layout of the palace, the large ground-floor hall decorated with stuccoes by Baldassarre Fontana and with frescoes by Paolo Pagani, and the construction of the great Italian-style garden, known as the Libosad, or 'flower garden', which was equipped with an exceedingly complex hydraulic system that fed the ponds, fountains, and complex water plays. The Bishop of Liechtenstein did not stop with the work on the castle; he gave fundamental impulse to the library and the art gallery: the library, with its 33,641 old volumes, including 304 manuscript codices, 180 incunabula, and more than 1000 sixteenth-century books, today constitutes one of the most valuable historic collections in the Czech Republic; the art gallery, which houses masterpieces of German, Flemish, and especially sixteenth-century Venetian painting, is presently the second-most important gallery in the country, after the National Gallery in Prague.

A fire broke out in 1752, damaging the castle and especially the rooms on the second storey, which then became the object of a new decorative campaign, marked by late Baroque and Rococo styles. The artists who worked on it were the Moravian painter Josef Stern, who decorated the ceiling of the library and the Chapel of Saint Sebastian, the Viennese artist Franz Anton Maulbertsch, who frescoed the *Apotheosis of the Bishops of Kroměříž* in the feudal hall, and Franz Adolf von Freenthal who, in collaboration with the stucco artist Martin Keller, decorated the ceiling of the dining hall which later became the Assembly Hall.

At the end of the eighteenth century, neo-classicism made its entrance at Kroměříž, manifesting itself in the classical forms of the Colonnade of Colloredo and especially in the great park that surrounds the castle: the architect Anton Alois Arche built there the classical-style rotunda known as the Pompeian Colonnade because it was adorned with ancient busts from the archaeological dig of the buried city in Campania. In those years, all the same, classicism was already finding itself obliged to coexist with the style of the nascent Romantic movement, which at the turn of the nineteenth century caused the construction in the park of Kroměříž of an English-style garden, with plantings of exotic trees. The northern fondness for orientalism was in part the inspiration for the Chinese Pagoda, still standing near the little lake, which can be reached along a trail that concealed a curious mechanism: when you stepped on a stick, little Chinese statues would greet the spectator with a bow, triggering general amazement.

THE FLAYING OF MARSYAS BY TITIAN

In the art gallery of the Castle of Kroměříž is housed the famous canvas depicting *The Flaying of Marsyas*, an absolute masterpiece from Titian's late period. The Venetian master painted it towards the end of his life, in 1570, with the shambling technique, in broad chromatic, almost incandescent, masses that was so typical of his last phase.

The painting portrays the satyr Marsyas being flayed by Apollo, after losing to the god in a musical contest. In offering this tragic subject, Titian meant to represent the end of the natural and primitive world embodied by Marsyas, and the advent of rational civilization, harmony represented by Apollo, an epoch-marking turning point that was viewed by the painter with a sense of dolorous melancholy. Evidence of this is provided by the sad and thoughtful pose of King Midas, who witnesses the scene helplessly, in the right of the painting. In the face of the monarch who could turn everything he touched into gold, a member of the defeated civilization, some have claimed to recognize a self-portrait of Titian: like the mythical character, the Venetian painter was also said to have the gift of transforming, with his paintbrush, any material into gold. The melancholy pose of Titian-Midas, then, seems an indication of an awareness that such a gift is temporary and meaningless in the face of violence and the tragic, ineluctable passage of human history.

On page 184
The Archangel Michael drives off Lucifer.

On page 185
Surrounded by splendid gardens, the castle of Kroměříž owes its general layout to the work of two Italian architects, Filiberto Lucchese and Giovanni Pietro Tencalla.

Two reception halls, decorated in the Rococo style, adorn the residence of Kroměříž.

On the facing page
Titian (Tiziano Vecellio),
The Flaying of Marsyas,
oil on canvas, 1570.

The Kremlin of Moscow

The Kremlin, with its massive walls, its cathedrals with gilded onion domes, and its towers, closes off to the north Moscow's vast and lively Red Square. Kremlin (*kreml'*), in fact, describes the 'fortified citadel', which, generally built on the site of the original settlement, ensured the defence of a community in case of attack or siege. Because it often contained the cathedral, the meeting places of the leading citizens, and the marketplace, it represented the heart of the public life of Russian cities. Even though it has been the symbol of power for more than 800 years, the Kremlin of Moscow is not the oldest one in the country: in the twelfth century, when the confederation of principalities known as Kievan Russia was at the height of its glory, the citadels of Kiev, Novgorod, Tver, and Vladimir were far more important.

The chronicles mention Moscow only after 1147. The foundation of the city is identified with the construction of the wooden palisade on the forest-covered highland that dominated the confluence of the Moscova River with the Neglinnaya River, built in 1156 in order to protect an existing building by Yuri Dolgoruky (George Longarm), the Prince of Suzdal. This marked the beginning of the long history of what would one day be the capital of Russia, a city whose importance surged suddenly when, in 1328, Moscow became the seat of the Prince of Vladimir and, as a result, of the Russian Orthodox metropolitan. In the face of the constant threat of fires and sieges, the defensive walls of the Kremlin – which Ivan Kalita had reinforced as early as 1339, replacing the pinewood palisade with a stouter palisade made of oak – were reinforced by the Grand Duke Dmitri (Demetrius) who ordered the construction of stone walls and towers between 1359 and 1374. From that point forward the bastions were reinforced and expanded many times, until they attained monumental dimensions, 6 metres thick, with their nineteen towers. Although, during the Mongol raid of 1382, the Khan Tokhtamysh succeeded in breaching the walls and destroying the ancient wooden fortress that stood within, the massive walls withstood enemy attacks on numerous occasions, including the Mongol siege of 1408–09, thanks to the cannons that defended them.

When Moscow, in the wake of the storming of Constantinople in 1453, became the seat of the Byzantine Church in Europe, the Kremlin was subjected to a substantial reconstruction. In 1474 Czar Ivan III the Great, who intended to make Moscow the 'third Rome', sent a mission to Venice in search of Italian architects. That was how the Bolognese architect Aristotele Fieravanti came to supervise the reconstruction of the Cathedral of the Assumption between 1475 and 1478, the Milanese architects Pietro Solari and Marco Ruffo were assigned to work on the walls and towers between 1482 and 1490, and the Piedmontese architect Alvisio Novi was entrusted with the building of the Cathedral of Saint Michael Archangel in 1505, the year of Ivan the Great's death. In order to construct these buildings, craftsmen from the West were employed, which helped to meld Byzantine-style architecture with the taste of the early Italian Renaissance. The intense construction activity of those years created three cathedrals, the Terem Palace and the Faceted Palace, more than 2 kilometres of new walls, the nineteen watch towers – including the Tower of the Sav-

The Kremlin of Moscow, seen from the Moscova River in a print from the nineteenth century.

On the facing page
The domes of the family churches of the czars.

Crown of the Empress Anna, preserved in the Armoury of the Kremlin.

iour, the principal entrance to the Kremlin – and, in 1485, the central gate, known as the 'secret gate', from which an underground corridor led to the river.

The south-central section of the Kremlin is known as the Cathedral Square because it is overlooked by the Cathedral of the Assumption, the Cathedral of the Annunciation, and the Cathedral of Saint Michael Archangel. Designed by Alvisio Novi, the Cathedral of Saint Michael Archangel houses the tombs, all in white stone and sheathed in copper, of forty-seven czars, from Ivan Kalita to Peter the Great. Its bell tower, the tallest tower of the Kremlin, was named for the czar who ordered the construction of the church, Ivan the Great, but it owes its present-day form to the determination of Boris Godunov to celebrate his own election as czar and his wish to leave a symbol of his pious devotion during the famine of 1600–03. Inside the bell tower, crowned by a cylindrical tower and a golden onion dome, there are thirty-three bells, all richly decorated in bas-relief, one of which, the 'czarina', weighs 218 metric tons and stands nearly 6 metres high.

Ivan III himself commissioned the architects Marco Ruffo and Pietro Solari, who had worked on the defensive walls and the towers, to build a residence worthy of his greatness. And so, between 1487 and 1491, the Faceted Palace (or Diamond Point Palace) was built, named for the limestone ashlar rustication of the façade, typical of the architecture of the Italian Renaissance. The building is renowned especially for its Feasting Hall (also known as the Golden Hall), a square room on the second floor, extending over some 560 square metres, covered by four basket-arch cross vaults supported by a single massive gilded central pillar. The vaults, the lunettes, and the walls of the hall are entirely covered with religious frescoes, executed at the end of the sixteenth cen-

On the facing page
*The Bell Tower of Ivan
the Great, built by Bon
Friazin at the turn
of the sixteenth century.*

*The ring of walls
of the Kremlin includes
nineteen towers.*

*View of the Great Palace
of the Kremlin seen from
the Moscova River, with
the Vodovsvodnaya and
Blagoveshenskaya
Towers.*

191

*The Cathedral
of the Annunciation
was the private church
of the czars.*

THE TOWERS OF THE KREMLIN

Of the nineteen towers that rise over the enclosure of battlemented walls surrounding the Kremlin, the largest and the most famous is the Tower of the Saviour, for five centuries the official entrance into the fortress from the Red Square. It was built in 1491 by Pietro Solari and takes its name from the image of Christ that stands above its portal. In the first few decades of the sixteenth century, the walls and the vault of the central arcade were adorned with an elaborate frescoed decoration. About a century later, Czar Mikhail Romanov entrusted the English clockmaker Christopher Halloway with the task of adding to the square Renaissance construction a spectacular late Gothic-style superstructure, which pushed the tower to its present height of 70 metres, with ten storeys occupied by a dense network of passageways and refined mechanisms to drive the clock and the bells. Symmetrical with the Tower of the Saviour is the Tower of the Trinity, a massive military structure which housed a prison deep within its bowels. A low bridge (once spanning the River Neglinnaya, which was filled in between 1818 and 1819) connects it to the Kutafya Gate, the ancient official western entrance to the Kremlin. Also to the west, but towards the south, the Pinewood Tower is the one that most faithfully reproduces the typical forms of Russian architecture: its square-based structure tapers through four ever-smaller storeys, enlivened by an exuberant decoration of mouldings and cornices that is reminiscent of the wooden churches of medieval Russia. The bell tower that looms above it, 60 metres tall and covered with green tiles, suffered terrible damage in 1812, when the Napoleonic army entered the Kremlin through the gate that runs through it. At the southern extremity stands the Water-Pump Tower which, through a complex network of lead pipes, provided water to the buildings and the gardens of the citadel; built in 1480, it was demolished and rebuilt in 1805, and then once again demolished seven years later by the retreating French troops. In 1817 Czar Alexander I entrusted its reconstruction to the architect Osip Beauvais, who gave it an Empire-style façade.

The Taynitskaya Tower, or Secret Tower.

The Vodovsvodnaya Tower, or Water-Pump Tower.

The Senatskaya Tower, or Tower of the Senate, separates the Senate building from the mausoleum of Lenin on the Red Square.

The Granovitaya Palata, the Faceted Palace (or Diamond Point Palace), commissioned by Ivan III from Marco Ruffo and Pietro Solari, is named for the limestone ashlar rustication of the façade, typical of the architecture of the Italian Renaissance.

On the facing page The majestic Feasting Hall, on the interior of the Faceted Palace, covered by four cross vaults resting on a single massive central gilded pillar, features vaults, lunettes, and walls entirely adorned by frescoes.

On pages 196–97 The Kremlin of Moscow is an imposing fortified citadel, surrounded by monumental walls that are as thick in some places as 6 metres.

tury but restored in 1668 by Simon Ushakov. The Golden Hall was, over the centuries, the setting for many important ceremonies and events: in 1552, Ivan IV celebrated the victory won over the Mongols at Kazan, and Peter the Great toasted there to his triumph over the Swedes, defeated in 1709 at Poltava.

In 1508, three years after the death of Ivan the Great, the first part of the Terem Palace, the most luxurious in the Kremlin, was completed. Surmounted by splendid golden onion domes and linked to the three court chapels (the upper cathedral, dedicated to the Redeemer, the Church of the Crucifixion, and the Church of the Resurrection), it contains portals, walls, and parapets, both sculpted and painted, beautiful stained glass and extremely refined majolica stoves. Between 1839 and 1849, it was incorporated into the project of the Great Palace of the Kremlin, prepared for Czar Nicholas I by the German architect Konstantin Thon. This magnificent imperial residence, extending over no less than 45,000 square metres, joined the Terem Palace with

the Faceted Palace and with the ancient Church of the Nativity of the Virgin (1393). The monumental central section of the Great Palace, built in the nineteenth century, has a long southern façade (125 metres) overlooking the Moscova River, enlivened by the chromatic interplay between the tufa stone of the base and the white stone of the window frames and the other decorations. In the interior are no fewer than three official reception halls, dedicated respectively to Saints Vladimir, Alexander, and George; the last hall, which preserves an exquisite wooden floor, is the most famous, since in the past it was used for government meetings.

Beginning with the reign of Ivan III, the buildings of the Kremlin became the privileged setting for the great historical events of the country: the ascent to the throne in 1533 of Ivan IV the Terrible, crowned czar over all the Russias in the Cathedral of the Assumption in 1547; the Polish occupation of 1610; the proclamation on the part of Alexi I of the supremacy of the state over the church during

the ecclesiastic council of 1666–67; the entire reign of Peter the Great (1694–1725), who completed the north wing of the fortress and, in expectation of a Swedish invasion, erected a new line of fortifications outside of the old walls. All the same, it was none other than Peter who cast a shadow over the ancient citadel by building Saint Petersburg (1703–23) as Russia's 'window' on the West.

In the north-western section of the Kremlin, on the site of the granaries destroyed by fire in 1701, Peter the Great had ordered the construction of the stern, classical construction of the Arsenal, which he hoped to turn into a sort of great museum of war. This project was never achieved and the official museum of the Kremlin instead was installed in the Armoury rebuilt in the nineteenth century by Thon a little further south, adjoining the Great Palace. Originally, and until the years in which the czar moved his court to Saint Petersburg, this building was the imperial arms factory and the workshop of the czar's goldsmiths and jewellers. Today it houses the crown treasures and the imperial insignia, historic weapons, carriages, armour, clothing, *objets d'art*, and objects of craftsmanship.

Even though the court had moved to Saint Petersburg, around 1745 a new palace was built in the Kremlin for Elizabeth I and, twenty years later, a radical renovation of the entire complex was planned by Catherine II the Great, crowned Empress in 1762 in the Cathedral of the Assumption. The enlightened and cosmopolitan czarina, eager to give the lie to the rumour that her coffers were empty, commissioned the young Russian architect Vasily Bazenov in 1768 to transform the decrepit and long-neglected fortress into an 'Eastern Versailles'. The project called for covering the existing buildings with colonnaded façades and creating a vast park criss-crossed with avenues, fountains, and gardens. But already in 1775,

THE CATHEDRALS OF THE ASSUMPTION AND THE ANNUNCIATION

The Church of the Assumption, an imposing square-plan building surmounted by five golden onion domes, was built from 1326, during the reign of Ivan Kalita, on the model of the medieval cathedral of Vladimir. It was the object of a massive reconstruction beginning in 1475 when the Bolognese architect Aristotele Fieravanti came to Moscow and created his masterpiece with this cathedral, merging the spatial equilibrium and the construction techniques of the Italian Renaissance with the traditional forms of Russian architecture which he had carefully studied. Work was completed in 1479, but in the decades that followed the cathedral was further embellished by a rich fresco decoration completed in 1515 – the work of the renowned Muscovite painter Dionisy with his disciples – and with luxurious furnishings, including the majestic five-order iconostasis, 16 metres tall, adorned with dozens of icons and sheathed with silver. In 1812, during the French occupation of the Kremlin, Napoleon quartered in this church his cavalry soldiers who melted down the precious objects that were contained in it, obtaining some 5 metric tons of gold and silver. The importance of the cathedral is documented, aside from the presence of the most sacred relics of the nation, by the fact that until the eighteenth century the patriarchs and metropolitans of the Russian Orthodox Church were buried here and that, from the sixteenth century on, all the czars of Russia were crowned here.

Taking inspiration from Fieravanti's design for the Cathedral of the Assumption, a group of architects from Pskov reconstructed in 1482, on the site of an earlier, existing church, the neighbouring Cathedral of the Annunciation. This is the smallest church in the Kremlin, because it was originally meant as a private chapel for the czar, but it is also the most exquisitely decorated. Open porticoes were built alongside the building, and Ivan the Terrible ordered that two new domes be added to the original three, then another four, until there was a total of nine copper-sheathed, gilded domes that still crown the cathedral today. On the interior, the church is decorated by an exquisite jasper- and agate-intarsiated floor, and by a series of frescoes executed by the renowned Russian painters Prokhov and Rublev.

On the facing page
The gilded onion domes
of the Cathedral
of the Annunciation.

View of the apse
of the Cathedral
of the Assumption,
designed by Aristotele
Fieravanti in 1475.

Detail of the southern
portal of the Cathedral
of the Assumption, with a
fresco of the Virgin Mary
with the Christ Child.

just two years after the start of construction, Catherine cancelled her ambitious urbanistic project, because the victory against the Turks had consolidated her personal power within the country and had given Russia renewed international prestige. The czarina settled for a more modest programme, commissioning the architect Matvei Kazakov to build a new palace for the Archbishopric and, especially, a new Senate building, a majestic classical-style building with a remarkable triangular plan, built between 1776 and 1787 in the north-eastern corner of the complex.

The serious damage done to the walls and the buildings of the Kremlin by the fires and the explosions that broke out during the Napoleonic invasion of 1812 made a new reconstruction necessary, for which the finest architects were hired, in particular Osip Beauvais, who oversaw the reconstruction of Red Square and designed the Aleksandrovsky Park along the west side of the Kremlin.

When in 1917 the last czar, Nicholas II,

abdicated and Lenin took power, Moscow became once again the heart of Russian politics. In 1918 it became the capital of the Soviet Union, and the Kremlin, despite the economic difficulties of the time, was restored at the express wish of Lenin. Relics of the long years of Communism include the transformation of the ancient Cathedral of Saint Basil into an anti-religious museum in 1923 and, beginning in 1925, the construction of a mausoleum in pink granite to house the cadaver of Lenin, at the centre of the eastern façade of the Kremlin.

Both of these buildings overlook the large rectangular space (75,000 square metres) of the Red Square, which runs along the wall of the citadel with which it communicates via the Tower of the Saviour. Despite what is generally thought, the square does not take its name (*Krasnaya Ploshad*) from the colour of the Communist flag that first flew during the October Revolution of 1917. Called *Torg* (marketplace) in the chronicles of the fifteenth century and, after the great fire of 1493, 'the site of the fire', it took this name around 1660, which in Russian not only means 'red', but also 'marvellous, beautiful, sparkling'. Over the centuries it has served as a market, a political meeting place, a parade ground, an open air construction area, functions that were so important to the country that Alexander I, after Napoleon's retreat, began his reconstruction of Moscow right there.

In the Red Square, on the opposite side from the eastern façade of the Kremlin, we find the GUM department store, a massive shopping centre that has become in the last decade a symbol of the free market in Russia. In the easternmost area stands the Place of Skulls, a sort of raised platform used over the centuries for religious services but especially for the public executions of rebels and political prisoners. Here, in 1547, Ivan the Terrible knelt and repented of his sins; here, in 1698, after the last revolt of the *streltsy* (a special corps of musketeers), Peter the Great ordered the execution of crowds of mutineers.

But the building that, with its nine multicoloured onion domes, dominates the Red Square, closing off its southern side, is the Cathedral of the Intercession, better known as the Cathedral of Saint Basil, symbol of Moscow and of all Russia. It offers a splendid example of Byzantine-Slavic decorativism, and it was built between 1553 and 1560 on the burial site of the saint, in order to celebrate Ivan the Terrible's great victory at Kazan. The building is in fact a cluster of constructions: a central church surrounded by nine auxiliary churches, eight of which are dedicated to as many other victories won by Ivan over the Mongols, and one extra church to contain the relics of Saint Basil. Legend has it that, when construction was finished, the czar ordered that the architects Barma and Postnik, who supervised the project, have their eyes ripped out, to keep them from ever matching this creation.

The Monastery of San Lorenzo at El Escorial

Built at the end of the sixteenth century in the period of the Spanish monarchy's greatest splendour, the Convento de San Lorenzo el Real de Escorial is an extraordinary synthesis of building types, corresponding to the various functions contained within: monastery, royal palace and private retreat of the sovereign, church and pantheon of the ruling dynasty. This character of the complex reflects the role of the Spanish monarchy in the age of the Counter Reformation, becoming a symbol of its efforts in defence of the Catholic religion. These buildings served to formulate a new architectural style, typical of the classical tastes and the Counter Reformation spirituality of Philip II. The array of paintings that enrich the monastery was conceived as an integral part of the original design and corresponds to a single iconographic programme, which celebrated the monarchy and the faith, militant and triumphant.

Various reasons led King Philip II to his decision in 1559 to found this royal monastery, named after and dedicated to Saint Lawrence (San Lorenzo). First of all, the king thus honoured one of the last wishes expressed by his father, the Holy Roman Emperor Charles V, who had ordered the foundation of a monastery in which he could be buried alongside his wife, Isabel of Portugal. The new foundation was also intended to commemorate the victory achieved in the battle of Saint-Quentin where, on 10 August 1557 (Saint Lawrence's Day), Philip II had defeated the French army; according to tradition, moreover, the sovereign had been obliged to fulfil a vow for having destroyed during that battle a church dedicated to Saint Lawrence.

In 1560, a site was selected for the foundation on farmland to the north-west of Madrid, where over time the city of San Lorenzo de El Escorial grew up around the monastery. The cornerstone of the construction was laid in 1563; in 1584, with the official conclusion of work, the buildings were occupied by the Girolamite monks who ran the monastery until 1885, when they were replaced by Augustinian monks. Currently, the Escorial is run by the Patrimonio Nacional (National Heritage of Spain); in 1963, the Nuevos Museos were installed in the Escorial, containing and exhibiting the art collection.

The plan of the Escorial corresponds to an impressively sized rectangle (207 by 162 metres); on the interior, the intersection of perpendicular structures creates a gridwork of courtyards, with a pattern that clearly evokes the instrument whereby Saint Lawrence met his martyrdom, having been tortured on a grate over red-hot coals. Built entirely out of grey granite, the building has four corner towers and can be divided into three parallel sections, each of which has its own access on the western façade. The central entrance consists of a monumental façade in an ecclesiastical layout, with two orders of stacked giant columns, and is topped by a pediment. The southern sector of the complex is occupied by the buildings of the monastery and is, in turn, divided into two zones of equal size. The first zone is arranged around a cross with four internal courtyards consisting of simple Tuscan colonnades, the Patios Chicos; at the intersection of the two arms of the cross stands a tower, in keeping with a pattern that is repeated symmetrically on the other side of the complex. Beyond the Patios Chicos opens up the great Patio de los Evangelistas, enclosed by two orders of arcades supported by Doric and Ionic half-columns. At the centre of this courtyard stands a small octagonal Doric temple (1586–91), covered with a dome and surrounded by four square pools; the building is adorned with four statues of the Evangelists (by Juan Bautista de Monegro) which, in the context of the surrounding garden, a symbol

Panoramic view of the Convento de San Lorenzo el Real de Escorial.

On the facing page *Luca Giordano,* Saint Lawrence in Glory, Adored by Charles V and Philip II, *fresco in the vault of the staircase (1692-1694).*

of Paradise, allude to the theme of the propagation of the faith. On the opposite side of the complex are situated, first, the seminary and the college, also arranged in the form of a cross adjacent to the façade, then the area reserved for the royal palace. Here a large courtyard, enclosed by a double order of Ionic and Doric pillars, is bounded to the east by two smaller courtyards, overlooked by the apartments of the officials and the courtiers.

The central structure of the Escorial is occupied by the most prestigious buildings: the Library, the rectangular Patio de los Reyes, the basilica and the private apartments of the king, arranged around the Patio del los Mascarones. The church, the genuine heart of the entire complex, is flanked by two towers and has, on its lower storey, punctuated by Doric half-columns, a deep portico with a triple arcade. On the upper floor, the pilaster strips that support the tympanum are faced with six statues, the sole decorative element of the entire complex. The structure of the tympanum is broken by an arched great window which provides light to the interior, along with the six rectangular apertures opening halfway up the wall. The church, which presents the typical characteristics of Roman classicism, has a central plan in the form of a Greek cross inscribed within a square. The narthex leads to a small public chapel, set beneath the choir of the monks, reserved for private use. In the main space, the arms of the cross are covered with barrel vaults and the space is punctuated by fluted Doric-order pillars, upon which rests the upper gallery which runs around the interior perimeter. The high dome that is set upon the intersection of the arms is covered on the exterior by a tambour, and constitutes the first example of this type of structure in the history of Spanish architecture. The presbytery is raised and is flanked by two chambers reserved for imperial and royal burials; the church con-

Panoramic view of the complex, with the imposing silhouette of the basilica.

Façade of the Library. Corresponding with the central entrance to the monastery is a monumental façade with an ecclesiastical layout.

On the facing page The exterior of the monastery, seen from the garden. The architectural style employed in the buildings is typical of the classicist taste.

PHILIP II

The son of Charles V and Isabel of Portugal, Philip II (1527–98) ascended to the throne of Spain in 1556, following his father's abdication. Once he had established, with his victory at Saint-Quentin and the subsequent peace treaty of Cateau-Cambrésis (1559), Spanish domination over much of Europe, Philip turned his attention to fighting against the spread of heresy in his own states, relying on the assistance of the Tribunal of the Inquisition. In his war against the Turks, who were threatening Catholic Europe from their position in the Mediterranean, the king achieved the great victory of Lepanto (1571), where Spain was the leading combattant. Later, Philip was obliged to face the revolt that erupted in the Netherlands, which ended with the *de facto* independence of the Protestant provinces. Educated in a learned milieu that was open to humanistic culture, the king inherited from his mother a passion for collecting and especially for Flemish art. He was a patron of the arts and he assembled at the Escorial an extraordinary collection of paintings, which included works by Hieronymus Bosch, Tintoretto, and Veronese. Part of this collection was transferred in 1939 to the Museo del Prado.

Titian (Tiziano Vecellio), Portrait of Philip II, *oil on canvas. Florence, The Palatine Gallery of the Pitti Palace.*

On the facing page *El Greco*, The Dream of Philip II. *The painting is also known with the titles of* Adoration of the Name of Jesus *and* Allegory of the Holy League, *and it celebrates the role played by the Spanish king in religious politics.*

cludes with the rectangular *sagrario* and is connected directly with the king's private apartments, which overlook the main altar.

The general layout was established by the royal architect Juan Bautista de Toledo, entrusted with the project in 1559: the gridwork design, which had been fairly well defined in 1564, was maintained practically unchanged in the various construction phases that followed over the next twenty years, during which the construction of the Escorial was supervised by numerous other figures. In particular, an early plan for the church, which called for four towers with domes, among other things, was harshly criticized by the Urbino-born architect Francesco Paciotto, who had been summoned to Spain by Philip II as a military architect. The Italian architect revised various aspects of the original design by Juan Bautista, suggesting a square plan with a transept and introducing numerous other modifications. In 1563, the council of architects who were overseeing the project of the Escorial approved the overall plan of the Spanish architect, but with the modified church by Paciotto. Later Juan Bautista himself returned to the problem of the church, developing a new proposal until when he died, in 1567, work entered into a phase of stagnation. That same year, a variety of plans for the basilica, including those by Juan Bautista, were sent to the Academy of Design in Florence, and a number of Italian architects were contacted to obtain their opinions and suggestions: among them, Pellegrino Tibaldi, Galeazzo Alessi, and Andrea Palladio sent plans for the church. Finally, having viewed all of the various plans, Jacopo Vignola developed a new plan which was submitted to Pope Gregory XIII and then sent to Spain in 1573. In the meantime, around 1570, work on the Escorial had resumed with the appointment as director of the architect Juan de Herrera who, in 1574, laid the cor-

Private gardens of Philip II at the Palace of the Monastery of San Lorenzo with an 'Italian-style' loggia.

Small Doric temple on the Patio de los Evangelistas. The octagonal temple, clearly inspired by the models of Italian classicism, is covered with a dome and surrounded by four square basins.

THE ARCHITECTURAL MODELS

Numerous critical studies have been produced to identify the formal models and the symbolic references of the Escorial. The general layout has been traced back to various possible precedents, including the Palace of Diocletian in Split (former Yugoslavia); among the more immediate references we should mention the Ospedale Maggiore by Filarete in Milan and a number of cross-vault hospitals built during the early sixteenth century in Spain. As for the specific motifs set forth in the individual buildings, there is a clear reference to the Italian models of the Renaissance and Mannerism, beginning with the plans drawn up by Michelangelo for Saint Peter's, reflected in the first design for the basilica. In the façade of the church, we can find clear influences of the architecture of Leon Battista Alberti in Mantua, but also references to Bramante and the Vitruvian sketches done by Cesare Cesariano. For the Patio de los Evangelistas, we find references instead to the Palazzo Farnese by Antonio da Sangallo the Younger. The various symbolic interpretations suggested for the Escorial all lead back to the same overriding concept, which is that this is a material expression of the spirit of the Counter Reformation, a complete manifestation of the precepts of piety, *gravitas*, and decorousness in artworks. Some scholars have tried to portray it as a hermetic depiction of the Temple of Jerusalem or of Saint Augustine's City of God, if not an actual allusion to the construction of the Tower of Babel, with a final identification in the writings of Herrera of the idea of a Christian architecture that began with Noah's Ark and culminated in the Escorial, both of these structures being direct emanations of divine wisdom.

ITALIAN ARTISTS AT THE ESCORIAL

The intensive participation of Italian artists in the decoration of the Escorial reflects the tastes of Philip II who was the most enlightened patron of Titian, with whom the king was already on close terms by 1554: at that date, it is documented that the painter sent the monarch a number of paintings with mythological subjects, including the splendid *Danae*. In the later years of his career, Titian painted almost exclusively for Philip II, executing a substantial number of canvases for the Escorial. In the sacristy, we find a *Christ on the Cross* by Titian, while his *Glory* for the chapter hall is now at the Prado; aside from the *Last Supper* for the refectory, we should mention the large and impressive *Martyrdom of Saint Lawrence* (1564–67), which was originally displayed on the main altar of the basilica.

With the assignment of commissions for the frescoes of the Escorial, a number of the most important artists of late Italian Mannerism arrived in Spain. The Lombard Pellegrino Tibaldi (1527–96), painter and architect, left Milan for Madrid in 1586, after having worked as the leading figure in the reformation of ecclesiastical buildings theorized by Saint Charles Borromeo. Federico Zuccari (*c.* 1542–1609), who came to Spain in 1585, had been a successful painter in Rome, working on a variety of decorative series. He linked his reputation to the refoundation of the Accademia di San Luca and his treatise *The Idea of the Sculptors, Painters, and Architects* (1607). The Genoese painter Luca Cambiaso (1527–85, at the Escorial from 1583 on) was an immensely learned artist, who updated the influence of Michelangelo upon an entire generation of Italian painters with Venetian influences and the style of Correggio, as well as displaying notable skills in the areas of perspective and composition. Leone Leoni (*c.* 1509–90), who worked on Philip II's monastery along with his son Pompeo, had already enjoyed the protection of Charles V, when he executed for the imperial family a series of portraits in which there prevailed a tone of celebratory magnificence and styles inspired by ancient bronze-work and the examples of Cellini and Sansovino.

Pompeo Leoni,
The Family of Charles V
at Prayer (1592–1600).
The statues, executed in
gilt bronze, compose
the funerary monument
of Charles V, and are set
within a temple-shaped
niche next to the
presbytery of the basilica.

The Library, located in the central structure of the palace, is decorated with allegorical frescoes by Pellegrino Tibaldi.

On the facing page The tapestry of The Crockery Pedlar, *based on a cartoon by Francisco Goya, and executed for the royal apartment of the Prince of Asturias,* *was woven at the Real Fabrica de Tapices de Santa Barbara (Royal Manufactory of Tapestries) at the Palacio Real (Royal Palace) in Madrid.*

View of the basilica. The high dome that rests above the intersection of the arms of the transept is covered on the exterior by a tambour, which constitutes the first example of this type of structure in the history of Spanish architecture.

Ezechias, one of the monumental statues depicting the monarchs of the Bible, crowning the entrance to the Church of San Lorenzo.

nerstone of the church which was concluded in 1584 and consecrated in 1586. Aside from any questions of attributions concerning the credit due to each of the two architects, the complex as a whole is marked by a considerable stylistic consistency which, through the use of classical orders, geometric abstraction, and formal simplification, attains results of extraordinary sobriety and monumentality. We see here a clear delineation of the so-called *estilo desornamentado*, of Italian origin, which is distinguished from the previous *plateresco* tradition by its great austerity.

The last two decades of the sixteenth century witnessed the construction of numerous annexes, service buildings designed in part by Herrera himself. The most important addition was built at the behest of Philip III, who commissioned the Roman architect Giovanni Battista Crescenzi to design the Panteón de los Reyes (1617–18): in this subterranean octagonal chamber, decorated with marble and jasper inlay and embellished with gilt bronze capitals, an ornamental style was introduced to the Escorial that was extraneous to the austere character of its original architecture. The hall contained a crucifix by Gian Lorenzo Bernini (1654), later replaced with another crucifix by Domenico Guidi. Other buildings followed in the late eighteenth century, by the neo-classical architect Juan de Villanueva (the Casita de Arriba and the Casita de Abajo); the final construction was the

Panteón de los Infantes (1862–88), built at the behest of Isabel II.

The monastery was endowed at its very creation with a considerable number of paintings, frescoes, sculptures, altars, and reliquaries, as well as collections of books and manuscripts; over time, many of these objects have been transferred or lost, but what remains is enough to show that the Escorial was endowed by Philip II with a remarkable treasury of artworks. One of the sites that received the greatest effort in terms of decorations was certainly the church: in 1576 the king commissioned thirty-two altarpieces (depicting pairs of saints) from Juan Fernández de Navarrete, who is traditionally said to have studied in Italy with Titian; only seven of the canvases in this important series were completed because Juan died young in 1579, leaving the project to be finished by other Spanish artists. Five other canvases were painted by Luca Cambiaso, Pellegrino Tibaldi, and Romolo Cincinnato, three of numerous Italian artists that Philip II summoned to work on the project of the Escorial. In the vaults of the church, Cambiaso painted a number of compositions with Marian subjects, while the frescoes with *Stories of Saint Lawrence and Saint Jerome* in the choir were executed in collaboration with Cincinnato. In the *sagrario*, the scenes from the Old Testament by Pellegrino Tibaldi (1586–87) alluded to the theme of the Eucharist, as in the evident case of the *Manna Falling from Heaven*. On either side of the presbytery, two oratories contain the funereal monuments of Charles V and Philip II, depicted with other members of the royal family intently praying. The gilt bronze statues (1592–1600) were executed by Pompeo Leoni and set in temple-shaped niches designed by Herrera. On the main altar is a rich *retablo* (1579–89), also designed by Herrera and executed in Milan in the workshop of Leone Leoni with the contribution of various artists. Built of marble and jasper, with pedestals and capitals made of gilt bronze, it is decorated with monumental statues of saints, evangelists, and Fathers of the Church and with a *Christ on the Cross Between the Virgin Mary and Saint John.*

Another important decorative episode is that linked to the Patio de los Evangelistas, painted by Tibaldi and his assistants with sixty-two episodes from the Lives of the Virgin Mary, Jesus Christ, and the Apostles. In the immense Library, located on the west wing, Tibaldi painted a series of allegorical subjects (1587–92). The vault is occupied by personifications of the Liberal Arts and the Sciences, seen from below and surrounded by giants; in the lunettes were depicted historical figures that were representative of these disciplines. In the Escorial there were also distributed a great many paintings with devotional subjects, largely Flemish or Italian, taken from the collection donated by the king to the monastery between 1571 and 1598. In the seventeenth century, more decorative series were executed by Diego Velázquez (chapter hall, sacristy, and scriptorium) and Luca Giordano (vaults of the main staircase and of the church).

Hieronymus Bosch, Hay Wagon Triptych, central panel. This painting was part of the collection of paintings of Philip II, housed in the Escorial and abounding in major Flemish works.

213

The Alhambra in Granada

In Granada, Andalusia, the fortress of the Alhambra constitutes, along with the neighbouring garden of the Generalife and the Moorish quarter of the Albaicín, an exceptional complex of great artistic and historical value and the sole surviving document of the final phase of Arab domination in Spain. Built in the thirteenth century as a full-fledged fortified city-palace, the Alhambra was until 1492 the headquarters of the Nasrid sultans, whose residence was placed, along with the seat of government, within the ring of its walls. The fall of this dynasty, the last bulwark in the face of the onslaught of the Christian *reconquista*, marked the end of Muslim rule in the Iberian Peninsula.

The Kingdom of Granada was founded in 1237 by Muhammad ibn Yusuf ibn Nasar, a provincial prince of little importance who managed to take advantage of the crisis of the Spanish Almohads, proclaiming himself the Sultan of Arjona (1232) and extending his own dominions to the Mediterranean coast of southern Spain. During his reign, reconstruction was begun on an existing fortress that was already known by the name of Alhambra (Red Rock) and which was located on one of the three hills of the city, the Sabika. The first phase of construction, documented by a number of buildings and continued by the successors to the founder, resulted in the building of a ring of defensive walls fortified with towers, corresponding in its extent to the existing one. The current appearance of the Alhambra was further defined over the course of the fourteenth century, when the Sultans Yusuf I (1333–54) and Muhammad V (1362–91) enriched it with luxurious buildings of great prestige.

The perimeter of the fortifications, extending more than 1,700 metres, enclosed an area of more than 10 hectares and is punctuated by some thirty towers with various functions and sizes. Developed as an independent city structure, the Alhambra had four main gates, two to the north and two to the south: the oldest existing gate is the Puerta de las Armas (thirteenth century), overlooking the Albaicín and the lower section of the town, which was the main point of connection with Granada. Its structure is typical of fortified Hispano-Islamic gates: beneath a horseshoe arch, the passageway twists and winds so as to make it easier to defend. The most monumental gate, on the other hand, is the Puerta de la Justicia (1348), which preserves on its interior richly painted vaults. Within the circle of the walls a welter of streets and internal gates identified three different quarters, which could be isolated from each other in case of attack and which served entirely independent functions.

At the western extremity, on a ridge overlooking Granada, stood the Alcazaba, which housed the garrison that defended the fortress: the layout of the quarters is documented by the remains of the foundations and brick floors which are still in place. There are also two major constructions with a defensive function: the Torre de la Vela, a four-storey watch-tower, and the Torre del Homenaje, which probably dates back to the time of the fortress's foundation. At the far end of the walls, on a slightly inclined terrace, extended the *medina*, which could be reached through the Puerta del Vino, built at the turn of the fourteenth century: in this urbanized complex lived the members of the court and the royal administration, as well as the artisans who worked to maintain and embellish the Alhambra. Running through the quarter was the Calle Real; this included not only houses and shops, but a mosque, the cemetery of the sultans (Rauda), plazas and public baths, cisterns for the water supply, and possibly a *madrasa* (Koran school). The most significant remains of the *medina* were constituted by the Torre de la

Panoramic view of the Alhambra. The perimeter of the fortress encloses three separate quarters and features rich palaces, residential areas, and the seat of the government of the Nasrid sultans.

On the facing page Patio de los Arrayanes *in the* Cuarto de Comares. *The courtyard is almost entirely occupied by a smooth basin of water, in which the surrounding buildings are reflected.*

THE GENERALIFE

To the north-east of the Alhambra, the Nasrids owned a huge country estate where Muhammad II (1273–1302) ordered the construction of a palace known by the name of Generalife (corruption of the Arabic *giannat al-arifa*, or garden of the architect). Currently this complex, laid out on terraces, is directly linked to the fortress by a series of gardens built in the twentieth century in keeping with the style of Muslim tradition. Set in an immense expanse of farmland, the Generalife consisted of four gardens (parts of which are still cultivated) and a private palace, immersed in an ornamental garden. The building, which is similar in structure to the Alhambra, has interior decorations similar to those of the other royal residences, but executed with less lavish materials, such as plaster and brick. The building's most interesting feature is the patio, through which runs a long watercourse; the perimeter of the courtyard is lined with four flower-beds and, in the narrow passages that run along the flow of the water, there spurt forth high jets of water that feed the pond, thus becoming the chief ornamental motif of the whole. Water, for that matter, is the fundamental element in the design of a Muslim garden, which is traditionally considered as a prefiguring of the paradise described in the Koran: a luxuriant and shaded place, abounding with fruit and embellished by fountains, a universal symbol of life and prosperity.

*On the facing page
Patio de los Leones.
At the centre
of the courtyard stands
a marble fountain
supported by twelve
carved lions, each
depicted in a different
way.*

*View of the Palace
and the Garden
of the Generalife.*

Patio de los Leones.
*The slender marble
columns that surround
the courtyard are
arranged in a complex
alternation of individual
elements and groups
of multiple pillars.*

Patio de los Arrayanes,
*seen from the north.
The seven arches
of the portico, supported
by slender columns, have
decorative stucco panels
with diamond motifs.*

On the facing page
Vault of the Sala
de Dos Hermanas.
In the muqarnas *vault,
numerous small plaster
niches create a beehive
surface of great
decorative effect.*

Cautiva (fourteenth century) and by the later structure known as the Torre de las Infantas, set on the city walls and later converted into residences. The architectural structure of the two buildings is similar and features a small entrance surrounded by round arches set on pillars, from which one enters the side alcoves and the main room; the upper floors of the towers, which culminate in a terrace, were also occupied by homes. In the Torre de la Cautiva, we should mention the wall decorations, which consist of glazed ceramic mosaics composed into geometric motifs (*alicatado*) and stuccoes, which were originally coloured to imitate the effects of tapestries and carpets.

The central section of the Alhambra contained the buildings reserved for the sultan, who had in these palaces both the seat of his government and his own private residence. Nowadays, this area, the best preserved section of the entire fortress, is a cluster of juxtaposed constructions, which since the sixteenth cen-

tury has been known by the name of Casa Real Vieja (Old Royal House), to distinguish them from the adjoining Renaissance palace built to the south of the Arab palace by Charles V (Casa Real Nueva, or New Royal House). In the Cuarto de Comares and in the Palacio de los Leones, which constitute the two main sections of the Casa Real Vieja, the fairly simple exteriors contrast with the precious appearance of the interior courtyards and the decoration of the rooms: here a phantasmagoric array of light and colours, spread over the walls and ceilings, is accompanied by the sense of movement of the columns, which are the main structural element. The sumptuous interiors of the Arabic residences were substantially respected and left intact by the Christian kings, who lived in them and adapted them to their own requirements.

The palace complex opens with a sequence of courtyards and public spaces that culminates in the Sala del Mexuar, decorated with

THE CASA REAL NUEVA

The history of the Alhambra following the Christian *reconquista* had its most important phase in the architectural works ordered by Charles V (1500–58). The emperor commissioned the painter Pedro Machuca to build a new royal palace (1526–68), which would stand next to the palace of the Arab sultans on a line with the Patio de Comares. Inspired by the models of Italian classicism, this building (which was left unfinished) featured a square plan, with a snubbed-off corner occupied by an octagonal oratory and four entrances each set at the centre of one of the sides. In the middle of the square was a large round courtyard, surrounded by a two-storey portico: the columns of the two orders (Doric and Ionic) are surmounted by a straight-line trabeation, which replaced the traditional succession of arches. The façade is presented as an original revision of the so-called 'House of Raphael', a Roman project by Bramante (*c.* 1510), with the rusticated ashlars on the lower storey and the motif of the twinned columns on the upper level. In early sixteenth-century Spain, the palace of Charles V must have had a singular importance and innovative dimensions, even if its influence was not immediately felt: its direct successor, in fact, can be seen in another royal palace, even more alien in its austerity from the extravagances of the *plateresco* style: the Escorial. For the fortress of Granada Charles V also ordered the construction of the Puerta de las Granadas (*c.* 1546) which was placed as a triumphal entrance at the south-western extremity of the outside walls.

Pedro Machuca, Casa Real Nueva: the courtyard. In the middle of the great square plan of the palace is a large round courtyard, surrounded by a two-storey portico.

Pedro Machuca, façade of the Casa Real Nueva. The rusticated ashlar facing and the motif of the twinned columns are inspired by Bramante's 'House of Raphael' in Rome.

THE CALLIGRAPHIC DECORATIONS

Numerous rooms in the royal palaces
of the Alhambra feature, alongside the countless
decorative elements, ornamental calligraphic
inscriptions, for the most part containing verses from
the Koran or poems about the hall in question or the
sultan who ordered its construction. In the Muslim
world, a special significance was accorded to writing,
since it represented the means whereby the sacred
scriptures were diffused, and writing is therefore
considered as a religious act. It was used for
decorative purposes in all artistic genres, in some
cases linked with ornamental plant or animal motifs.
In the Sala de Dos Hermanas an inscription
reproduces twenty-four verses written by the court
poet Muhammad Ibn Zamrak, in which the room
and the adjoining courtyard are compared to
the constellations: the stars of the sky, in fact, would
prefer to be in this room, which has both manifest
and hidden beauties in its 'brilliant' vault, while the
arches of the courtyard rest upon columns adorned
with light, like the celestial spheres. Likewise, in the
inscription placed upon the Fountain of the Lions, the
verses form a specific commentary to the symbolism
of the architecture: 'I think of a carved monument,
whose veil/of splendour consists of pearls,/and
which adorns the place with/the light of gems'.

Detail of a calligraphic inscription.

Detail of a wall covering in azulejos, *enamelled ceramic tiles, used for wall decorations.*

stuccoes and polychromatic tiles. In the Cuarto de Comares were distributed the private apartments, which ran back from a façade (1370) that was harmoniously punctuated by geometric decorations and ornamental vine clusters. The residence is arranged around the Patio de los Arrayanes, almost entirely occupied by a basin of water in which the surrounding buildings are reflected: the water enters from two sources set on the short sides and spreads out placidly, leaving the surface of the pool always smooth. The walls of the portico are adorned with a tiled plinth and the seven arcades, supported on slender columns, have stucco panels decorated with diamond patterns. The Sala de Comares, which contained the throne, is the most impressive room of the entire Alhambra: above a plinth with multicoloured tiles, the walls are entirely covered with stucco slabs arranged geometrically and carved with plant motifs and calligraphic ornamentations. In the ceiling, a true masterpiece of Islamic woodwork, a remarkable composition of wooden polygonal boards designs a starry sky, a cosmic and eschatological representation created in honour of the sultan. Another noteworthy space in the Cuarto de Comares is the Turkish bath, which could be reached from the patio through a narrow stairway: the most spectacular room in the complex of the Baño was the Sala de las Camas, flanked by two alcoves and lit by a lantern, beneath which ran an ambulatory which served the rooms that were once set aside for the care of the body. The whole space is adorned with stuccoes, tiles, fountains, and columns.

The Palacio de los Leones was built in the second half of the fourteenth century (Sultanate of Muhammad V) as an independent construction adjoining the Cuarto de Comares, and it constitutes the high point of the architecture and the decorative art of the Nasrid era. In the main courtyard (Patio de los

Detail of a small room with blind, polylobate windows.

Decorative detail of the Sala de Dos Hermanas.

On the facing page
Sala de las Camas
in the Baño de Comares.
*The room of the alcoves
(or bedchambers)
is adorned with
stuccoes, tiles,
fountains and columns.*

Leones) pride of place belongs to a marble fountain, set at the point of intersection of two small perpendicular channels; the basin is supported by twelve carved lions, all depicted in different ways. The patio is surrounded by slender marble columns, in a complex alternation of single elements and groups of two or three shafts, until it reaches, in the two pavilions that jut from the short sides of the portico, clusters of four shafts. On the eastern side we find the Sala de los Reyes, a room surrounded by five alcoves, the middle of the five featuring a painted dome: the paintings, done with a technique similar to that used in the miniatures on sheepskin fastened to the ceiling, portray a group of ten noblemen intently discussing something among themselves. In the two external domes, as well, we find paintings that depict court scenes. The palace was completed by two independent residential units, the Sala de Dos Hermanas and the Sala de los Abencerrajes, which have some of the loveliest *muqarnas* vaults in the entire complex: numerous little plaster niches, receding and arranged according to geometric patterns, shape the structure from the pendentives down, creating a beehive surface with a stunning decorative effect. Finally, on the side of the garden, is the Mirador de Lindaraja, which has exquisitely fashioned decorations and ceiling.

The Palace
of Drottningholm

The Palace of Drottningholm stands not far from Stockholm, on the island of Lövo, in the Lake of Mälaren. It is a massive and magnificent complex, comprised of seven chief clusters of buildings, as well as pavilions and gardens. Built as the summer residence of the royal family, and later transformed into the official royal residence, it documents with its form the refined and spectacular tastes of its illustrious founders, who embraced the fashions and aesthetic trends that held sway between the seventeenth and nineteenth centuries on the European continent, and especially in France.

The first construction campaign began in 1662, under Queen Eleonore, who assigned the project to the Swedish architect Nicodemus Tessin the Elder (1615–81). Construction stretched out over four decades, until 1703, a period during which the initial Baroque forms of the building, extravagant and spectacular, were brought into closer compliance with the more sober and harmonious forms of the French architectural models which influenced Nicodemus Tessin the Younger (1654–1728) who had replaced his father. Belonging to this phase of construction are the royal bedroom and the atrium-vestibule from which the main staircase rises. In 1744 Queen Luise Ulrike commissioned the architect Carl Harleman to build the four lateral wings that run out from the main structure and, at the same time, the French architect Jean Eric Rehn to build the sumptuous library.

Around the middle of the eighteenth century, when the intermediate wings, originally one-storey tall, were given a second floor, the building took on its present appearance. Expansion and renovation went on over the decades that followed as well, leading to the creation of new ancillary buildings, the radical restructuring of the throne room and, during the reign of King Oscar II (1829–1907), of

the Bernadotte Dynasty, an extensive campaign of decoration intended to make the palace adhere more closely to the eclectic and Rococo tastes of the king.

The changes and shifts in styles and fashions also affected the gardens: the French garden, which surrounds the complex entirely, designed by Nicodemus Tessin the Younger in 1681 on the model of the Baroque park of Versailles, with bronze statues by Adriaen de Vries, hedges with surprising shapes, and flower-beds, bushes, waterfalls, fountains, and artificial ponds; and the English garden, built in 1778 to the north of the French garden, to plans by King Gustavus III and the architect Adelcrantz, reflecting the new preference for a more lively and 'picturesque' landscape.

Among the pavilions scattered throughout the park, aside from the Chinese Pavilion, especially interesting is the pavilion of the Court Theatre, or Royal Theatre, which houses one of the best preserved Baroque stage sets in all Europe. It was built in 1764, at the behest of Queen Luise Ulrike and to plans by the architect Adelcrantz, on the ruins of a building intended for the same purpose but destroyed by a fire two years earlier. It was enlarged with the construction of the Dining Room in 1791, that is, during the period of great splendour and magnificence which coincided with the reign of King Gustavus III (1771–92), who was himself an actor and the author of historic dramas. The exterior of the construction has architectural forms that combine the decorativism of French Rococo with neo-classical simplicity, while the interior has preserved its original eighteenth-century form and functions: the stage, the dressing rooms, the storerooms, the scenery, and the large orchestra, capable of seating 400 spectators. Also preserved is the theatrical machinery, designed and built by the Italian Donato Stoppani, and still functioning.

In front of the Palace of Drottningholm is the French-style garden.

On the facing page
The official bedroom.

*Surrounded by
the French-style garden,
in which the fountains
are embellished by the
bronze statues of Adriaen
de Vries, the Palace
of Drottningholm is
composed of seven chief
sections, built between
the eighteenth
and nineteenth centuries
by the various sovereigns
who lived here.*

*The Court Theatre,
which contains a splendid
Baroque stage set,
has on the exterior
architectural forms
of neo-classical simplicity.*

THE CHINESE PAVILION

The wooden structure of the Chinese Pavilion
(Kina Slott) of Drottningholm, built by the architect
Adelcrantz, provides an exemplary incarnation
of the vogue for oriental decoration that spread
throughout Europe in the eighteenth century.
Built in 1763, it replaced the pavilion that had been
designed and built ten years earlier by the architect
Carl Harleman and by King Adolphus Frederick,
as a birthday present for Queen Luise Ulrike.
It has a two-storey central structure, joined
by curving galleries to two lower constructions.
Surrounding the buildings are four smaller pavilions,
in which the effects of oriental art are blended
with the Rococo style, and a small garden,
also Chinese in inspiration.
The decorations of the interiors, as well, combine
Rococo with exotic imagery, predominantly trees
and dragons. Restored many times, without any
modification to the structures or decorations, these
rooms contain a number of artworks from the royal
collections, just as they did in the eighteenth century.

*The constructions
that make up
the Chinese Pavilion
of Drottningholm, built
in 1763, combine
the evocative aspects
of exotic art with
the forms and decorative
motifs that are distinctive
of European Rococo.*

The Abbey of Saint John the Baptist at Müstair

The Abbey of Saint John the Baptist at Müstair, in the Swiss canton of Graubünden, constitutes one of the most exquisite pieces of surviving documentation of the architecture and painting of the Carolingian Age. According to tradition, it was Charlemagne himself, upon his return from his coronation in Lombardy, who founded it at the end of the eighth century and entrusted it to the Benedictines. It became a convent in 1163, and throughout the Middle Ages it attained great power and wealth. In fact, it stood in the central-eastern area of the Alpine arc which, criss-crossed by the roads that linked the Adriatic regions and Lombardy, on the one hand, and Bavaria and the Rhineland on the other, then played a major strategic, political, and economic role.

The monastic complex is a unified nucleus of buildings distributed around two cloisters and enclosed by an external ring of walls. The most important construction is the church, dedicated to Saint John and erected during the Carolingian period. Formed by a simple rectangular hall some 20 metres long, it is concluded to the east by three tall semi-circular apses, adorned on the exterior by blind arcades. During the Gothic and Baroque periods, it was subjected to major modifications, like the rest of the complex: two rows of columns divided the interior into three aisles, a matroneum was installed, and the original wooden ceiling was replaced by a vaulted roof; on the exterior, in the fifteenth century, adjoining the right-hand side of the church, a stout tower with a square plan was built, a tower-house for the abbess of the convent.

The frescoes that decorate the interior of the church, executed around the fourth decade of the ninth century A.D., represent the most extensive cycle of paintings from the Carolingian era that still survives, and therefore constitutes a priceless documentation of the fun-

damental artistic and cultural rebirth known as the 'Carolingian Renaissance'. The wall paintings, set in ninety-one panels arranged on five registers, depict *Stories from the Old and New Testament* in a sequence that is not chronological but scriptural, intended, that is, to juxtapose the scenes of the Old Testament with the evangelical events for which they were thought to be a foreshadowing. The panels are framed with painted strips of garlands and ribbons, and culminate towards the top in a large cornice that illusionistically reproduces an architectural feature. Sadly, the cycle has suffered considerable damage, both because of ill-conceived restorations, and because of the repainting of the apses, which probably took place between 1165 and 1180, while the frescoes on the side walls, with the *Stories of David*, were removed and placed in the Landesmuseum in Zurich. One thing that was preserved, however, is the magnificent scene of the *Last Judgement* on the counterfaçade, the first example of the placement of this subject in this location.

The frescoes of Müstair are characterized by an attention for the placement of figures in balanced and symmetrical compositions, and by a capacity to create magnificent rhythms and complex architectural backgrounds. Likewise, the rapid application of paint, using a few bright hues set within broad juxtaposed bays, enlightened by quick highlights, reveals the complex and sophisticated culture of the executors of the frescoes. The evident link between the frescoes of Müstair and the famous cycle in the Lombard Church of Santa Maria di Castelseprio, has led scholars to believe that the artists working on the Swiss convent might have come from that region, or that at the very least, there was a direct and profound familiarity with the painting that was done there.

Other precious artworks preserved in the Benedictine complex date from successive cen-

Detail of the frescoes executed on the interior of the Church of Saint John in the fourth decade of the ninth century; the mural paintings represent the most extensive series of paintings to survive from the Carolingian era.

On the facing page *View of the abbey complex, with the three semi-circular apses of the church, dating back to the higher Middle Ages, and the massive structure of the tower-house, built in the fifteenth century for the abbess of the convent.*

turies: dating from the Romanesque period are, aside from the frescoes preserved in the church's apse area, the large statue in painted stucco depicting Charlemagne (1165), located in the choir, and on the left wall of the same room a fine Romanesque relief depicting the *Baptism of Christ* (1087); a number of fragments depicting the *Crucifixion* and the *Deposition of Christ* preserved in the cloister (dating from the end of the eleventh century); and, in the cemetery to the right of the church, the *Heiligkreuzkapelle* (Chapel of the Holy Cross), a small three-apsed building erected in the thirteenth century and enriched in 1520 by an elegant wooden ceiling. At the end of the eleventh century the Chapel of Saints Ulrich and Nikolaus was also built, a two-storey building adorned with major reliefs from the Carolingian period that, in the refined interlacing decorations, are reminiscent of those of Cividale del Friuli. The other rooms in the abbey, which for the most part date back to the eighteenth century, stand around the main cloister and contain documents, models related to the religious complex, reliquaries, outfits, and objects of sacred art, dating from the thirteenth to the eighteenth centuries. In the interior, which contains the Gothic and Renaissance furnishings, special attention should be paid to the Baroque Fürstenzimmer, or 'Prince's chamber', built in 1659, which provides a further documentation of the political function that the monastery served for many centuries after its foundation.

The large stucco statue from the Romanesque era (1165), placed in the choir of the church, depicts Charlemagne who, according to tradition, founded the monastery at the end of the eighth century, entrusting it to the Benedictine monks.

On the facing page Detail of a fresco depicting a monstrous figure.

GROENLANDIA

ALASKA

RUSSIA

TURKEY

GEORGIA

KAZAKISTAN

MONGOLIA

JAPAN

CYPRUS

ARMENIA

AZERBAIJAN

Haghpat

UZBEKISTAN

NORTH
KOREA

Himeji-jo

LEBANON   SYRIA

TURKMENISTAN

KYRGHYZSTAN

SOUTH
KOREA

ISRAEL

IRAQ

Isfahan

TAGIKISTAN

Beijing

IRAN

CHINA

Great Wall

KUWAIT

AFGHANISTAN

Wudang

SAUDI

BAHRAIN

QATAR

PAKISTAN

Lhasa

TAIWAN

ARABIA

UNITED
ARAB
EMIRATES

Agra

NEPAL

BHUTAN

YEMEN

OMAN

INDIA

BANGLADESH

MYANMAR

PHILIPPINES

Konarak

LAOS

VIET NAM

THAILAND

CAMBODIA

MALAYSIA

BRUNEI

Dambulla

SRI LANKA
(CEYLON)

INDONESIA

MALDIVES

SINGAPORE

REPUBBLICA
DEMOCRATICA
DI TIMOR EST

Borobudur

ASIA Asia

The Monastery of Haghpat

The Monastery of Haghpat, which is located in the northern region of Armenia known as Tumanyan, is the largest and most important architectural complex to have survived since the Middle Ages in that country. Of the original vast construction, which over the centuries has undergone destruction and plunder, there survive only the main buildings, gathered in a compact block surrounded by an enormous fortified enclosure, a fortress, a hermitage, and a fountain (1258).

The monastery was probably founded around A.D. 976 when, at the behest of Queen Khosrovanush, wife of King Ashot III (who reigned from 952 to 977), the main church was built and dedicated to the Holy Cross (*Sourb Nshan*). The construction was completed in 991 at the behest of the two sons of the founder, King Smbat (who reigned from 977 to 989) and Gurgen, the Prince of the little local realm of Lore, probably under the supervision of the Armenian architect Trdat. The church, a typical example of Armenian ecclesiastic architecture, with a cross plan, has a conical dome that was restored between the eleventh and the twelfth centuries, set upon a cylindrical tambour through pendentives and arches that are set upon pillars with flanking columns. The façades are embellished with high V-shaped apertures, arranged in pairs. On the eastern façade, the rectangular niche under the pediment features a relief depicting the two brothers who commissioned the church in the act of holding up a small architectural model of it, crowned in keeping with their respective rank: Smbat wears the voluminous turban, the symbol of royal power conceded to Armenian kings by the caliphs, while Gurgen wears a sort of helmet.

The narthex (in Armenian, *gavit* or *zhamatun*) that stands next to the western wall of the church was built in 1185 in the shape of a rectangular gallery to be used as a mausoleum for the descendants of Gurgen. In 1210 it was expanded towards the west, until it was larger than the church itself, though it stood on lower ground. It contains the oldest and most admired example in Armenia of a vaulted roof held up by pairs of crossing arches, supported by pillars flanking the walls. The traditional dome with the central aperture is here replaced by another system of cross vaults.

The other monastery buildings, all made of basalt and austere in form, are clustered to the north-east of the church. The bell tower, standing alone and set atop a small hill, was built in 1245 when Hamazasp was the abbot. Its form is quite original: it is in fact constituted by two floors, surmounted by a small rotunda; the lower storey, with a cruciform plan, has four splayed jambs at its corners, supporting the second storey with its octagonal plan. Hamazasp himself ordered the construction of a *gavit* (1253–57) linked to the northern façade of the church through a gallery, singular for its placement across from a small chapel and not, as is more customary, on a line with a church. This is the most important surviving example of an Armenian four-storey building covered with a dome with a central aperture. Adjoining the south-eastern corner of the *gavit* is the monastery library, built in 1262 but subsequently transformed into a storeroom.

The Monastery of Haghpat contains many *khatchkars*, slabs of stone with a cross carved in the centre, especially in the gallery that crosses the church and which leads to the other buildings. A *khatchkars* of special importance is the one of the Amenaprkich (1273), which depicts in bas-relief a *Deposition* over which looms a *Christ in Majesty* and which is framed on either side by the figures of the Apostles.

The Monastery, restored in the seventeenth century, was restituted to the Armenian Church in 1989 so that it could return to use as a place of Christian prayer and devotion.

The relief set on the eastern façade of the Church of the the Holy Cross depicts the two brothers Smbat and Gurgen, the former with the royal turban, and the second with a helmet, in the act of donating a small architectural model of the church.

On the facing page
The buildings of the monastery, made of basalt blocks, surmounted by the distinctive conical roofs.

The Great Wall

Along the outer edge of the city walls the functionaries, who until the night before had sipped cups of wine together, reciting poetry and waiting for the wax of the candles to burn down entirely, took their leave, after having been assigned to different areas of the imperial territory. It is such a scene that Li Bai, one of the greatest Chinese men of letters of the eighth century, evoked in some of his verses.

Beyond another bastion, the Great Wall of China, a meeting was taking place, instead of a separation: a meeting between a Chinese princess sent as hostage to the nomadic tribes who were pressing along the northern borders in order to pacify them, and her future husband, a barbarian, the misunderstood member of a different culture. If nothing else emerged from these political marriages, they did obtain the effect of bringing together the cultures of the steppe and Chinese culture, and the cunning ministers of the Middle Kingdom knew very well that, by sending a daughter of the emperor to the 'barbarians', they were instilling in them a slowly growing desire to settle down. And leaving their *yurts*, saddles, and stirrups to move to the city was tantamount for the barbarians to defeat.

Perhaps more than a Great Wall, we should speak of a number of Great Walls. In 221 B.C., in fact, Qin Shi Huangdi, who financed the project of the terracotta army in present-day Xi'an, in the process of reunifying the country also encouraged the task of joining together various stretches of walls built over the preceding centuries for defensive purposes. During the 'Springs and Autumns' period (770–476 B.C.) and in the period, with a significant name, of the Warring States (475–221), the various feudal powers of the badly fragmented Kingdom of the Zhou family worked feverishly to build walls to halt or slow the raids of neighbouring

states and the nomadic soldiers from the north. Among the seven dukedoms along the Huanghe (the Yellow River) who contended for power during the Springs and Autumns period, it was the Chu Dukedom that first began to reinforce its borders; later, the states of Yan, Zhao, and Qin, having experienced repeated combat with the nomads along their northern borders, also decided to start work on their own 'Maginot Lines'.

The unification of these existing stretches of wall and their expansion, carried on even during the Han period, led to the creation of a line of defence extending 5,000 kilometres, from the bay of Liaodong in the east, all the way to Lintao, in Gansu, in the west.

The chief purpose was the defence of the Hexi corridor (the "zone to the west of the River", which meant the Yellow River), a narrow strip of irrigate land that ran from Gansu all the way to Lop Nor, in the heart of the Xinjiang (the region of the Uigurs, or Chinese Turkestan), in an area rich in minerals and criss-crossed by the northern Silk Road. The wall pretty much followed the Hexi, running slightly to the west of it. It is therefore natural that the history of the Great Wall of China should run parallel with the progressive encounter and fusion of the various central Asian cultures that bordered the Silk Road.

The Han and pre-Han walls have almost entirely vanished under the erosion of the wind, or they have been buried by sand. In any case, they were not all built in masonry: in the desert sections the builders were satisfied with earth embankments that have collapsed over the centuries. All the same, we know that steel tools were used to optimize the labour, and the ancient winding route of the walls can still be followed from the air, because of the remaining scars of pounded earth or stands of cane that follow their route.

As early as the sixth century A.D., the walls

Aerial view of the stretch of wall at Simatan, some 120 kilometres from the capital, to the north of Miyun.

On the facing page
At Badaling, 60 kilometres away from Beijing, the wall has a foundation of stone slabs, but then it rises upward with a brick structure.

The Great Wall does not
meet the sea until it
reaches Shanhaiguan
(the Pass of the Sea
and the Mountains),
to the north-east
of Qinghuangdao,
in Hebei Province.

*On the facing page
A guard-house
at Badaling, two storeys
high: for troops
and for weapons.*

had deteriorated to the point that they had become useless. It was not until the fourteenth century, under the Ming Dynasty, that the wall was rebuilt, but this time for propaganda purposes. Perhaps, from that point on, the wall served more to keep the subjects in than to hold the enemies out: a sort of immense symbol of national unity in a period when the empire chose to close in upon itself. A curious destiny befell the Ming Dynasty: just after having financed the greatest maritime expeditions to explore and survey the Indian Ocean, led by Admiral Zheng He (1371–1433), the sovereigns chose to return to the interior of their boundaries; and it was then, in a sort of unconscious chase, that Europe began the Age of Discovery. The Great Wall of China was transformed into a sort of buffer zone, to be praised in the imaginations of the subjects of the empire.

It is no accident that this sort of public work should have been undertaken by those same emperors who, in Chinese history, paid the most attention to the management of their own image: Qin Shi Huangdi of the Qin, Gaozi of the Han, Wendi of the Sui and Gaozu of the Tang all lavished resources upon other "great works" and infrastructures: not only palaces, but also canals, roads and state granaries to protect the people against famine.

This jewel of the poliorcetic construction of defensive engineering required almost two centuries to complete. All the same, no military strategist would be so naïve – and the Chinese have never been known for their naïvety – as to believe that it is possible to build an invulnerable wall. The wall was not built in the hopes of halting all nomadic invasions: it was meant to slow them, hinder them, render them easier to deal with; in particular, the very long strip of wall that ran lengthwise, like a scar, across the Middle Kingdom, served two functions considered much more useful by the Chinese than that of a mere military bastion. First of all, the paved surface on the top of the wall allowed the passage of horses, and therefore constituted a sort of elevated superhighway for the rapid

*The garrison towers,
in Badaling, now house
wood-carvers.*

Aerial view of the Great Wall in the Jixian district.

Towers for the garrison at Badaling.

deployment of troops where needed, as well as facilitating the transport of provisions for the garrisons and trade in all sorts of goods. In the second place, from the towers that punctuated the path of the great wall at regular intervals, it was possible to transmit signals that could then be passed along, like a long telephone cable: by night, signal fires were used, and by day, a wisp of smoke, so that it was possible to warn the nearest garrison of the approach of enemy forces.

The towers that we find along the bastions are of two different sorts, because they serve two purposes: some served as dormitories for the troops of the garrisons, as well as storehouses for weapons and munitions; the others, the "smoke piles", were elevated observation points, shelters for sentinels.

From the Han to the Ming, in reality, the wall shrank considerably: in the second century A.D., the bastions extended into the Gobi Desert as far as Lop Nor, while under the Ming they extended no further than Gansu.

The most significant restorations were done on a line with Badaling, the Shanhai Pass and the Jiayu Pass, in the Gobi Desert.

The fortress at the Jiayu Pass, 40 kilometres to the west of Jiuquan, was completed in 1372 and could house a garrison of 400 soldiers. It was abandoned not long afterwards, and was not restored until the sixteenth century. The enclosure wall stands 10 metres tall, as compared with the 7–8 metres average to the north of Beijing. The core of the wall is pounded earth, covered with bricks. On the last stretches of the wall is a solemn inscription that in four characters offers the first greeting to a traveller arriving from Europe.

Even today, there is no agreement on the overall length of the surviving stretches of wall, but it has been calculated that if we re-utilized all of the bricks to build a wall that stood 5 metres tall and 1 metre thick, it could run ten times around the Earth at the equator.

BLOOD, SWEAT, AND WALLS

Legend has it that the construction of the walls under Qin Shi Huangdi required a decade or so, involving 300,000 individuals in exhausting and brutal waves of forced labour. Three years after the beginning of work, Meng Jiangnu was desperately waiting her husband's return. She decided to go herself to bring him clothes that she had made with her own hands. She got as far as the Shanhai Pass, near present-day Qinhuangdao, in the province of Hebei, at the point where the walls, meeting the coast, seem to plunge down into the Pacific Ocean. Meng overcame unspeakable obstacles before she finally reached her destination and learned that her husband had died. She could not even pay her respects to the corpse of her beloved, since it had been incorporated into the wall to build up its structure with every last bit of mass. Meng Jiangnu, then, wept. She simply wept. But she wept for so long that 400 kilometres of wall collapsed in sympathy, returning her husband's corpse to the light of day so that she might honour it fittingly.

*Graffiti along
the Great Wall.*

241

The Potala in Lhasa

There is another 'White House' in the world, which towers, unthinkably, thousands of metres higher than the one in Washington D.C., and tens of thousand of kilometres away from it. It is the Potrang Karpo, or 'White Palace', which, along with other buildings, forms the Potala, the site of the religious and secular power of the Dalai Lama. The valley of the Kyichu, the river that runs around Lhasa, is already at an elevation of 3,600 metres; the Potala is a dizzying acropolis upon an acropolis, looming over the cityscape on a cliff rising to a height of 130 metres.

'The road from Netanga to Lhasa rises and falls along the rocky ridge that plunges down to the River Kyichu, then it rambles along sleepily in the water-drenched plain that is weighed down with heavy sand banks; where the road comes to a turning, a pile of rocks as high as a hill marks the place where, for the first time, the adoring eyes of the pilgrims are able to gaze upon the gilded spires of the Potala: a prayer and a rock tossed onto the growing pile, an anonymous relic of devoted souls. ... Toward noon I walk under the Potala: more than a palace, it is another hill that continues the rock, asymmetrical and capricious like some creation of nature, and yet built with an internal consistency so that you expect to see every angle and every line appearing exactly as it is, creating the appearance of regularity where everything is in fact arbitrary. It grew with the stone like a diamond attached to a matrix: ... the white frames the red central structure and above it there is a glittering array of golden domes and spires. The caravan winds along beneath the Potala, it scatters in confusion at the sight of an elephant, a gift from the Maharajah of Nepal, which suddenly emerges, solemn and immense, turning down towards the river and coming to a halt in the Ghiavolinca, a park shaded by willows and poplars.'

These were the first impressions recorded, on one of his numerous expeditions to Tibet, by Giuseppe Tucci, the brilliant and polymath Italian orientalist, in 1948. The Potala can only be reached, today as 1,300 years ago, by foot. There are no elevators to ease the way, amidst the 'basso continuo' of the Buddhist chants and the aroma of yak butter, used as fuel for the lanterns in the chapels.

In the seventh century A.D., the Emperor Srong-brtsan-sgam-po (Songtsen Gampo) would withdraw into the grottoes of these cliffs, the 'Red Hill' (*Marpo Ri*), to meditate. It was thought that the Bodhisattva Chenresi (Avalokitesvara) had done so before him, inconceivably long ago, and always with the indulgent complicity of time Songtsen Gampo was in turn considered to be a reincarnation of Avalokitesvara.

Songtsen, in Chinese, King Zhanpu (Shuzhan Genpu), was responsible for the creation of the Kingdom of Tufen, in Tibet, with Lhasa as its capital. The Tang Emperor, in the context of a cunning matrimonial policy with respect to his neighbouring kingdoms, in 614 sent him his daughter, the Princess Wenchen, as something midway between a hostage and a bride.

In order to ward off any sense of inferiority towards the munificent Tang Empire, Songtsen launched the programme of construction of the Potala, as the administrative centre of his newborn kingdom: thus the first components of the palatial complex were built. Already, this first phase of construction led to the creation of 1,000 rooms. Only the 'Grotto for the Prince of Dharma' and the Main Hall, the Pagbalhakhang, have survived the events of the centuries: fire, lit either by lightning or else by yak butter candles, has whimsically destroyed the rest.

The reconstruction of this complex could only take place once the economic conditions

The Potala dominates the cityscape of Lhasa.

On the facing page
The Potala reflected in the Kyichu, the river that runs past Lhasa. The Kyichu runs at an elevation of 3,600 metres, and the Potala rises 130 metres above the city.

The golden roofs of the Potala frame the Main Hall, dedicated to Avalokitesvara.

The White Palace: you can see the two Halls of Dawn, the Eastern and the Western Hall.

On the facing page
A fresco depicting Tara
(White Star).

to undertake a project of this scale had been established; specifically in the late seventeenth century during the reign of Lozang Gyasto, the fifth Dalai Lama and founder of the Gelugpa theocracy. The ruins of the seventh-century construction were incorporated into the foundation of the larger complex, which still stands today. Work began in 1645, involving 7,000 labourers and 1,500 craftsmen. After three years, the fifth Dalai Lama moved from the Zhaibung monastery to the Potrang Karpo, or White Palace, which was already finished, while the Potrang Marpo, or Red House, was added between 1690 and 1694.

The configuration of the complex remained virtually unchanged until 1922, when the thirteenth Dalai Lama, a political figure of considerable importance, restored a substantial part of the White Palace and added two storeys to the Red Palace. Very slight damage was done by the Tibetan revolt against the Chinese occupation in 1959; the Potala miraculously escaped intact from looting by the Red Guard – luckier by far than so many other Chinese archaeological sites – due, it appears, to the direct intervention of the Prime Minister of the time, Zhou Enlai.

The name of the complex owes its identity to the first patron of the architectural occupation of the red rock, Songtsen, with Avalokitesvara: one of the homes of the god, in fact, is a mountain in southern India that bears the name of Potala, and the fortress and the palace are ideal depictions of that mountain.

With its 130,000 square metres – set in a total area of 360,000 square metres – with 360 metres on the east-west side and 270 metres on the north-south side, and rising 119 metres on thirteen storeys, the Potala is the tallest ancient palace on earth. An immense architectural complex, perhaps even excessive, with its 1,000 rooms, it was created and grew as a sort of compromise. The Potala was built –

AVALOKITESVARA: WHO WAS HE?
In a specific cosmological vision, Adibuddha
Mahavairocana Mahavira (Primordial Buddha, Great
Splendour, Great Hero) is depicted in a central
position, surrounded by four Buddhas, one for each
of the cardinal points of the compass: Amitabha
is the Buddha of the Western Paradise. His most
important acolyte is Avalokitesvara (Lord of Mercy).
The devotion of Avalokitesvara made reference to
a simple message of salvation, and it was therefore
quite effective with even the simplest population,
but it did not constitute a great attraction for more
speculative intellects. Salvation, according to this
school, could be attained through the mere repetition
of the name of Amitabha, thousands of times.
This practice led to the development of a specific
hymnology and a liturgy, which survives even now.
In Tantric Buddhism the Buddha is depicted
in a mystical union with his female complement,
representing Wisdom. Femininity is rendered in fact
by a slight outward turn of the hip and by a graceful
pose of the hand, often held towards the face.
When it arrived in China, the female version
of Avalokitesvara was readily accepted, since
it could easily overlap with an existing native divinity,
Xiwangmu, the Queen Mother of the West.
The Chinese name of Avalokitesvara is Guanyin.
The depiction of 1,000-armed Guanyin is the oldest
one: we find it in the frescoes of Dunhuang, along
the Silk Road, when the deity still showed masculine
features. The eleven-headed and 1,000-armed
version might derive from:
– a corporeal representation of the Vishnucakra
(the disk, the most important weapon, of Vishnu);
– the image of Siva Nilakantha (with the midnight
blue neck);
– the mixed form of Harihara.
On each palm we find a painted eye, because
the meaning of Guanyin is '[she who] contemplates
the voice [of those who suffer]'.
From the eleventh century, the following
iconography took root:
– a hand with a flagon containing the nectar
of Doctrine;
– a willow branch to scatter it upwards, that it might
rain upon the people;
– a pearl necklace;
– the Buddha of the Paradise of reference,
the Western Paradise, among the hair
(this is Amitabha, the Buddha of Infinite Light);
– a white outfit: the whiteness of the garb may
derive from the iconography of Tara (white star),
transcendent Bodhisattva born of a tear of none
other than Avalokitesvara, which developed
from the sixth century A.D.

Panoramic view of the Potala.

The western section of the Potala, with the Hall of the Earth Mother and the Excellent Monastery, restored in 1675–76.

On the facing page
The Portal of the Perfect Convergence, decorated with the propitious symbols and the seven lions, emblems of royalty.

The Portal of the Western Hall of Dawn. Often friezes were hung at the doors, with stripes similar to those of the tiger, which were symbols of authority.

at the intersection of history and legend – because of the encounter between Tibetan and Chinese cultures, between a newly established king and the princess of a 1,000-year-old empire, and so it reflects on a structural level the blending of the two cultures. It is a syncretic structure, an architectural compromise between stone and wooden sentinel towers, typically Tibetan, but with exquisitely Chinese audience halls.

With its maze-like plan, the Potala eludes any attempt to define it: how should it be considered? It contains 1,000 rooms and 1,000 functions: it is the residence of the Dalai Lama and his court, it is a political think-tank, the seat of the Government of Tibet and site of its state ceremonies, a school for the training of monks and administrators, without forgetting that it is also the last resting place of the bodies of the previous Dalai Lamas, and it is therefore the destination for pilgrimages for the Buddhist religion, with its stupas.

The chapels held in greatest esteem by the crowds of pilgrims are found in the White Palace: these are the two small halls, the Phakpa Lhakhang and the Chogyal Drubphuk,

which date back to the earliest architectural occupation of the mountain in the seventh century A.D. In fact, the Phapka Lhakhang houses the most venerated statue, the Arya Lokeshvara.

Even now, two palaces coexist in one in the Potala: the White Palace and the Red Palace. The former, built as we have seen in 1645–53, develops out of the original 'Hall of Guanyin' along the east-west axis, and includes white-walled monastic halls (hence the name). The axis of vertical extension should not be overlooked, given that the palace has seven full storeys, the fourth of which houses the religious nucleus of the Potala, the Coqenxag or 'Eastern Hall', which extends over an area of 717 square metres, punctuated by thirty-eight pillars: this fabric of columns is the setting in which the Dalai Lama is officially consecrated to his position, at the age of eighteen.

On the fifth and sixth floors are the Dalai Lama's residence and the offices of the ruling prince; the seventh floor, with its enormous windows, opening to the sunlight, is the monarch's 'winter palace'. In this symbolic ascension, floor by floor, you pass by gold dishes and bowls, and jade goblets, until you reach the terrace of the 'Hall of Light', jutting out over Lhasa. From there, your gaze can embrace the distant mountain chains, the River Kyichu, with the fields and rows of trees that punctuate the faraway villages, as far as the Jokhang monastery.

The Red Palace, built in 1690, is also an enormous three-dimensional emblem of the past coexistence of the Middle Kingdom and the Kingdom of Tibet: the Kangxi Emperor of the Qing Dynasty, a non-native Manchu Dynasty, offered the use of 100 of his artisans, Han, Manchu, and Mongols, to take part in the construction. Alongside the throne of the Dalai Lama you will see the curtains given as a gift by Kangxi and a good-luck inscription from Qianlong, two of the greatest emperors of the Qing Dynasty: midway between a respectful gift and a silent warning, emblem of the *longa manus* of the Chinese empire.

The Red Palace also conceals in its interior Buddhist chapels, with eight stupas of previous Dalai Lamas. The funerary monument for the fifth Dalai Lama is wrapped in gold foil of 110,000 taels, with 18,677 pearls, gems, amber, agate, and coral fragments studding it. The largest hall, which is almost 725 square metres, is the Sixipuncog, or Eastern Hall. In the westernmost section, on the other hand, we find the Hall of the Sacred Stupa for the thirteenth Dalai Lama: it stands 14 metres tall, and it boasts a mandala of 200,000 pearls; on the walls, one can admire the fresco of the meeting between the Dalai Lama and the Emperor Qing Guangxu and the Dowager Empress Ci Xi in Beijing.

And what does the Potala represent today? Like a weary dinosaur, venerable if for no other reason than its extraordinary essence, memorious of long-vanished past eras, today the palace is an immense museum, with 50,000 square metres of frescoes, with themes ranging

from the life stories of religious and secular personages to historical events. In the eastern hall, for instance, is depicted the meeting between the fifth Dalai Lama and the Qing Emperor Shunzhi in 1652.

In the Red Palace, there are 1,000 Buddhist pagodas, 10,000 statues of the Buddha, tangka paintings, pattra leaf sutras, golden certificates attesting an endless array of appointments and nominations, seals made of jade or gold, warranties of ongoing exchanges with the Ming and Qing emperors, collections of wool carpets, baldaquins, curtains, silks, sacred hangings in gold and silver, porcelain, and stone.

A structural restoration of the Potala – the greatest undertaking of this sort that the Chinese Government had assumed since the Liberation of 1949 – was inaugurated on 11 October 1989, to the sound of horns, by the young Lama of the Sera monastery, Gyain-

cain Qoinjor, chosen in the strictest observance of the ancient divinatory methods: both his parents were still living, and he himself had been born in a year that was considered favourable. In September 1994, the restoration project was completed, at a cost of 53 million Renminbi.

For the Chinese it is a monument that comes in handy: a memento of the gap separating the Tibetan theocratic élite and the popular rulers. At the time of the rule of the fourteenth Dalai Lama, 95 per cent of all Tibetans lived in conditions bordering on slavery, or servitude, without human rights. Today the marvellous frescoes on the walls clash with the shopping for souvenirs offered by the little sales booths within the halls themselves. Again a compromise, again a contrast between the military uniforms of the guards and the few elderly monks who lead tourists through the palace, describing its beauties.

A lion guards the courtyard of the Potala from high atop the pitched roof.

On the facing page
The amazing silhouette of the roofs of the Potala.

A corridor linking the dormitories of the White Palace.

The Forbidden City
in Beijing

In each of the four corners of the enclosure walls of the Forbidden City, there stands a watch-tower with a six-pitched roof.

On the facing page
Bronze crane, on the terrace of the Taihedian (Hall of Supreme Harmony).

To the chance passer-by who may happen to linger at sunset along the slopes of Coal Hill, to the north of what was once the Forbidden City, a collection of buildings that is now legitimately penetrated by thousands of tourists every day, the setting sun and the craftsmanship of generations of men will afford a blinding spectacle. The last rays glance off the alternately concave and convex terracotta tiles of the golden yellow roofs topping the myriad of palaces and buildings that make up the ancient imperial court, instilling its fiery light and setting off a bright orange wildfire thanks to the translucent glaze that covers all the roof tiles. At that hour, the plan of the court appears to the eye in all its symmetry, like a magnificent symphony in which we can recognize every section of the main theme, though it may be declined in ever varying forms; at the same time, the Chinese Versailles manifests itself in all its longitudinal expanse, like a procession of palaces that never seems to come to an end.

Today these spaces are used as exhibition halls, an immense museum with a storeroom containing more than 900,000 items. But even before the fall of the empire, in 1911, the Forbidden City had finally become – or perhaps it had always been destined to be – a museum of itself and, at the same time, a network of symbols. As we stroll through its courtyards and its great halls, we must realize that every object – in its location, form, name, and relationship to its setting, even its numerical relationship – necessarily referred to another meaning, indeed various further meanings, intertwining levels of understanding with that which surrounded it and referring inevitably to a far more eternal court, made of jade, the Celestial Court of which the earthly court was only a projection – faded and imperfect, perhaps, but unique. As a result, in foreign policy, any state with which China had relations could be noth-

ing other than a vassal state, to the point that 'empire', in Chinese, takes the name of *tianxia*, '[as much as lies] under Heaven'.

When in 1368 Zhu Yuanzhang had defeated and indeed routed the Mongols, freeing China from one of the very few foreign dominations that it ever underwent, he shifted the capital from Khanbaliq – city of the Khan, which is to say, present-day Beijing – with all of the memories of foreign domination that it carried with it, and undertook an architectural programme for the construction of a new court far to the south, near the site of the 'southern capital' Nanking (*Nanjing*, in Chinese), in keeping with the direction of development towards the seas of South-East Asia, one of the most prosperous areas of trade for the Middle Kingdom.

Zhu, of avowed peasant birth, was opposed to luxury, and the simplicity of his tastes was to be reflected in the treatment of the wall paintings that celebrated his victories.

Nanking, therefore, placidly began to serve the role of the capital of the new dynasty – the 'splendour', or the Ming – and that is how things still looked almost forty years after the collapse of the Yuan, the 'origin' dynasty created by the Mongols. But the followers of Zhu Yuanzhang had not taken into account the ambitions of Zhu Di. He was, in fact, a member of the imperial family, but he had not been named by Zhu Yuanzhang as an heir to the imperial succession. Zhu Di, as the Prince of Yan, possessed the feud within which lay Khanbaliq, and in order to outflank his competition he decide to resume construction of a new capital there in 1403. Khanbaliq in Chinese translated as Dadu, the 'great capital', or better, the 'capital of the Great [Khan]'.

Zhu Di's decision was to prove, in the medium term, a strategically good one: the location of the northern capital allowed him to keep a closer watch over the northern bor-

ders from which the worst problems tended to come, that is to say, raids by nomadic tribes. Some three centuries later, however, the court decided to move a little further away from the Great Wall, and it fell easy prey to the irresistible invasion of the Manchu.

The definitive transfer to the new northern court finally took place in 1420; construction work was completed six years later. In the reconstruction of the complex, the imperial architects took into account, first and foremost, the existing situation that they had encountered, that is, the plan and the immense amount of material available for recycling from the earlier Yuan Palace, and they undertook a massive extension along the north-south axis, recovering courtly models from the Song Dynasty, the next-to-last dynasty, the last truly Chinese dynasty prior to the Mongol invasion, and therefore in the spirit of a 'restoration'. They also built a defensive moat that ran all the way around the external perimeter of the court, and with the landfill they built an artificial hill to the north of the complex to protect it from evil influences, in keeping with the dictates of geomancy, or *fengshui*; the layout of the moat and the hill recreated the favourable natural elevation of the first court, back in Nanking, though on a smaller scale, probably in order to quell the objections of those who raised preferences for the location of the old capital. To the west of the palace, two man-made lakes came into existence, along with an imperial park, restoring the layout of the court of the Jin era (twelfth-century dynasty).

To the south of the little man-made hill, known as Coal Hill (Meishan), there spread out 720,000 square metres of palaces and courtyards, with a total of 9,999 halls. The number nine, according to Chinese numerology, expresses the greatest possible power of *yang*.

If we imagined ourselves floating high

View of the Zhonghedian, or Hall of Perfect Harmony, and of the Baohedian, or Hall of Preserved Harmony.

The first of the three main halls of the Forbidden City, seen from overhead.

On the facing page The Hall of Supreme Harmony, the point from which all imperial power radiated outward.

COURT APPAREL

The clothing worn by court functionaries was influenced by the Manchu style, determined by the long practice of riding horseback among this nomadic people: they seem like greatcoats worn by cavalry officers, with their narrow sleeves which flare at the bottom, the split in the side, a horseman's hat, and boots. The dragon with five claws worn on the chest was a privilege exclusive to the emperor alone. Often the dragons were portrayed in pairs, face to face, and they would be struggling for a pearl, the symbol of power. Along the outfit were clustered the twelve motifs created by the legendary monarch Shun as early as 4,500 years ago: the mountain, a sign of determination and stability; the dragon, symbol of vigilance; the pheasant, symbolizing warlike combativeness; the goblets for the rites for the household gods, symbol of purity and altruism; the flame, which represents zeal, honour, and virtue; rice, which the emperor must procure in plenty for his people; seaweed, a respect for the equilibrium of the open seas; the axe, symbol of justice.

The *chaozhu*, the ceremonial necklace, was more or less like the soldier's stripes. The colour of the silk threads that joined the various parts of the necklace revealed the status of whoever wore it: radiant yellow was the colour of the emperor, his wife, and his concubine; gold for the family members and the princes; turquoise for all others.

The necklace derived from the rosary of Buddhism, a religion that – influenced by the Mongols – the Manchu had adopted. The 108 beads punctuated the process of eliminating the ten impure desires. After every twenty-seven beads there was a larger bead, the 'Buddha head'. The Buddha head that lay in the centre of the back of the neck had a pendant, the 'dorsal cloud', with a miniature stupa. The material of the beads changed, not only according to who was wearing them, but also in relation to the purpose of the ceremony: when the priest was sacrificing to Heaven, the necklace was made of turquoise beads; for sacrifices to the earth, amber beads; for the Temple of the Sun, the beads were made of coral; and they were made of malachite for the Temple of the Moon.

The numerology of the necklace can also be viewed in a different way: the number 108 could refer to the temporal-meteorological breakdown of the world into twelve months, twenty-four atmospheres, and seventy-two climates. In the past, Buddhist bells rang 108 times in the morning and 108 times in the evening, to ward away evil. Now bells are only rung 108 times on the last day of the year and on special occasions, to ward off the 108 worldly concerns of the old year.

STUPA

Upon the death of the Buddha, his body was cremated on a funeral pyre; the few remaining bones were distributed among his disciples who scattered over the length and breadth of India. When they reached a territory where their preaching took root, they would bury the relics of the Buddha and build a cenotaph – an 'empty tomb' – atop the spot in commemoration, a *stupa*, around which would develop the monastic community.

The form of the reliquary tower, that is, what is commonly called a pagoda from a mistaken reading of the Chinese *dagoba*, derives from the fusion of the Indian *sikhara* with the Chinese *lou*, a synthesis that took place from the third century A.D. The *sikhara* is an Indian reliquary tower; it derives from the hypertrophic development of a pinnacle atop the stupa. A stupa is a mound tomb built for great political or spiritual leaders, such as the Buddha. The *lou* is a Chinese military watch-tower.

The circular platform, which is evocative of a brick wall, supports eleven worshippers or monks in attitudes of prayer. The depiction functions according to a metonymic process, using a part to represent the whole. The area of the monastery is reflected in the simple citation of the *gatha* [gate], of a fence, of the monks, of two symmetrical trees and three flowers. The tree is one of the possible aniconic depictions of the Buddha, as is the pagoda itself, for that matter. The bells in the acroteria on each roof send out prayers whenever the wind blows sufficiently to make them ring. What we have here, then, is a synthetic, metonymic depiction of a monastery, and at the same time, of the Buddhist *ekklesia*.

The origin of the pagoda as a reliquary tower is revealed in a minor detail: if you look inside the tower, you will discover a small coffer – it is the 'strongbox' containing the relic.

On the facing page
Portrait of the last Empress of China, enthroned.

View of the Palace of Celestial Purity, Qianqinggong.

The Wanchunting, or Kiosk of the Ten Thousand Springs.

One of the portals leading from the central axis of the Forbidden City to the ancillary and lateral palaces.

On the facing page Bronze lion set to guard the Hall of Supreme Harmony.

above the city of Beijing, we would be able to see that the city plan resembles a set of Russian nesting dolls whose inner core is represented by the imperial palace, the *gugong*, surrounded by the complex of the purple Forbidden City, the *zijincheng*, which occupies the northern section of the present-day metropolis, and that is in turn immersed in what was once called the Mongol City, the array of shops and homes of artisans and merchants who made their living by providing secondary services to the court.

But why on earth a 'purple' Forbidden City? The colour purple symbolizes, in Chinese astrology, the Pole Star, or the constellation *Ziyuan* (meaning, 'original purple constellation'), of the emperor. The eclipse of *Ziyuan* is therefore an evil occurrence.

The perimeter of the first wall, the one that is surrounded by the moat, extends 960 by 760 metres; the second wall contains an area extending 2,500 by 2,750 metres; the third wall, long since levelled and nowadays only an imperceptible scar, extends for 6,650 by 5,350 metres. The Mongol City had a perimeter of 7,950 by 3,100 metres.

Along an imaginary continuation of the north-south axis of the court, but outside of it, stand the temples of the fundamental pre-Confucian divinities, to whom the emperor made annual sacrifices: the Temples of Heaven, Earth, and Agriculture, nowadays set snugly in the large urban fabric. The horizontal rhythm of the parks that surround them imposes a halt on the spasmodically rising verticality of the 'rising city', and the people of Beijing love to linger there, perhaps playing squash against the temple walls.

A number of scrolls survive that depict court processions with such an abundance of details that nowadays we are capable of reconstructing the protocol with great precision. The Forbidden City reveals itself in these scroll paintings to be much more than a piece of architecture: it is an articulation of space, meant to accommodate and punctuate a rite

that was meant to be very precise and to perpetuate itself, never changing, over time, like a
propitiatory dance.

If we were to imagine bringing our noses
very close to the surface of these paintings and
– victims of our own excessive curiosity –
falling right in, we would begin our itinerary to
the imperial threshold from Tiananmen
Square, the Gate of Heavenly Peace, which in
reality is made up of five gates; the symbolism
of the number five boasts exceedingly ancient
roots in China, and we will find it immediately behind the portal, when we find ourselves obliged to cross five little marble bridges,
or *huabiao*. On the little columns of the rail-
ings, subjects could affix requests and com-
plaints, hoping to attract the emperor's interest.

In the network of references and correspondences that is the Forbidden City, the
longitudinal extension is punctuated by Wumen, the Meridian Gate, meaning the southern
gate, where to the north echoed the drum and
bell that signalled the opening of the gates giving access to the court.

Nothing is simple in the Forbidden City,
and the southern gate is actually articulated
into five pavilions, five 'ventricles' that would
filter visitors according to their rank. Each
rank had its own privilege: when a tourist ar-
rives in a leisurely manner from Tiananmen
Square and enjoys a direct view of the court,
he or she may not realize that they are making
use of a 'route' that was once available only to
the emperor. Only two other classes could enter the court through the central ventricle of
the Wumen: the empress on one single day of
her entire life, the day of her wedding; and
the three laureates of the state examinations
who – having received their official appointments from the emperor – could only exit
through that gate. The eastern pavilion was
reserved, instead, for functionaries, while the
western pavilion was reserved for soldiers. In

Interior of the Hall of Perfect Harmony, Zhonghedian.

The main chamber of the Chuxiugong, one of the six western palaces, in which the Dowager Empress, Ci Xi, also resided.

short, tell me how you enter and I will tell you who you are. It was at the Wumen Gate that the emperor sat to witness military triumphs or to issue a new calendar.

The Western eye might soon weary of the way that space is laid out and punctuated on the interior of this complex: if you proceed from south to north, you will encounter a series of palaces that are extremely wide and not very deep, creating as many courtyards, bounded to the east and west by a procession of secondary palaces. In reality, this simple rule of composition is violated in thousands of ways, even though it is possible to identify clearly a first part, for the distinctly political functions (*qianchao*, palaces in front), and a second section (*neiting*, inner court), the residence of the imperial family and their assistants. The further north you go, the more selective access to the palaces became: only a very few indispensable servants were admitted to the *neiting*, the Chinese executive offices.

The most important buildings of the *qianchao* are the Taihedian (Hall of Supreme Har-

mony), or the throne room, the room of the morning audiences, the decision-making room, the administrative heart of the Middle Kingdom; the Zhonghedian, the room in which the emperor rested before the Taihedian, where the ambassadors were received; and the Baohedian, where the annual banquet was held with the high-level functionaries and the vassals of other races, as well as the final oral examination of the laureates of the civil service competitions, on a three-year schedule.

The *neiting*, on the other hand, developed according to three areas: the central axis, with three palaces; the imperial garden, which lay before the northern gate (an oasis of greenery extending over 7,200 square metres); and finally the six western buildings and the six eastern buildings, devoted to a wide array of functions: pavilions, galleries, gardens, Buddhist and Taoist temples.

The Taihedian was first built between 1406 and 1420; it was rebuilt in 1669, and it was further restored in 1775 to the version that we see today. In order to reach the throne on its interior, you must climb up a series of stairs that represent a sacred mountain, but the building itself stands on a high base, which makes it necessary, in order to enter, to undertake three flights of stairs. The central staircase was reserved for the emperor alone, and it features a number of dragons flying amongst the clouds: the bas-relief is carved on a single block of granite, measuring 16.57 by 3.07 metres, and weighing 250 metric tons.

At solemn ceremonies, the aristocratic spectators would take their places on the facing terrace, the orchestra on the eastern side, the percussion instruments (gongs, cymbals, and drums) on the western side. The presence of the music served, first and foremost, to orient and choreograph the movements of the attending dignitaries. At the centre of the adjoining courtyard – which extended over 30,000 square metres – the foreign ambassadors would array themselves. Along the axis of the emperor's passage, as he advanced in his jade carriage, the honour guard would lay, instead of the red carpet that we might use, animals that symbolized power (lions and turtles) made of gold and silver. The dignitaries, during their morning audience, could not look the emperor in the eye: they remained waiting on the terrace out front and entered only when they were summoned.

The Chinese do not like to give directions using the concept of left and right: they prefer the terms east and west, and therefore it would be a good idea to carry a compass with you wherever you go, remembering however that a Chinese compass always points south. All the same, along the routes through the Forbidden City, a series of symbols will remind you constantly of the direction in which you are headed: all that you need to do is un-

The main hall of the Palace of Celestial and Terrestrial Union, or Jiaotaidian.

Interior of the Hall of Middle Harmony, with the imperial throne.

The focal point of the Forbidden City: the Hall of Supreme Harmony.

Bronze tortoise, on the terrace of the Taihedian.

veil those symbols. And so it may be useful to observe how the emperor set himself in a veritable 'plan of the cardinal points of the compass': once he sat on his throne, he turned his face towards the river of golden waters (*jinshuihe*), which tourists cross over five bridges, to the south, indicated by a vermillion bird; his back, instead, was turned towards the north, whence came all negative forces. For that reason, a great screen was spread out behind the back of the Son of Heaven; similarly, behind the back of the entire Forbidden City, we have seen that Coal Hill was raised, and it is no accident that it has five peaks; an austere symbol of the north is the shell of the black tortoise. And so, the emperor's left side was facing towards the east, indicated by a blue dragon; al-

so towards the east was the headquarters of the civil ministries, known as the house 'of the Blooming Letters'. To the west, a cardinal point of the compass marked by a white tiger, were located the military ministries. The vertical axis also bore its own very precise array of symbols: on the ceiling, above the emperor's head, there was a caissoned hemispheric vault, representing the vault of Heaven, with a dragon carved in the centre. There are dragons and then there are dragons: the imperial dragon extends its five-clawed paws and it is golden yellow in colour. The screen of the nine dragons, for instance, is a wall extending 31 metres by 6 metres tall, with nine dragons in different colours on a background of 270 enamelled tiles which form the waves of the

View of the Golden Canal at the Wumen (Meridian Gate, or Southern Gate).

Nocturnal view of one of the buildings of the Forbidden City, emblazoned with the image of Mao Tse-tung.

sea in the lower register and the clouds of the sky in the upper register.

It is worth allowing your gaze to linger on the acroteria, the tiles that occupied the forward-most position on the roof. This is a 'critical' position for many cultures, not only Chinese: a point through which evil spirits could easily intrude into the lives of the residents. Best to entrust the apotropaic task of warding off the evil and unwelcome guests to monstrous figures. To decorate these acroteria, as early as the Ming era, the *sancai* (three-colour) technique was used, with production systems that have basically remained unvaried to the present day.

The decorations in enamelled ceramics were made of stoneware: baked at a tempera-ture of 1400 °C, then glazed, it was extreme-ly tough and withstood the ravages of time.

Entrance to the *neiting* was not only lim-ited to certain persons; it was limited to certain items of furniture. The court ordered kilns to provide specific moulds for vases on a monopoly basis to ensure that no single piece could be reproduced: no one else in the Middle Kingdom could therefore claim to handle works similar to those enjoyed by the Son of Heaven. There was one exception to this rule, a genre over which various Qing emperors were besotted: mechanical clocks, especially those made in Saxony, which crowded the imperial collections in their dozens and hundreds, and are still prominently displayed in the palace.

The Wudang Mountain

Mi Fu (1052–1107), one of the greatest calligraphers that the Middle Kingdom ever produced, defined the Wudang Mountain in a simple, austere, powerful three-character inscription: *Di yi shan*, the 'Number One Mountain'.

The Wudang – known also as Taihe – is far from being a simple mountain: it is a chain of more than seventy peaks, embracing a roughly circular area 400 kilometres in diameter in the north-western part of Hubei province, to the south of the cities of Shiyan and Danjiangkou.

In so much space, it is natural that the widest array of religious traditions should be found: it would seem that the site attracted an early construction of very simple huts, with straw roofs, as retreats for Buddhist meditation. And so the earliest occupation of the site was Buddhist; but it was Taoism that gave this mountain chain its greatest renown, and specifically the popular belief that these peaks were the site of the ascetic retreat of Zhenwu, who won immortality here, rising to the heavens as a deity of the northern regions.

The mountain was the site of a Taoist monastery complex as early as the Tang Dynasty (618–907), when the Temple of the Five Dragons was built under Zhenguan (627–49); the expansion of the structures continued under the Song Dynasty (960–1279) and the Yuan Dynasty (1271–1368). Most of the religious buildings erected until then were however destroyed during the conflicts that led to the overthrow of the Yuan Dynasty, just after the middle of the fourteenth century.

The decisive step that brought Wudang into the sphere of architectural legend, however, was the work of the fourth son of the founder of the Ming Dynasty (1368–1644): Zhu Di. He skilfully usurped the throne from his nephew, who was the designated heir; when in 1403 the coup d'etat was accomplished, in order to si-

lence the objections of his subjects, he found himself obliged to finance a major public work thanksgiving to Zhenwu, with whose good auspices he claimed to have undertaken his rather unorthodox climb to the throne.

Three hundred thousand artisans and carpenters were assembled for twelve years, from 1412 to 1424, on the ridges and the watersheds of the Wudang mountain chain: the halls had to be built on the edge of steep cliffs, high amidst the perennial clouds wreathing the mountain summits, in the full respect of the silhouette of the landscape, with a sufficient density of construction; in short, as we might say today, with absolutely no environmental impact, in keeping with the devotional attitude towards nature that is traditional in Taoism. It should be admitted that the highest peak, despite the name of Tianzhu, Pillar of Heaven, is hardly a Matterhorn or an Everest. It is barely 1612 metres tall; but the 70 kilometres of paved trail that run from the entrance portal up to the peak are not child's play, especially if we take into account that along the route you will pass, and presumably stop at, a plethora of religious buildings of an exceedingly high architectural level: eight palaces, two temples, thirty-six monasteries, seventy-two cliff temples, thirty-nine bridges, and twelve pavilions. There is a maze of peaks, sheer drops, natural and channelled mountain torrents, artificial basins, wells, little lakes. As the Chinese love to count, and adore fitting reality into so many slots in numerological relationships, they have identified seventy-two peaks, thirty-six sheer drops, twenty-four mountain torrents, three basins, nine wells, and ten lakes: in most of these cases, everything revolves around multiples of nine, the number that expresses the power of *yang*.

Indefatigable, Zhu Di – better known to the history of art with the dynastic slogan of Yongle – promulgated some sixty decrees to

The Xuanyue Portal, at the beginning of the sacred itinerary.

On the facing page
View from above of the Bixia Temple: built in the year 1009, under the Zhenzong Emperor of the Song, it remains today a masterpiece with minimal environmental impact.

deal with the demands of the labourers, to express his preferences on the plans to be built, and to convey materials to the site (with an abundance of gold and silver, donated by the imperial family). In 1424, 1.6 million square metres had been built or restored, still housing nine sanctuaries, nine monasteries, seventy-two temples, and thirty-six convents; and Zhu Di's successors continued to embellish the site, selecting it as a temple for their family household gods.

At the beginning of the sacred itinerary, the pilgrim walks through the Xuanyue Portal, whose arcades rise 20 metres high, with five registers of carvings.

The Yuzhen Temple, which is just 1 kilometre from the portal, houses a bronze statue of Zhang Sanfeng, a great patriarch of the Wudang Taoist order. The Yuxu Temple is the largest in the complex, with 2,000 rooms. In the five-storey Fuzhen ('return of truth') monastery, a pillar actually supports 12 different roof beams. Sheer above the Nanyan cliff stands the Tianyi zheng wanshou stone sanctuary, from the Yuan Dynasty (thirteenth to fourteenth centuries). From here a stone beam, 30 centimetres in diametre and almost 3 metres long, extends like a horizontal flagstaff over the void. On its surface is carved a writhing dragon, upon whose head can be inserted a stick of incense. Pilgrims would risk their lives in the attempt to light the incense over the dizzying drop, in order to prove their devotion.

The Zixiao Palace, at the foot of the Zhanqi Peak, to the north-east of Tianzhu, was built in 1413. The main hall, the Zhixiao, was erected on a three-level terracing; it features a

The Golden Hall of the Tianzhu Peak: to build it required more than 100 tons of gilded bronze.

The complexity of the wooden arm structures that enable the arch of the roof pitches dates a building, in much the same way as Western archaeologists are able to date the style of capitals.

On the facing page Tubular tiles and acroteria of the Zhongtianmen, the Portal Standing Midway Along the Road to Heaven, on the Huangjian Ridge.

The Xuanyue Portal, standing 20 metres tall and 13 metres wide, at the beginning of the sacred road, paved with stone, that leads to the summit of the Wudang mountain chain.

double cornice, supported by an interplay of nine load-bearing beams, and it offers an acute chromatic contrast between green tiles and red walls. The breathtaking turquoise blue of the clear sky was taken into consideration by the Chinese architect as one hue in the palette with which he was able to play.

Through the city of Zijin and its enclosure walls – one and a half kilometres of perimeter consisting of hewn monolithic slabs weighing half a ton each – you will reach a granite basement, upon which extends a procession of tiles, beams, ridge beams, rafters and joists, and bronze entrance doors, at a total weight of more than 80 tons. This is the Golden Hall, also known as the Crown Hall. Work on it be-

gan in 1416 and it measures 5.54 metres in height, 5.8 metres in width, and 4.2 metres in length. The Hall – perched high atop the Tianzhu Peak, the last station of the pilgrimage – is made of gilt bronze, though it faithfully imitates the similar wooden constructions. Before a lightning rod was installed after construction, every bolt of lightning caused huge blasts of light around the pavilion, without ever damaging the interior.

In the 400 kilometres of peaks and valleys of the Wudang there is room, as we have said, for other traditions as well. For instance, in the Jiudaohe area, there runs a pilgrimage route for Buddhists called, in an understatement, 'the divine rear door', even though it stretches for 'only' 10 kilometres. Moreover, Wudang is an astonishing open-air herb garden: this had been perfectly well understood by Li Shizhen who, during the Ming era, composing his *Compendium of Materia Medica*, had selected here no fewer than 600 of its 1,800 medicinal herbs.

But most of all, for millions of fans, Wudang is synonymous with the martial arts. Under Hongzhi (1488–1506) of the Ming, the Eight Masters of the Zhixiao Sanctuary, on Wudang, created a syncretic combination of the Taiji Thirteen Postures in the version of the Wudang School, Taiyi Wuxing quan (Martial Art of the Five Elements) by Zhang Sanfeng, a great Taoist figure under the Northern Song Dynasty, with the *qigong* (breathing exercises) of Hua Tuo: this gave rise to the *Neijia quan* (Martial Art of the Inner House), which even now rivals the Shaolin School, the best known southern school.

The main bell, a masterpiece of chased metal, in the Temple of Lao Jun.

Aerial view of the Golden Palace, perfectly integrated with the slopes of the mountain.

The Castle of Himeji-jo

Until the fifteenth century, the fortresses of powerful warriors, in Japan, were defended by simple, if stout, wooden palisades. But Japanese poliorcetics, the 'science of fortifications', was destined to undergo an unexpected acceleration caused by an entirely chance occurrence. In 1543 a Portuguese ship heading for China, desperately trying to avoid shipwreck, took refuge in the port of Nagasaki, on the island of Kyushu; the Lusitanian mariners were immediately condemned as *namban* or southern barbarians. The Europeans brought with them trade, evangelization, and muskets. The muskets, in particular, appealed to the Japanese spirit of observation, and they immediately copied the technology and began to use it in their own wars.

The advent of firearms brought about a radical rethinking of the systems of defence, and it was only natural that in this field as well the Japanese should have turned to the Europeans: whoever brought the illness should also know its cure. In an early period, the castles were called *yamajiros* and they stood on hill-tops, so as to be able to survey the countryside. In the period of the civil wars in the late sixteenth century, instead, the large castles (*hira-jiro*) stood on elevations of the land in river valleys, to protect the rice paddies and the irrigation canals upon which individual lords based the nourishment of their armies. But we should immediately note that the Japanese donjons were not very effective. Suffice it to consider that the best one was close to Osaka, the general headquarters of Hideyoshi: it barely withstood a first campaign carried out by Tokugawa, but it yielded to the second massive attack, after a month-long siege.

Japanese castles are based first and foremost, as one would expect for a defensive military architecture, on deceit and disorientation. The path to a castle was labyrinthine, a continuous succession of unexpected curves; once an unfortunate visitor made it past the moat, he would find before him, rising on a natural hillock, a massive stone plinth upon which stood the *hommaru*, the heart of the castle, consisting of the residence of the general, the main donjon, plus a series of smaller donjons and fortified corridors. The castle also housed storerooms for provisions and munitions; the roof had two or four pitches.

The complex was roofed with a wooden superstructure painted with white lead, whose silhouette was given a dramatic appearance by a two-pitch roof that rose above a tympanum. The module of the two-pitch roof was repeated abundantly, and often performed no true structural function: these were, in other words, false roofs. They were intended to fool spies into believing that they had divined the internal structure of the castle from outside, so that invaders, once they made their way inside, would be completely disoriented: they would enter through the roof of the fifth floor and find themselves on the floor of the seventh storey.

The donjons have a likely precedent in an architectural typology that is as far as can be from the military requirements of Japanese architects, that is to say the Chinese belvedere pavilions from the Song Dynasty (c. twelfth century). The smaller donjons, located at the corners of the outside walls, were probably influenced by the model of the typical watchtowers found on Chinese city walls.

The castles were at the same time strongholds and displays of power: when a general lost a battle, he would usually raze his castle to the ground before killing himself. The castles were also destroyed extensively by the bombardments of the Second World War: Himeji was subjected to air raids in 1945.

At the end of the Muromachi period (from the name of the general headquarters of the

Aerial view of the donjon of the White Heron.

On the facing page
An acroterium seems to continue guarding the city.

ruling clan of the Ashikaga: 1336–1573), the importance of Kyoto had begun an ineluctable decline; the period of time that encompassed the years of the civil wars, 1573–1615, takes the name of the Momoyama period, from the site of the Castle of Fushimi which belonged to Toyotomi Hideyoshi, near Kyoto.

Already at the turn of the sixteenth century, Japan was in the hands of some 250 feudal lords, or *daimyo*. Oda Nobunaga, born in 1534, following a series of victories over other *daimyo*, began the process of unifying the territory under a sole political administration, and in 1568 won a key victory by conquering the region of the capital. He entered Kyoto under the pretext of wishing to restore power to the fifteen-year-old *shogun* Ashikaga Yoshiaki.

The fiercest rivals proved to be not so much the other *daimyo*, but the private armies of the Buddhist monasteries, powerful with the economic support of the faithful and absolutely unwilling to lose their independence and their privileges. Oda was a person of sound principles: he had a very special respect for the emperor (he needed him as a puppet to justify his own overweening ambition) and for those sanctuaries that had done nothing to hinder his objectives. In 1571 he massacred 3,000 people and razed to the ground the Enryakuji on Mount Hiei. In 1574, at Nagashima, impatient with the surrender negotiations, he surrounded 20,000 people, soldiers, women, and children, and burned them to death.

Savagery doesn't always pay and in 1582, while he was in the company of his confederates in a sanctuary in Kyoto, Oda Nobunaga was killed by one of his own generals, Akechi Mitsuhide, who hoped to take his place. The murder opened the door to bitter conflict among the various 'condottieri', resolved with the nomination as successor of Toyotomi

Although it is an example of military architecture, Himeji-jo misses no opportunity to use elegant details, such as this beautiful rhythmic flow of rooftops.

View of the imposing defensive structure.

On the facing page
The structure with false levels of one of the donjons of the fortress.

Hideyoshi (1536–98). In this period, Nobunaga dominated Osaka, Sakai, and Kyoto. As was the case of the seigneurs of the Italian Renaissance, this period associated an exceedingly violent military cynicism with an incomparable flourishing of architecture and the arts: every general surrounded himself with a court in the intent of rivalling the other warlords as patrons of the arts.

Hideyoshi had specific ambitions: in 1591 he expressed his intention to invade Korea, with a view to then creating a breach of vulnerability in the Ming Empire. It was a project that bled the kingdom of men and means, lost in the guerrilla warfare mounted by the Koreans and then utterly defeated by the Ming army. In 1598, by this stage on his deathbed, he was obliged to order a general retreat.

But Hideyoshi had had enough time to pass a few key reforms. At the time, many samurais devoted themselves 'part-time' to farming, with the result of a disturbing concentration of weapons in the villages; Hideyoshi oversaw the domestication, as it

were, of the samurais, obliging them to swear an oath of loyalty to their *daimyo* and requisitioning their weapons in an operation known as the 'sword hunt'. Even more significant was the tributary revolution: Hideyoshi sponsored the compilation of specific tax rolls, so that for each taxpayer it would be possible to calculate the equivalent value in terms of production of bushels of rice. These data were used in order to be able to evaluate at any given time the resources available for military campaigns. Upon his death, Hideyoshi left a son, Hideyori, who was little more than a child; five of his warlords hastened to name themselves as regents.

Among them, Tokugawa Ieyasu (1542–1616) was the first to lay personal claims that could threaten the continuity of the Toyotomi. In the battle of Sekigahara, on 15 September 1600, 160,000 soldiers fought savagely from eight o'clock in the morning until two in the afternoon: Tokugawa emerged as the winner. Ieyasu made a different choice than that made by any of his predecessors, who had all them-

*The city of Himeji
as seen from one
of the castle roofs.*

selves named imperial regents: he wanted for himself the office of shogun, the maximum military title, in order to have his hands free to create a military government that would be independent of the court. In order to consolidate his power, he was obliged to annihilate the Toyotomi clan, and he did it in the most literal meaning of the word, in keeping with finest Japanese traditions: he physically eliminated the entire clan, so as to rule out the danger of any subsequent claims. With great political cunning, he retired after just two years and made way for his son to ascend the throne, in order to create a dynastic precedent: and so the shogunate remained a secure possession of the Tokugawa, and it was destined to remain theirs until 1868. But that two-year period was enough time for Ieyasu to transfer the *daimyo* so as to destroy their power base, confiscate their goods, and destroy their authority: the samurais, left without lords, became *ronin*, creating a delicate problem of public safety.

But why build a stronghold in Himeji of all places? A first castle had been built by the Akamatsu in the fourteenth century; Ashiba Hideyoshi had built a three-storey *tenshukaku* in 1580 and he also financed the foundations of the Castle of Himeji. In 1609, Ikeda Terumasa erected the five-storey tower that can still be admired today.

The city of Himeji stands in a particularly fortunate position: wedged between the mountains Masui, Hiromine, and Shosha to the north, its climate is rendered mild even in the winter by the Seto inland sea, just south of it. It is located in the fertile delta of the Rivers Ichi, Yumesaki, and Ibo, in the midst of a plain to the south-west of the Hyogo prefecture, not far from Kyoto, Osaka, or Kobe. Artefacts have been found that attest to the presence of human occupation in the area as far back as the ninth millennium B.C., but it was not until 1889 that it was recognized as an independent municipality, with just over 20,000 inhabitants. Today it is a city with a population of 460,000, with a large foreign component, and it has incorporated other

*One of the portals
leading to the defensive
parapet walks.*

*On the facing page
Details of one
of the façades: external
floors and internal floors
do not match up.*

smaller neighbouring villages. It has always constituted a crucial crossroads of traffic for the Nishi-Harima region, a marshalling yard for provisions and merchandise produced in the region, especially wheat and silk; today, alongside the textile industries, there are chemical industries that make Himeji the centre of the Harima industrial region.

In keeping with the tradition of disorientation so intrinsic to the Japanese castle, the Castle of the White Heron – in reality a complex of eighty-three buildings – 'reveals' only five storeys from the exterior, but on the interior there are seven storeys. Aside from the principal donjon, there are three lesser ones; the external superstructure consists of a wooden framework with a breadth of over 1 metre, reinforced on the interior by a core structure in bamboo canes and clay. The walls, punctuated with loopholes from which to shoot firearms, are plastered with lime to keep flames from spreading; the same paste was smeared into the crannies between the roof tiles in order to provide a waterproof covering.

The Japanese castle is an architectural model marked by contrast above all else: while on the exterior we see an understated opposition of textures and wefts (the white of the plaster, the daunting natural rustication of the stone plinth and the rhythmic layout of the pitches of the roofs), the interior allows itself the display of the greatest imaginable luxury. The Kano School specialized in the decoration of magnificent doors, painted with a gold foil background, perfectly suited to capture and reflect light.

The contrasts that permeate the Japanese castle can also be found in the personalities of the military commanders of the time: cruel in battle, monstrously ambitious, they also proved to be radical in their search for moments of harsh palingenesis, such as the austere tea ceremonies of the late sixteenth century.

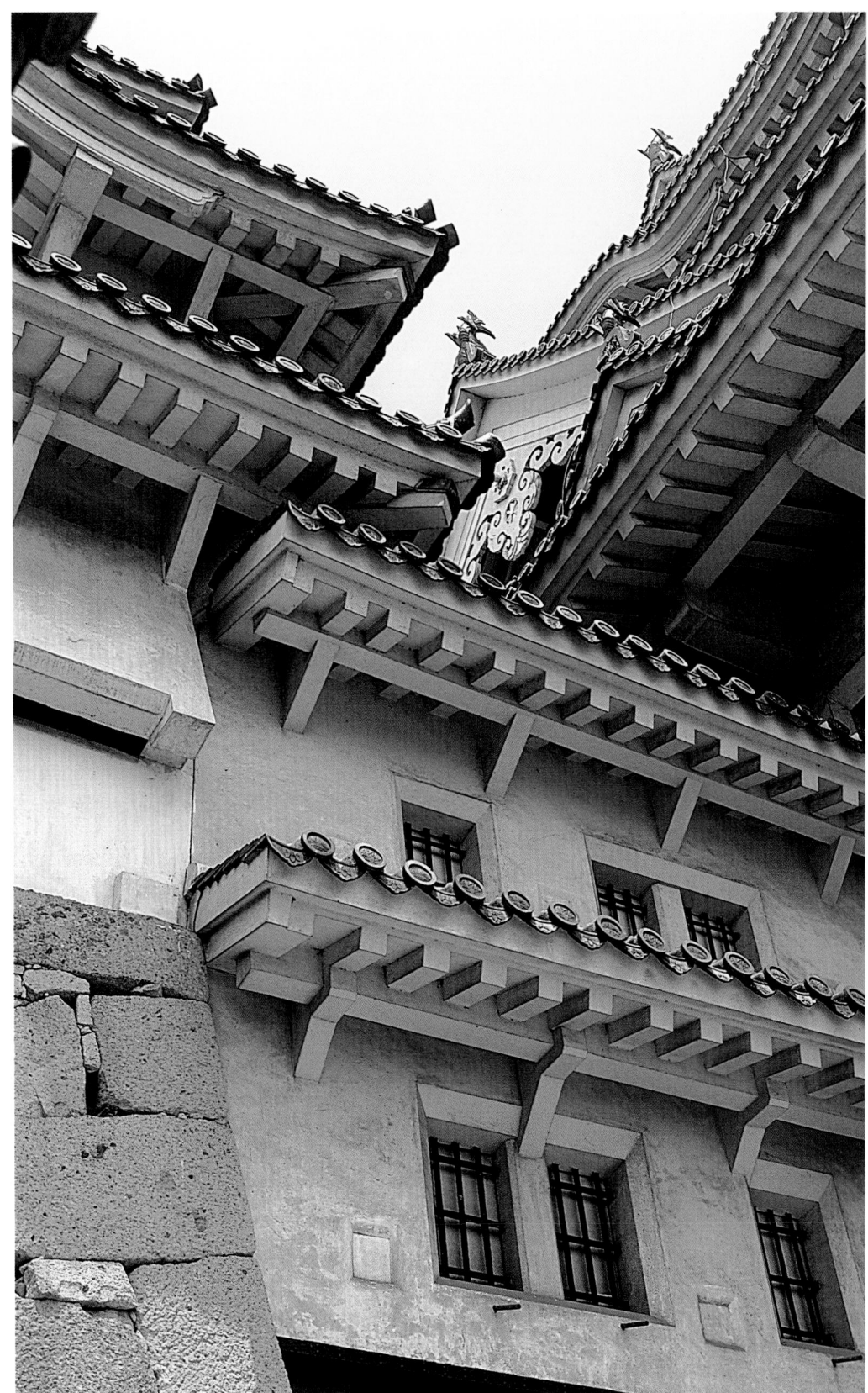

The Taj Mahal in Agra

The Taj Mahal, the masterpiece of Muslim art in India and the recognized symbol of the entire nation, is certainly one of the best known and admired monuments on earth. It was built at the behest of Shah Jahan, emperor from 1628 to 1658, who belonged to the Islamic house of the Moghuls; this dynasty descended from the Mongol tribes that in the previous centuries had spread terror throughout Asia and Europe. In 1526 their great warrior chieftain Baber, having failed to conquer Samarkhand, descended upon India from the great plains of Central Asia and quickly overthrew the Muslim dynasty that had reigned there for over three centuries, establishing an empire of his own. He established his capital at Agra, located 206 kilometres to the south of Delhi, not far from the desert of Rajasthan. In that city Baber immediately began work on a park that he named Rambagh (Garden of Loveliness), ordering the excavation of a great well and redirecting the waters of the River Jumna to feed canals, baths, and fountains. With its sprays of water, its symmetrical paths, and its expanses of flowers, the Rambagh became the prototype for all later Moghul gardens, including the gardens of the Taj Mahal. All the emperors who succeeded Baber on the throne carried on his project, lavishing money and labour on the construction of the imperial city.

It was not merely a respect for tradition that led to the construction of the Taj Mahal; underlying the creation of this great work of architecture was one man's great love for a woman. Shah Jahan in fact built this masterpiece as a mausoleum for his wife Arjumand Banu – better known by the title, which gave the building its name, of Mumtaz Mahal (the 'favourite of the palace') – who had died in 1629, after seventeen years of marriage, while giving birth to his fourteenth child, a daughter.

The chronicles of the period described the emperor's grief and despair; he shut himself up in his palace suite for eight days, refusing all food and drink. Six months after the death of the queen, which had taken place in Burhanpur, her body was transported to Agra; in 1631 it was temporarily placed in a crypt close to the site that had been set aside for her permanent burial place which, Shah Jahan had made up his mind, was to be the most extraordinary monument ever built in honour of a woman.

Reports that the emperor was looking for the right architect for the magnificent project brought hordes of designers and craftsmen hastening to Agra from southern India, Burma, Ceylon, Transcaucasia, and Persia. No document from the period tells us the name of the architect who built the Taj Mahal, but tradition has it that he was a certain Ustad Isa. It is said that when work on the Taj Mahal was completed, Shah Jahan ordered that the master craftsmen's hands be cut off, the calligraphers' eyes gouged out, and the architect himself be beheaded, so that none of them could ever build a similar monument. Recorded under various names, indicated as a native of a variety of locations and a member of countless different nationalities (Arab, Christian, Russian, Indian, or even Jewish), Ustad Isa may have been a character invented to satisfy the curiosity of the English tourists who came to Agra in the nineteenth century.

Equally unfounded are the hypotheses that the monument, in perfect Indo-Persian style, might have been designed by a European. Aside from any stylistic considerations and the questionable reliability of the sources upon which these attributions are based, we absolutely cannot accept the idea that a Christian architect could have been commissioned to build a structure to which, until the English occupation, non-Muslims were forbidden to enter, under pain of death. For that matter,

The Taj Mahal stands in the interior of a great garden with a square plan, the favourite form of Islamic architecture and a symbol of divine perfection.

On the facing page
The mausoleum is bounded at its four corners by minarets standing 42 metres tall.

The sarcophagi of Shah Jahan and Mumtaz Mahal are covered with mosaics and intarsias of precious stones.

An octagonal marble screen surrounds the tombs of the two monarchs in the funerary chamber of the mausoleum.

On the facing page View of the Taj Mahal at sunset from the octagonal tower of the Red Fort.

On pages 276–77 The geometric garden that surrounds the mausoleum is dominated by the great central fountain.

THE TOMB OF MUMTAZ MAHAL

At the end of 1631, as work was just beginning on the construction of the Taj Mahal, the body of Mumtaz Mahal was transported from Burhanpur to Agra, and placed in a temporary mausoleum near the site that had been set aside for her definitive burial. The queen's tomb, and the two mosques that were erected to guard it, were the first buildings in the complex to have been built. Probably the tomb took about ten years to finish, while another twelve years were required for the entire complex. When the tomb was completed, the emperor lay out on his wife's coffin the most precious diamonds from his treasury and extended over the sarcophagus a mantle of pearls. The mausoleum was girded by a golden balustrade and the floors of the entire chamber, now bare and worn by the passage of visitors, were covered with exquisite Persian and Moghul carpets. Hundreds of silver candelabra and golden lamps were hung on the walls, and the entry door was equipped with a solid-silver gate. Very little now remains of all the treasures, which were pilfered in the declining years of the Moghul era.

In the enormous octagonal space of the funerary chamber, where the light filters down from windows equipped with screens of marble fretwork, the queen's sarcophagus stands majestically and, alongside it, the tomb of Shah Jahan, placed here upon his death in 1666. Both the tombs, now empty because the bodies of the sovereigns have been moved to the crypt below, are surrounded by an octagonal screen of marble carved into an exceedingly delicate filigree. The mosaics of semi-precious stones that cover the two coffins are considered to be some of the most beautiful examples of such work on earth: at the centre of the mosaic on the sarcophagus of Mumtaz a quill is depicted, while on the tomb of the emperor we see an inkwell, symbols of the complementary natures of their souls.

The liveliness of the colours of the two sarcophagi contrasts with the sobriety of the calligraphic designs on the upper walls. The floral motif of the screen can instead be found in bas-relief on the lower walls of the central hall and of the four octagonal chambers that surround it, intended to contain the tombs of Shah Jahan's family, but never used. Because of their acoustics, which have proven to be perfect, these rooms are sometimes used to hold concerts of religious music. Under the dome, in particular, the weakest sound is amplified and reproduced to an astonishing degree.

*Panoramic view
of the Taj Mahal
from the terrace of
the monumental portal.*

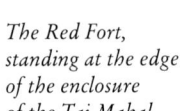

*The Red Fort,
standing at the edge
of the enclosure
of the Taj Mahal.*

*On the facing page
The brick structure of
the mausoleum is entirely
faced on the exterior
with slabs of white
marble, finely intarsiated
with semi-precious
and precious stones.*

the woman for whom the mausoleum was built, Mumtaz Mahal, as is indicated by the inscription that adorns her sarcophagus – 'Protect us, o Lord, from the race of unbelievers' – had been a fierce enemy of Christianity and had encouraged Shah Jahan to slaughter the Portuguese who had settled at Hooghly (on the site of present-day Calcutta).

According to some scholars, the most likely architect of the Taj Mahal is the Persian Ustad Ahmad Lahori, who had already been commissioned to design some of the emperor's most ambitious projects. According to others, the mausoleum was not designed by a single individual, but by a group of experts supervised personally by the emperor. The building's layout, for that matter, is anything but a complete innovation; indeed, with its domes and its minarets, it is reminiscent of many older Indian constructions, such as the Red Fort of Agra, enlarged and renovated many times at the behest of Shah Jahan himself, and the tomb of the second Moghul Emperor, Humayun, built in Delhi more than a

century before. Like that of its illustrious predecessors, the architecture of the Taj Mahal constitutes an harmonious synthesis between the rich architectural tradition of Persian Islam and the tradition of Indian decoration.

Long before the time of Shah Jahan, in fact, Indian stonemasons were famous throughout the East for their remarkable skills; when, in the fourteenth century, Tamerlane decided to embellish his capital, Samarkhand, he summoned from India the finest marble workers who became the pride of his workshops and, when he died, built for him the mausoleum of Gur-e Amir, also considered to have been one of the models upon which the Taj Mahal might have been based. Despite the well-established expertise of his local craftsmen, the emperor summoned to Agra for his ambitious project artisans from all over Asia: from Turkey, Ismail Afandi, who built the mausoleum's enormous dome; from Lahore, in present-day Pakistan, the expert jeweller Qazim Khan, whose task was to shape the gold on the pinnacle of the dome; and from Delhi, lastly, he sum-

281

moned skilled mosaic artists led by Chiranji Lal. But it was the artists who arrived from Persia, and especially from Baghdad and from Shiraz, the most numerous and generally most highly considered, who played the most decisive role in giving the Taj Mahal its singular mixed character, both Indian and Persian. In particular, from Shiraz was summoned Amanat Khan, the renowned master calligrapher who decorated the façade and the crypt of the mausoleum with inscriptions in Arabic characters. The inscriptions that covered niches, arches, domes, portals, and minarets had represented for millennia a distinctive motif of Muslim art (the religion forbade the depiction of the human figure), which employed the elegant forms of its script to define architectural space and, above all, to offer to the eyes of the faithful passages of the Islamic sacred scriptures. The importance attributed to the calligrapher's craft is documented in the case of the Taj Mahal by the immense amounts of money paid to Amanat Khan whose signature alone was considered worthy to appear on the walls of the mausoleum, where it is still visible on the interior, at the base of the dome, surrounded by verses from the Koran.

Construction, which began in 1631, continued uninterrupted for seventeen years and required the labour of 20,000 workers. In order to house those workers, a small city grew up in the space facing the construction yards, which took the name of Mumtazabad in honour of the dead queen. This city grew to be so prosperous that it was ultimately more important than Agra itself, and it appears that Shah Jahan even considered the possibility of transferring his official residence there. Caravans streamed into Mumtazabad, bearing construction materials: a red tufa stone excavated from the neighbouring quarries; white marble, transported on carts from the Makran region, at a distance of more than 300 kilometres; and semi-precious stones brought from even more distant regions, such as jade and rock-crystal from China, turquoise from Tibet, lapis lazuli from Afghanistan, chrysolite from Egypt, and sea shells, coral, and mother-of-pearl from the Indian Ocean.

The Taj Mahal was built on the interior of a vast garden, entirely surrounded by a wall with a square-plan perimeter (the plans of many parts of the complex are based on either the square – a geometric translation of the number four, a symbol of divine perfection for Islam – or the octagon, a multiple of four). On either side of the road that runs towards the outer gate, located in the centre of the eastern gate, there are two octagonal buildings: on the left is the one known as the 'tomb of the ladies of accompaniment', because it contains two sarcophagi, while on the right is a small mosque made of red tufa stone, which became a marble-cutters' workshop during the period of English occupation, and is therefore known as the 'stone-cutters' building'.

At the entrance, a long corridor full of shops leads to a courtyard where we find the inner portal, the genuine entrance to the Taj Mahal proper. The portal is a three-storey building faced with red sandstone, with a colossal arcade in the centre; the entrance opens in the building's south façade, which is decorated with verses from the Koran, beautifully executed in letters of black marble, growing in size towards the top, so that to someone looking up from below, they all appear to be the same size. The presence of a series of barriers which make up a building separate from the main construction is typical of Muslim architecture, and it served a dual function: it protected the riches concealed in the interior and it served to separate the holy space from the profane space. Unfortunately, we can no longer admire the silver portals that originally stood here, because they were taken apart and

The portal of the Taj Mahal is a three-storey building faced with red sandstone, with a colossal arcade in the centre, decorated with verses from the Koran, executed in black marble letters.

On the facing page View of one of the small mosques that flank the monumental tomb.

The mosque, made of marble and red sandstone, is decorated with arabesques in semi-precious stones.

The mausoleum of Mumtaz Mahal has a plan with a square base, rounded off at the corners, and dominated by the immense central onion dome.

On the facing page *Detail of the entrance door to the burial chamber of the mausoleum.*

The chromatic interplay
of the materials used
for the Taj Mahal
is enhanced by
the reflections from
the water and the
variations of light in the
various hours of the day
and under differing
weather conditions.

Detail of the intarsia
work in the upper fascia
of the enclosure that
surrounds the tombs
in the interior
of the mausoleum.

On the facing page
Small kiosk set
at the front of the terrace
of the mausoleum.

melted down during the rebellion of the Hindu faction of the Jatis in 1764.

This brings the visitor to the gardens, conceived according to an extremely strict geometric criterion. The green carpet of the gardens, which extends from the portal to the base of the main building, is in fact divided into four regular panels by marble channels that flow into the great central fountain, in whose waters is reflected the dome of the mausoleum. The park was clearly based upon the model of the Persian garden, which called for the introduction of the natural elements into an artificial, man-made structure. After the abandonment of the entire complex that followed upon the death of the direct descendants of Shah Jahan, and the decay and looting to which it was subjected for two centuries, the park was restored. Nothing remains of the animals, the wooded groves, the flower-beds, and the fruit orchards that once gladdened the complex, with the possible exception of an old *simal* tree near the mausoleum.

Thanks to the carefully planned placement of the garden and its situation upon a broad terrace at the northernmost extremity of the enclosure, the mausoleum seems to be very distant and tiny if it is viewed from the portal, while, by virtue of an inverse optical illusion, it becomes disproportionately large to the eye as one approaches. The building is set on a rectangular platform made of red sandstone, standing 7 metres high, marked at each of its four corners by minarets standing 42 metres tall, devoid of any practical function but built to confer a vertical thrust to the entire complex. It is flanked by two twin mosques made of marble and red sandstone: the western mosque, with its three domes and its pendentives framed by arabesques in semi-precious stones, has its interior ceiling covered with frescoes; the eastern mosque, known by the name of *ja-wab*, 'the answer', since it is perfectly symmetrical to the other one, has never been used as a place of worship and probably served a purely aesthetic purpose.

The mausoleum proper is the great central building, with a plan that involves a square base with its corners rounded off. It is dominated by the majestic central dome, with its 20-metre diameter and its distinctive Eastern onion-dome shape, which also recurs in the four smaller domes. The brick structure is entirely sheathed on the exterior by slabs of white marble that produce an effect of extraordinary luminosity. Forty-three types of semi-precious and precious stones compose refined intarsiated plant motifs, whose juxtapositions of colours are heightened in effect by the reflected light of the fountains in the garden and the changing light at various hours of the day and in various weather. At each of the four sides of the building there is a tall pointed arch which leads into an octagonal chamber, and from there one enters the funerary chamber located in the middle of the building.

The Temple of the Sun at Konarak

Upon his return from a series of especially successful military campaigns alongside his father, around 1238, the eighteen-year-old Ganga prince, the future *raja* Nrsimhadeva I, decided to follow the advice of his mother on the best way to invest his share of the plunder. Who can say whether he had any idea that the enterprise on which he was launching himself – the construction of a temple to the Sun God, Surya – would absorb all his time and energy for the next twenty years?

At the time an effort was even made to calculate the cost of construction: imagining that ingots could be cast in gold with the exact weight – little surprise – of the king himself, 1,000 ingots would be needed to finance the construction of the temple. The architects required six years and three months to plan the entire project, and a little more than twice as long for its construction. It might have taken even longer, but Nrsimhadeva I was anxious to inaugurate the completed temple on a Sunday that coincided with the birthday of Surya, which was something that occurred only once every seven years. Unwilling to bide his time until 1265, the king forced an acceleration of construction even during the rainy season, and officially commemorated the completion of the temple in 1258.

The iconographic programme was especially ambitious. Since the king had asked him to build a temple to the Sun God, the architect decided to immortalize in stone the chariot of the god, with a train of prancing steeds to draw it. The chariot was reminiscent, in its turn, of the *ratha*, that is, the wooden carts used to transport ritual statues in the processions held on the occasion of special ceremonies.

Nrsimhadeva was descended from a princess of the Cola Dynasty, Rajasundari, not to mention the fact that his wife herself was a Pandya. These family ties are sufficient evidence of the influence that was brought to bear on such a monumental project by the Cola and Pandya Dynasties, a pair of southern families. In fact, if we cast our attention on the Cola sites of Darasuram and Cidambaram, we find here as well the idea of the cart-temple.

The architecture in Orissa dates back to the turn of the seventh century, the result of a healthy sense of rivalry between King Sasanka of Bengala and Harsa of Kanauj and Pulakesin II, of the western Calukya, both patrons of the arts. Legend has it that Sasanka built the first Shivaite temple (which is to say, dedicated to Shiva) in Orissa, at Tribhuvanesvara. In reality, anecdotal evidence aside, nothing survives of the architecture from the period of Sasanka, nor, unfortunately, from the period of Harsa. We can only observe that most of the Shivaite temples in Orissa belong to the Pasupata School, the school that was preferred by none other than Sasanka.

Orissa constitutes for art historians a very fortunate conjunction of conditions. Here, the artists could rely upon full-fledged manuals, canons upon which they relied, establishing a consistent and well-structured lexicon. There was another even more important factor: these manuals have survived to the present day. The temple cella and the pronaos, the *vimana* and the *mandapa* in other parts of India, were known respectively in Orissa as the *deul* and the *jagamohan*. The *deul* presents a hypertrophic vertical development, a sort of turreted roof, called the *sikhara*. The *jagamohan*, on the other hand, had a *pidha* roof, with low platforms, like so many theatrical stages.

If we look carefully, we may note that the Temple of the Sun, leaving aside its disguise as a cart or chariot, is a fairly typical temple of Orissa, even though it is the largest one to have survived. In its construction, were assembled various solutions that had already

Panoramic view of the temple complex.

On the facing page
Detail of the frieze depicting the monumental Carriage of the Sun.

been undertaken independently and perfected in this structure.

The temple is first and foremost the house of the god, or of the god's iconic substrate. There are four key images of Surya: in the three niche temples and in the *sancta sanctorum*. In the icon to the south and the west, Surya is standing, immortalized with a slightly stereotypical and tense smile, which has none of the freshness of the earlier statuary; his arms – only two in number – bear lotus flowers, in a high-relief depiction that is so emphatic that it approaches sculpture in the round. To the north, he rides a horse, in accordance with an iconography frequently utilized to indicate the Son of the Sun, Revanta.

Four units in this architectural structure are easily distinguished along the vertical axis: on a high plinth (*pista*), stand the *bada* (wall), the *gandi* (proboscis: this is the pyramidal roof) and *mastaka* (highest crowning element). It is also possible to make out a number of horizontal units (*bhumi*), with horizontal ribbings (*amalaka*) to set them apart. This is the basic gridwork, but the planimetry was to become increasingly complex with the passage of time, with additions and subdivisions that attained a level of almost fractal intricacy. On the exterior, for instance, the layout is rendered more lively by the addition of ancillary temples, *ni sa*, on each side, with the exception of the eastern side. The *ni sa* temples contain secondary aspects of the deity to which the temple is dedicated. Preceding the whole array is a hall, now without a roof, but which – to judge from the remained pillars – was intended to support a fairly elaborate covering. It is a *natamandapa*, literally an 'antechamber for the dancing procession', decorated with plant motifs, especially lanceolate leaves.

But the aspect that we should not forget is the fact that the temple stands in a 'temple basin', a vast enclosed area, accessible through

The deul *presents a hypertrophic vertical development, a sort of turreted roof, called the* sikhara.

The jagamohan, *on the other hand, has a* pidha *roof, with low platforms, like so many theatrical stages.*

On the facing page
The key images of Surya are repeated four times.

In each wheel of the carriage, there are eight smaller spokes and eight larger spokes, at a diameter of three metres. Around the wheels of the cart were celebrated ceremonies for the equinoxes and the eclipses.

All around the plinth of the temple runs a frieze with a procession of elephants, as if they passed under the chassis of the carriage, among the wheels.

On the facing page Three types of stone are used in the temple, and none of them is found in the surrounding area: chlorite, laterite, and kondalite.

porticoes that punctuate the line of sight: in other words, it is anything but isolated – and generally, in Orissa, it faces west.

Three types of stone are used in the temple, and none of them is found in the surrounding area. In terms of materials as well, the monument thus becomes a display window for the incomparable sumptuary possibilities of the royal client. We can distinguish chlorite, 'the green stone', especially soft and therefore easy to carve, for pediments and important images; laterite for the assembly of stairways and basements; and kondalite for the rest. The *jagamohan* and its porticoes are made of pink sandstone, the panels are made of soft green stone; the central image of Surya is in fact made of green stone. In assembling statues composed of different pieces, the sculptors used no mortar, but instead headless tenons to join the stones; the decoration was then expected to cover the joints. This was

an innovation in this period, because earlier sculptural tradition seemed to be perfectly comfortable with leaving the joints fully visible.

When Caitanya, the Bengali Vishnuite 'saint' (1486–1533), came to Konarak, seven stone steeds halted in front of him, drawing a cart with twelve pairs of wheels. He barely had time to glimpse the solid-copper terminal steeple of the *sikhara*, before it was carried off as plunder in the sixteenth century, along with the gold and the precious stones of the interior decoration. This is a dimension that is now lost on the contemporary spectator, unaware that he is looking at a wondrous carcass that has been looted over the centuries. On the interior, long since sacked, there existed metal statuettes, that were 'portable'. The cult icon of the temple was in fact too heavy to be carried in a procession, so 'surrogate-images' were created, three-dimensional delightful little figures made of metal. One has survived, and is housed in the Jagannatha in Puri.

But if we wish to glorify further Nrsimhadeva I's sponsorship of the arts, we need look no further than the exceedingly precise external ornamentation, which does not pause for breath in any given square centimetre of space; a decorativism that never rests and, above all, remains absolutely perfectly balanced in every aspect and element.

The iconographic programme of the Temple of Konarak is deployed over three registers: the first, obviously, has to do with the Sun God, with planets, the steeds drawing his chariot or cart, the houses of the Zodiac; another has to do with the events of the lifespan of the monarch; finally, the Pandya wife, mentioned above, was named Sitadevi, a name that could hardly help but summon memories of the artists entrusted with the decorations of Sita, the wife of Rama and the protagonist of one of the most renowned sagas of the Indian subcontinent: the *Ramayana*, or 'voyage of Rama'. The similarity of the names made it possible to conjecture a link between the founder of the dynasty, Nrsimhadeva and the brave and powerful Rama himself. The royal couple thus became a projection of the epic couple.

The sovereign, in fact, appears more than once in the structure's immense frieze. We find him depicted in the pose of an archer, prostrate before the gods Shiva, Jagannatha, and Durga. Other metopes immortalize him presiding over symposiums of poets, or swinging on a luxurious swing in his harem, or even accepting a gift of a giraffe from foreign ambassadors. Next to the right foot of the main image of Surya we see a character in the pose of *añjali mudra*, that is, with his hands joined in a sign of devotion and respect. Perhaps this too is Nrsimhadeva I. For the image of the king as an archer, the Ganga sculptor Mahapatra was paid with silk outfits, two earrings,

On the facing page
Detail of one of the seven
stone steeds, responsible
for pulling the temple, in
an imaginary dimension.

Out of chlorite, the skill
and artistry of the Ganga
sculptors extracted
the massive strength
of a pachyderm.

and five gold ingots. This story has the twofold value of elevating an artist out of the shadows of anonymity – the normal condition in India – and of providing us with the monetary value placed on his work.

In each wheel of the carriage, there were eight smaller spokes and eight larger spokes, at a diameter of three metres. The twelve pairs of wheels might mark the passage of the sun through the zodiacal belt, or, more simply, the twenty-four half-months. We know that around the wheels of the cart were celebrated – aside from the annual rites for the birth of the sun – everyday ceremonies, monthly ceremonies, and ceremonies for the equinoxes and the eclipses. A certain pair of wheels was emphasized in each period of the year: the passage of time may have been linked to the passage of the sun through the various houses of the zodiac, and the wheels therefore came to constitute an immense and tangible liturgical calendar. The seven stallions might represent the seven rays of the sun that precede its rising, or else the seven days of the week.

All around the plinth of the temple runs a frieze with a procession of elephants, as if they passed under the chassis of the carriage, among the wheels: this is an ingenious solution, because the elephants appear to be – and are – tiny when compared with the similar frieze at the Kailasanatha Temple in Ellora, but it is for precisely this reason they exalt the relative size of the carriage!

The trabeation over the threshold depicts the *navagrha*, the nine 'planets' or really, we should say, the nine celestial bodies, since they correspond to Mars, Mercury, Jupiter, Venus, Saturn, the Sun, the Moon, the Waxing Moon, and the Waning Moon. This is a fairly standard iconographic choice for an exit in Indian temple architecture, even though it is especially appropriate for a temple to the Sun. If there is any astonishing aspect to this, it is

A detail from one of the three iconographic levels of the Temple of Konarak, the one regarding the biography of the sovereign Nrsimhadeva.

Nrsimhadeva appears repeatedly in the immense frieze of the temple: below, one of the metopes that immortalize him.

On the facing page Statues in the round find shelter in the nooks and crannies of the deul.

that the trabeation is a single piece of especially dense-grained chlorite. A piece of chlorite of this sort is not too hard to carve, but it is sufficiently strong to capture every smallest detail; it is a stone much beloved by sculptors when they wish to portray lovingly every detail of the jewellery of a deity, or the deity's physical and facial features, but it is incredibly heavy to lift. We are helped in this aspect by the texts, which inform us that such a heavy load was hoisted with the assistance of pulleys drawn by elephants.

Each personage is seated in a niche, each in turn similar to a miniature temple. Let us take the case of Ruha, the 'Waning Moon': the Indians imagined that he periodically devoured the moon, thus causing lunar eclipses. His body is swollen; his face is broad and smiling, like a fissure; his hairstyle is towering and vertical; his jewellery is miniaturistic.

On the roof of the *jagamohan*, arranged on three terraces as if they were actors in procession on three different stages, stand monolithic full-round sculptures. They depict a series of musicians and a pair of *bhairava*: these were benign or terrifying (*anugra* and *ugra*) protectors of the site, with their four faces and

six arms, dancing in perfect equilibrium upon a boat – and not just any boat, but the *samsarapota*, the Boat of the World. Of decidedly friendlier appearance were the musicians: they, in turn, were idealized feminine types, tending towards the divine; we know from a recorded anecdote that the supervisor of construction decisively rejected all statues based on actual models, and one sculptor tried in vain to slip one past that had been based upon his wife in the hopes of immortalizing her.

The walls, instead, are enlivened, in a continual interplay with the dodging light of the sun, by statues of copulating couples, in a broad variety of positions: these are the so-called *mithuna*. At Konarak, with respect to the rest of the decoration, their importance is decidedly marginal. Why did Indian artists feel a need to adorn the walls of their temples with depictions of this sort? Some have ventured the idea of special cults of the planet Sani (Saturn), but perhaps we should simply surmise that they represent *kama* (physical desire or love) transformed into *preman*, the flexibility that cannot be attained through renunciation or denial, but only through sublimation.

The Temple of Borobudur

The Sailendra Dynasty arrived in Java from the first empire in South-East Asia of any real importance, the Funan Empire, at the precise period when that empire's power was collapsing, in the middle of the sixth century A.D. King Vishnu began construction of Borobudur near the modern-day Magelang, in Kedu Province, about 40 kilometres from Yogyakarta, in A.D. 778; the monument was later completed in 825 or 842 by his grandson, Samaratunga. We find these dates not from any foundation inscriptions – none seems to have survived – but rather from the palaeography of the epigraphs left by the workers.

In this area there is an abundance of andesite, a dark grey rock of volcanic origin, which provided plenty of building material for the monument: in fact, the region has an elevated level of volcanic activity – a condition that, as we shall see, was hardly favourable to Borobudur.

The temple, initially, must have been a Hindu temple – and after all, Buddha can be considered a Hindu deity as well, since he was absorbed by Hinduism as one of the ten incarnations (*avatara*, 'descents') of Vishnu. Perhaps Borobudur was originally meant to serve as an immense tomb for King Indra (782–812), but no traces have yet been found of his ashes in the probes taken from the subterranean section.

In its shape, the complex is a compromise between the typology of the central Asian step pyramid, the *ziggurat*, and the Indian stupa. It should come as no surprise that the *ziggurat* was familiar to the Javans: Stutterheim was the first to realize that ancient Javan texts already documented a familiarity with step pyramids.

Shortly after the first few levels had been completed, *mahayana* Buddhism displaced Hinduism as the dominant religion of the region. The iconographic programme therefore needed to be reinterpreted, and Borobudur took on its present-day appearance: a massive monument, oriented towards the east, which takes advantage of the natural topography, covering and surrounding a natural elevation with nine or possibly ten declining terraces. Nowadays, there are still six upper terraces with a square plan and three lower terraces with a circular plan. If there were nine terraces, they may have referred to the nine previous lives of Siddhartha Sakyamuni Gautama before attaining Nirvana and becoming the Buddha; if, on the other hand, the levels were originally ten, they might have been a reference to the stages of existence required of a Bodhisattva in order to become a Buddha. Around the terraces run five kilometres of galleries with over 2,000 bas-reliefs and hundreds of images of the Buddha; crowning the structure rises a colossal seated Buddha.

In 856, just a few years after they had financed the completion of the project, the Sailendra Dynasty was overthrown; and about a century later, the centre of power in Java shifted from the middle of the island to the eastern area. The number of visitors declined markedly, and the volcanic eruptions of Merapi and the rapid growth of the tropical jungle did the rest: obscuring all recollection of the monument, of which nothing more is recorded until the chronicles of the eighteenth century. It was not until 1814 that the British colonel, Sir Thomas Raffles, then Governor of Java, literally unearthed the complex, freeing the temple from the strangling tangles of jungle plants and lava accretions, but because this first intervention did nothing to protect the complex, its net effect was to open the doors to tomb robbers.

Things did not go much better when the Dutch decided to take care of the site. In 1900,

The ziggurat *of Borobudur: from above, the temple looks like a lotus ready to bloom, floating on the earth.*

On the facing page *Clustered on the highest level are 72 bell-shaped stupas, standing 3.5 metres tall.*

a commission was appointed for its preservation, headed by the engineer Thadeus Van Erp. Van Erp soon found himself faced with a very urgent situation: in 1907, after seven months of excavation, he realized that the external walls were at grave risk of collapsing and the entire structure might soon collapse in upon itself; he therefore hastened to lay down a slab of cement on to the gallery floor in order to reinforce it. It became necessary to place a stone retaining wall around the plinth in order to strengthen further the structure, and even now that wall makes it impossible to view the lower level of the bas-reliefs.

In the early 1960s, the resumption of restoration, made necessary by the seepage of water which threatened to collapse the structure, was hindered by two earthquakes. In 1973 an association of twenty-seven nations, the Government of Indonesia, UNESCO, and a few private donors launched a decade-long restoration that cost US$ 25 million, an effort comparable to the rescue of Abu Simbel in 1966 from the flooding caused by the Aswan Dam.

The name of Borobudur is often translated as 'temple on the hill', but the term actually constitutes an abbreviation of Bhumisan Brabadura, 'the ineffable mountain of the accumulation of virtues': Borobudur was meant, therefore, beginning with its very silhouette, to echo the idea of a mountain – and not just any mountain, but a mountain of initiation, which offered an itinerary of formation, from the many to the one. The unusually large stupa is meant as a replica of the universe in keeping with the cosmological vision of *mahayana* Buddhism: Borobudur is an example of a three-dimensional *mandala*.

This microcosm is organized on three decorative registers: the first, *kamadhatu*, the 'sphere of physical love', represents the world of desire influenced by negative impulses, and

The temple basin of Borobudur rises like a man-made mountain of andesite.

View of the decorative frieze running along the walls of the seventh level of the temple.

On the facing page *The face of this meditating Buddha boasts the full features typical of the Gupta aesthetic.*

Each of the 72 stupas
on the highest level
contains a life-sized
Buddha.

The Buddha is celebrated
in 504 statues, each no
less than 1.5 metres tall.

On the facing page
The scenes depicted
on the lower terraces
are more worldly
and everyday than
the hieratic figures
of the highest level, even
though they continue
to express a moral
and didactic significance.

is partly buried; the middle one, *rupadhatu*, the 'sphere of form', depicts a state of existence, more than a geographic space, where man succeeds in controlling his negative instincts and makes good use of his positive ones; and the top register celebrates a world in which man is no longer bound by physical desires.

In order to observe all of the metopes in their correct order, you must begin from the southern staircase on the eastern façade, keeping the building on your right and walking towards your right, in a clockwise direction, which is to say, following the course of the sun. This activity in fact takes the name of *pradaksinapatha*, 'a circumambulation towards the south', and in the Indian culture is an act of devotion towards the object around which one turns. At the end of the walk, you will have taken ten full circles or circumambulations around the stupa, covering a total of 5 kilometres, comprising 2,500 square metres of bas-reliefs, distributed over 1,460 metopes of 2 metres each.

Each terrace is surrounded by open-air patios, with strips of bas-reliefs. The scenes depicted in the lower terracings are more earthly, and tend to have a didactic and moralizing intent; the higher you go the more rarefied the narrative becomes, giving way to a static, hieratic, epiphanous representation of the figure of the Buddha. The panels of the lower terraces are valuable sources of information on the objects of everyday life between the eighth and ninth centuries in Java: buildings, ships, weapons, musical instruments, and tools.

Probably, all of the bas-reliefs were originally stuccoed and coloured; even now they show fragments of colours, probably however to moss and lichen which, with the encouragement of the climate, settle on the surfaces, slightly altering the perception of

the bas-reliefs. The silhouettes of the reliefs are rounded and full, in keeping with the canons of Indian classical Gupta art.

The paths are organized in galleries 2 metres wide, which encourage seclusion and meditation. The view follows the succession of bas-reliefs until you reach the seventh level, in the open air. The transition from the claustrophobia of the lower levels to the landscape that overlooks the ridges of the volcano Merapi and the fields of rice on the Kedu plain is an experience of great dramatic power for the spectator. The pilgrim reaches a space no longer enclosed by walls, an open, circular structure, which transmits to him a sense of freedom, a surrogate for Enlightenment. Clustered on the highest level are seventy-two bell-shaped stupas, each 3.5 metres tall, each with a life-sized Buddha inside it, which surround and foreshadow the colossal

central stupa: with its 30 metres of height it launches the ultimate challenge of verticalization. It is the 'sphere of formlessness', or the 'heaven of non-form', the *arupadhatu*.

From an aeroplane, the temple seems like a lotus ready to blossom, floating on the ground. And it is more than a mere impression, because in all likelihood, all around it, 1,000 years ago, there was a lake: geologists have in fact verified that all of the surrounding villages, including the Temples of Pawon and Mendut that are in the same area, stand at a height of 235 metres above sea-level.

Just the stone landfill that surrounds the plinth alone amounts to 11,600 cubic metres; crowding the perimeter of the terraces are about 100 spouts for water to run off; the Buddha is commemorated in 504 statues, each standing no less than 1.5 metres tall, in the middle terracing, the *rupadhatu*. Each of the façades features ninety-two stupas with a Dhyani Buddha on the interior, posed in a different *mudra* in order to mark the cardinal points of the compass, of which there are five according to Indian tradition: indicating the east with the *bhumisparsa mudra* (the *mudra* of the 'summoning to testimonial of the Earth'); the south with a gesture of benediction; the west with the *mudra* of meditation; the north with the *mudra* of 'have no fear'; and the centre by showing the gesture of teaching.

The Temple of Borobudur measures 123 metres at its base and it originally rose 42 metres in height; today, partially covered by earth, it rises no higher than 31.5 metres. With its 55,000 cubic metres of stone, equal to 1 million pieces of stone each weighing 100 kilograms, not only does it rival in size the complexes of Pagan in Miyanmar (Burma) and Angkor in Kampuchea (Cambodia), but it is in absolute terms the largest ancient monument in the southern hemisphere, a testimonial to the massive workforce upon which the Sailendra Dynasty could rely.

If you cannot easily make your way to Indonesia, you can always settle for the new stupa of the monastery of Amaravati, which despite its name stands in the quiet countryside of Hertfordshire, in the United Kingdom. Acolytes have been working for more than ten years to build a small-scale replica of Borobudur.

The panels of the lower terraces are valuable sources of objects of everyday life between the eighth and the ninth centuries in Java: buildings, ships, weapons, musical instruments, and tools.

Borobudur was meant, beginning with its silhouette, to echo the concept of an 'initiatory mountain': this is an example of a three-dimensional mandala.

The Mosque of Isfahan

The reason why Isfahan is now so highly regarded is because it represents a fundamental source for the study of Islamic urbanistics, in as much as the layout of its buildings is as well preserved as anything else in the Muslim world; and that is without considering the fact that the architecture of Isfahan was fairly conservative, since it remained substantially impervious to extra-Persian influences until the seventeenth to nineteenth centuries.

The Great Maidan, the central square of the city, may have existed as long ago as 1504: it covers an area that is fully 521 metres long and 160 metres wide, bounded along its entire perimeter by a double order of loggias that house shops, on the square side and on the portico side. The central space was left free, to serve now as a temporary market, now as a polo field, or else as an arena for theatrical performances or for public executions. It was marked off from the loggia by a canal, long since filled in with earth, and by rows of trees.

The central axis of the square, running north-south, leads to the 'Boulevard of the Garden in Four Lots' (Cahar Bagh), the main promenade, which cuts across the city towards the river where a bridge – built by a general who was a favourite of the emperor in 1600 – connects it to the 'garden of the twelve terraces', extending over one full square mile. Since the royal residence stood on one side of the river and the gardens on the other, the Zayanda was spanned by the Pol-i Khadjou (1641–66), a particularly elaborate bridge, with a central passage open to cart traffic and two pedestrian loggias along the sides.

We understand a great deal about the importance that Abbas I attributed to the intense programme of new constructions when we read about the forced removal of the inhabitants of Gilfa. From this village in Armenia, the Safavids forcibly recruited 50,000 labourers. Because the men of Gilfa were excellent builders, the Safavids intended to hoard their skills, and prevent Gilfa from falling into Turkish hands. Among the ranks of the Armenians there were also wealthy merchants who had secured the privilege of preserving their Christian faith: as they travelled the trade roads towards Europe and India, they found themselves working as commercial agents for the Shah. In order to worship as Christians, the Armenians were even allowed to build numerous churches, of which the Cathedral of the Holy Saviour still survives, a splendid outpost of Byzantine art in which Iranic and European motifs have an opportunity to mingle. Even today, the Christian ghetto, on the other side of the river from the main palace, still bears the name of the village from which the Armenians were originally taken.

In the artworks that they commissioned, the Safavids emphasized simplicity, in part to distinguish themselves from the chromatic explosion of their predecessors, the Timurids. Safavid art is not marked by any particular innovation: it harkens in general terms to the forms of the previous dynasty, though bolstered with new decorative forms, with continual ceramic sheathing. Already, the Timurids had used majolica tiles, in enamelled ceramics; but those tiles, though they were manufactured in various colours, bore only a single colour per tile. In the first decades of the seventeenth century, however, the *hast rang*, the 'seven colours', began to appear: each enamelled tile featured seven shades of colour, which increased the speed of decoration. The disadvantage? A drop in the precision with which the colours were thus distributed. But the majolica decoration of the Safavids fulfilled an architectural criterion easily visible to the Western eye, which is the cunning repetition of the same pattern. If the city deserved its moniker of 'the other half of the world'

View of the Great Maidan and the entrance to the Masjid-i Shah.

On the facing page
The polychrome majolicas of the inner portals of the Mosque of the Shah are reflected in the ritual waters of the basins.

An architectural element
behind the portal
of the Masjid-i Shah,
the Mosque of the Shah.

The two slender minarets
and the dome of
the Cahar Bagh Mosque.

WORDS OF ISLAMIC ART

Iwan: loggia, vaulted space, overlooking a courtyard; when it takes a monumental form, it calls for a portal, which then takes the name of *pitaq*.

Madrasa: was the public school, for various subjects, not necessarily and not only religious subjects; it later became the centre for higher Muslim teaching, specializing as a Koran school.

Muqarnas: arch with niches like stalactites, or a beehive, in any case with a distinctly fractal taste, a decorative function. There are various theories about its origin. A plausible antecedent could be the mausoleum of Arab Ata at Tim in Transoxiana, dating back to 977–78; still earlier (eighth to ninth centuries) are a number of concave stucco elements, with flat bottoms, found during the excavations done by the Metropolitan Museum at Mashapur: they may have been part of a *muqarnas*.

Mihrab: niche that indicates the direction of Mecca in a mosque.

Sahn: the courtyard of the mosque.

Ulama: term sharing the root of *mullah* and a plural form of *alim*, 'learned man' (in theology and jurisprudence). From among the *ulama* are chosen the *sheiykhs*, the *imams*, the *kadis*, and the teachers of the Koran schools.

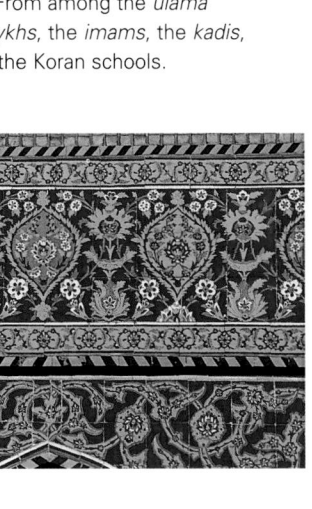

The frieze over a muqarnas.

The ceiling over one of the almost 500 bays of the Friday Mosque, eleventh to sixteenth century.

bestowed upon it by Western merchants, it was precisely because of the speed with which those merchants watched the city grow every time they came back: new *madrasas*, mosques, and bridges were built and covered with 'seven colour' tiles, perhaps less precise, but very decorative indeed. Safavids decorators played with two key colours: the ochre of the earth and the light blue of the sky. The most ancient monument from the Safavid era that still survives is the Mosque of Ali: some parts made of brick alternate with parts made of ceramics, with a decorative solution similar to that of the Blue Mosque in Tabriz.

The Palace of Ali Qapu is a building with a curious history. Structurally speaking, it is no more than an entrance portal to the royal palace, as its name ('high gate') would suggest; the building already existed even before the arrival of Shah Abbas. But when the time came for Abbas to develop an architectural plan for his future residence, he took the forms of the portal to heart and made it his favourite residence. And so he was obliged to reinvent its fundamental structure, integrating it into a much grander vision. The park boasted basins

with sprays of water that danced and sparkled even then, through the operation of a piece of hydraulic machinery pulled by a pair of oxen. The frescoes in the throne room and the adjoining rooms featured female figures that were clearly of Chinese derivation, in order to remind the spectators of the time the importance of Isfahan as a major crossroads on the Silk Road. On the upper storey, the sharp-eyed can pick out niches frescoed with distinctly erotic scenes: this was the banqueting hall, and those niches once held silver urns, inset with pearls.

But the masterpiece of the reign of Shah Abbas is indubitably the Masjid-i Shah, the Mosque of the Shah, which stands on the southern side of the Maidan with a monumental entrance that was completed in 1616, as is stated in the inscription over the portal. Construction of the complex began in the spring of 1611, under the supervision of Master, or Ustad, Abu'l-Qasim. The master builder stopped construction for a couple of years in order to allow the foundations to settle in to the earth. We know that construction was still under way in 1638.

A niche in the ceramic decoration of a wall.

From the perfect simplicity of a point, cascading outward, the kaleidoscopic image of a muqarnas *is generated.*

On the facing page
The dome of one of the mosques of Isfahan, faced with majolica tiles.

Standing before the mosque is a sort of domed vestibule. The mosque must have jutted out on to the square, which already existed but which was oriented to the north. The religious building, nonetheless, could not ignore the imperative of being on an axis with Mecca; and so a sort of domed octagonal vestibule was built in front of it, making it possible to articulate the two, diversely oriented layouts. The portal also served the role of inviting one to enter, creating a cushion space, somewhere to decompress from the chaos of the marketplace in the adjoining square.

The two panels on the walls on either side of the entrance are the ceramic version of two tapestries. The eye may be overwhelmed by the decoration of the *muqarnas* at the entrance: these are niches that resemble stucco grape clusters or beehives, a fractal decoration, symbol of the multiple vacuity of reality, in which the gaze could lose itself. The *muqarnas* are set in the corners of the walls of the arches.

Even if the façade of the mosque, for much of the day, lay in shadow, it still catches the light of day because of its ceramic sheathing. Indeed, the use of majolica coverings, for a mosaic and tile decoration, makes the façade of the mosque glow with a turquoise light. The bulk of the building soars in a daunting effort at verticality, the material counterpart to the yearning of the faithful towards the divine: like hymns elevated ever upward, there is a succession beginning with the external portal, rising to a height of 27.4 metres; the *pitaq,* which rises to a height of 30 metres; the two minarets in the front, reaching heights of 45 metres; and the pair of minarets of the sanctuary, standing higher still and further soaring because of the spiral motif that runs through their length, culminating in the little wooden balconies that crown them. Overtopping this sequence of pinnacles that rise like a succession of organ pipes, stands the dome, 55 metres above the ground. The Masjid-i Shah thus outdoes in height its immediate model, the Mosque of Gawhar Chad at Mashad. Everywhere you can see the calligraphy of verses from the Koran: particularly fascinating in the relationship between sheer power and elegance are the inscriptions along the tambour of the dome.

The mosque occupies a place at the mouth of the 1,000-year development of the four-

iwan mosque, where all the elements line up in perfect equilibrium. In the interior, the sanctuary receives the light of the sun all day long thanks to two large windows, to the west and the east. The central hall, through broad apertures, communicates with two rectangular halls. These apertures take on the form of ribbed vaults set on arches, which in turn are based on stone pillars. The side rooms served as mosques in the winter; atop one of these secondary sanctuaries stood the *godalsteh*, the little pointed building from which the faithful were called to prayer. During the summer, instead, the faithful would gather in the *sahn*, the courtyard of the mosque, which featured rooms with roofs, supported by very high single arches that would break the rhythm of the two-storey *riwaqs*. The direction of Mecca, necessary in order to orient one's prayer, was marked by the *mihrab*, made of marble and porcelain.

Every kind of architecture exudes, from its interior, a sort of rhythm, a music, through the agreement and the reciprocal arrangement of its various elements. Mosques and churches have very different kinds of music, directed towards diametrically opposed objectives: the Christian basilica has a path that moves the faithful towards the altar; the mosque, instead, is intended to cause the faithful to halt, in order to be able to contemplate the revelation.

On both the left and right sides, the mosque is bounded by courtyards intended for religious education, with two-storey porticoes where the students would live; there are still a few original doors. In an arid highland like Iran, every garden is seen as a heaven on earth; as a sort of counterweight to the landscape that merchants would encounter on their way to Isfahan, the garden was meant to be an inspiration to abundance. This is a constant of Iranian architecture; for that matter, it is no accident that the Greek word *paràdeisos*

*Sky, majolica, wood:
the elements of
the natural elegance
of the Safavids.*

*The ceramic calligraphies
of the dome and the
minaret seem to call and
respond to each other.*

On the facing page
*The Safavid decorators
made use of two key
colours: the ochre
of the earth and
the light-blue of the sky.*

was used to describe the garden of the Emperor of Persia. The garden of the mosque fully lives up to this tradition: in a courtyard with four *iwans*, the colour that dominates is turquoise, found as well in the vaulted ceilings of the niches; in the basin for ablutions were mirrored both the sky and the mosque, in an ideal conjunction between the faithful and the Divine.

The religious centre of Isfahan, before the royal mosque was built, was the Friday Mosque, Masjid-i Jami: the sanctuary of the *mihrab* dates back to 1022, and therefore to the Seljuk period (during the reign of Malek Shah); the site had already contained a mosque in the Abbassid period, but it later burned down. The complex, then, appears as a sort of construction site in operation from the eleventh to the seventeenth centuries: the central courtyard is surrounded by columned halls; the mosque, which still boasts two splendid wooden pulpits (*mimbar*), has incorporated, in its development, an independent building, the *gubad-i khaki*, a domed pavilion.

Safavid architecture was not purely religious, but only three instances survive of creations in a 'civilian' context. The first of them

is the Chehel Sotun, the 'Forty Columns'. The peristyle that constituted this building in reality boasted only twenty columns, all exceedingly slender, with a typically Iranian leonine base; but their number is doubled by the image reflected in the basin of water at their feet. This is an exquisite example of an architectural model that is fairly common in Central Asia: a wooden portico adapted to mansions, temples, and mosques, as well as to ordinary private dwellings. The *talar* is its basic module: this is a portico with a flat ceiling, attached to the façade of the building in question. In the Chehel Sotun, which served as an immense open-air reception hall, the basic module of the *talar* was embellished by ceilings with polychromatic paintings and mosaics, stalactite decorations in the corners, and fountains. The wall paintings responded to an uninhibited taste for the erotic, too explicit for the successors to the Safavids, the Afghan and Qajar governors, who had these scenes covered over with a layer of paint. Only recently have restorers managed to remove this coat of 'censorship', bringing back to the light of day the joy of life that characterized these frescoes.

The Golden Temple
of Dambulla

The village of Dambulla is located in the north-central section of the small territory constituted by the Singhalese island-state, about 12 miles to the south-west of the Castle of Sigiriya, along the road that links Matale, an English fortress and monastery, to the old capital Anuradhapura. The inhabited section of the village is located upon a giant cliff (*rangiri*, or 'golden rock') marked by numerous peaks and looming 160 metres over the surrounding plain, a vast grassland covered with tall green plants beyond which the gaze reaches as far as Sigiriya.

On the highest part of the rocky highland is the Golden Temple. Of all the rock temples in Sri Lanka that form the *Raja Maha Vihara*, the voyage in which the Buddha visited three places, the Temple of Dambulla is the most spectacular. The history of these buildings seems to date back to about the third or second century B.C. This dating is derived from the typological study of the letters found in the inscriptions written in Brahmi. When King Valagam Bahu (Vattagamini Abhaya), fleeing the Tamil armies, left Anuradhapura and took refuge in these caverns for fourteen years, from 103 to 89 B.C., the place was consecrated in eternal gratitude once the king regained his throne. The earliest buildings date back to the first century B.C.

The destination of pilgrimages for the past twenty-two centuries, then, this cliff-side sanctuary consists of five separate grottoes. The monumental entrance is built in the style of the façades of colonial churches: a long corridor, created by basket arches supported by simple smooth columns and covered with a tile roof, it extends jutting structures linked by stairways to the plaza in front of the building. Each entrance is decorated with various motifs in relief and statues; the upper section culminates in an attic upon which stands a triangular pediment or, in the case of the main

grottoes, a semi-circular fronton. The white of the structure contrasts against the green of the vegetation and the dark grey of the moist rock.

The interiors are lit only by candles, which reveals the gold and cobalt blue of the statues and paintings that adorn them, creating a mysterious and almost magical atmosphere. Of particular interest are the Buddhist-style wall paintings, which cover a total surface area of 2,100 square metres, and the 157 statues of the Buddha. Both of these arrays of artwork offer documentation of the degree of the island's cultural development over the course of the centuries, characterized by the reciprocal influences of Buddhism and Hinduism.

In the first grotto, the frescoes on the walls and ceilings date back to the period from the fifteenth to the eighteenth centuries, depicting episodes from the life of the Buddha. The fairly narrow structure of the site has made it possible to create, carved directly into the living rock, a statue of the sleeping Buddha, 15 metres in length, which appears all the more gigantic because of the necessity of admiring it up close. It is accompanied by other statues of the Buddha, reclining or meditating.

In the second grotto, Maha Vihara, the largest one, which is entirely frescoed, there are more than sixty Buddhas, either alone or else accompanied by statues of a number of Hindu gods, such as Vishnu and Ganesha; some of these date back to before the twelfth century, when the new religion first reached the coasts of Sri Lanka. Also housed here are two depictions of the Buddha in meditation, surrounded by monks who are about to attain Nirvana, and statues depicting the kings present in the frescoes which recount the history of the island.

In the third grotto, the ceiling is entirely covered with very colourful frescoes of the

View of the continual portico that links the entrances to the five sacred grottoes.

On the facing page
The Sleeping Buddha, *15 metres long, carved along the wall of the narrow corridor that forms the first grotto.*

Buddha meditating, repeated thousands of times.

The fourth grotto, usually closed to visitors, was a little temple that contained the jewels of the queen, wife of King Valagam Bahu: the site was plundered by thieves in 1981. The fifth grotto, less interesting than the others, seems to offer visitors a moment reserved to the discovery of themselves, a little meditation in order to regain inner peace.

The complex is completed by a temple from a recent period and by the monastery of Buddhist monks. A large new white Buddha, like the one in Kandy, should welcome the future pilgrims to Dambulla as well.

The Golden Temple was added to the World Heritage List in 1991.

THE HISTORY OF SRI LANKA

According to the texts of the *Mahavamsa* (Great Genealogy), which date back to the sixth century A.D., the Aryan colonization of Sri Lanka took place in 483 B.C., with Prince Vijaya from the Ganges valley, in whose veins ran the blood of a fierce lion, or *sinha*, hence Singhalese. The Aryans introduced new metallurgical techniques for working iron and advanced methods for farming, such as irrigation. Vijaya married Kuveni – Princess of the Vedda, the earliest nomadic inhabitants – and founded the Singhalese Dynasty. Two centuries later, the Tamils arrived from southern India by crossing the Palk Strait. From that day forward, for almost 1,800 years, the island was governed in a sort of feudal system by various Singhalese Buddhist dynasties and by Hindu Tamils, who battled in an incessant struggle for power. The alternation of the capitals (Anuradhapura, Polonnaruwa, and Kandy) that marked this period is a marker of the chaos into which the island was plunged. In 1507, Sri Lanka was occupied by the Portuguese, who established a monopoly upon the spice trade. In 1658 the monarch of the Kingdom of Kandy asked the Dutch for help in expelling the Portuguese. Sri Lanka thus became a Dutch trading emporium governed by the Singhalese people, even though the area was continually subject to the actions of the British East Indies Company. In 1795, the island became a British possession and, in 1835, a British colony. Gradually the country, which was called Ceylon under British rule, regained its freedom: in 1948 it became independent and in 1972 it was proclaimed a republic with the name of Sri Lanka.

On the facing page Details of the wall paintings depicting musicians in a ceremonial procession.

One of the 157 statues of the Buddha: in this case, we see the canonical iconography of the Buddha meditating, seated with crossed legs.

MOROCCO

TUNISIA

A L G E R I A

L I B Y A

EGYPT

Memfi

Abu Simbel

WESTERN
SAHARA

MAURITANIA

M A L I

N I G E R

CAPE
VERDE

SENEGAL

GAMBIA

GUINEA
BISSAU

GUINEA

SIERRA LEONE

IVORY
COAST

GHANA

TOGO

BENIN

Abomey

BURKINA
FASO

NIGERIA

C H A D

ERITREA

S U D A N

DJIBUTI

E T H I O P I A

S O M A L I A

LIBERIA

EQUATORIAL GUINEA

SÃO TOME
AND
PRINCIPE

GABON

CAMEROON

CENTRAL AFRICA
REP.

CONGO

Z A I R E

UGANDA

KENYA

RWANDA

BURUNDI

T A N Z A N I A

SEYCHELLES

ANGOLA

ZAMBIA

MALAWI

MOZAMBIQUE

COMOROS

Ambohimanga

MADAGASCAR

MAURIT

NAMIBIA

ZIMBABWE

BOTSWANA

SWAZILAND

LESOTHO

SOUTH AFRICA

AFRICA Africa

The Royal Palaces of Abomey

According to legend, the dynasties of the kingdoms located to the south of the present-day Republic of Benin come from Tado, a city in modern Togo, and they descend from a mythical couple: Princess Aligbonon of Tado and a leopard. In 1625 two of their descendents, Ganyé Hessou and Dako of the Fon people, founded a new kingdom: Danhomé, overlooking the Gulf of Guinea. The second King, Houégbadja (1645–85), established the legal foundations and the great principles upon which the kingdom functioned, such as the rules of succession and the political objectives of the sovereigns. In this period, the extension of the kingdom was limited to the highland where the capital, Abomey, stood. In the eighteenth century, King Agadja (1708–40) expanded the frontiers of Danhomé all the way to the Atlantic coast, conquering the Kingdoms of Allada and Savi thanks to his extraordinary military power. A strong internal cohesion, reinforced by a clear linguistic and cultural identity and a respect for hierarchies, gave the Fon their strength. From that moment on, Danhomé began to take an active part in the trade in black slaves, making use of the port city of Ouidah, capital of Savi, and enriching itself considerably with the sale of prisoners of war, political dissidents, criminals, and other innocent victims sold as slaves to Caribbean plantations in the New World. The kingdom reached its apex during the nineteenth century under King Guézo (1818–58). The politics of the tenth king was based on the centralization of state power through a strong army, which warred against neighbouring kingdoms, imposing heavy tributes to be paid by their subjects. Obliged by the anti-slavery movement, Guézo made reforms in order to develop the agriculture and convert the economy of Danhomé, replacing the export of slaves at least in part with the export of such agricultural products as bananas and palm oil, and introducing new crops, like corn and tobacco. The new economic climate made it possible to establish profitable exchanges with the French Government. At the end of the nineteenth century, despite the fierce resistance to European penetration with an intense guerrilla warfare waged under King Gbêhanzin (1889–94), the kingdom finally lost its independence and dissolved into the French colony of Dahomey. The sovereign was captured and deported to Argel, and was replaced by a designated king named Agoliagbo under a French protectorate incorporated in the colonial territories known as French West Africa.

From 1625 to 1900 twelve kings succeeded each other as the rulers of the Kingdom of Abomey, and each of them built a palace of his own, with its own service structures, sanctuaries, and tombs, not far from the residence of the previous king, in all covering an area of 44 hectares. Only King Akaba (1685–1708) kept his lodgings separate, creating a second zone on the interior of the ring of walls that protects the royal quarters. The layout of the royal residence, identical in each and every palace, was based on a building surrounded by a wall overlooking three courtyards with different functions: the outermost one housed military parades and religious ceremonies; opening on to the second one were the reception rooms and common rooms; while the third opened on to the private lodgings of the sovereign and his wives.

The simple structure in unfired brick, finished with teak, bamboo and straw roofs, is embellished with architectural decorations, paintings, clay sculptures and polychrome reliefs. For a society without written documents, these bas-reliefs served the function of recording past events. An important documentation of the development of the Fon people and

Courtyard of the Cannons, the great parade ground where the army would gather on the eve of each battle.

On the facing page
At Zingpoho, the historic museum preserves the carved wood and the fabrics that are typical of African art.

their empire, the art records their myths, customs, and rituals, glorifies their military triumphs, and depicts the power of the king. The small reliefs in brightly painted sun-dried earth depict scenes of war, illustrate mottos, reproduce royal heraldic emblems and mythical animals which symbolize the characteristics of the various kings and their power as rulers. The walls show that the military power of the kingdom was based in part on platoons of women warriors, who rivalled their male counterparts in fierceness and courage.

Currently, some of the buildings are occupied by descendents of the royal dynasty, while another zone has been transformed into an ethnographic museum which houses and preserves the artworks, sculptures, textiles and paintings of African art.

The main façade of the Palace of King Guézo (1818–58), still undergoing restoration.

Alongside the Palace, King Guézo built his own tomb.

One of the polychrome bas-reliefs that decorate the outer walls of the Palace of King Guézo.

PRESERVATION EFFORTS

The site was inscribed simultaneously on the World Heritage List and on the Endangered Heritage List in 1985, after a cyclone hit Abomey on 15 March 1984. According to the report developed at the time, the royal monumental complex and the museums, the Guézo Portico, the Throne Room, the tomb of King Glèlè, and the Hall of Jewels all suffered damage. Since then, numerous restoration programmes have been put into effect on behalf of the site. In 1994 UNESCO moved to seek help from various states and institutions in order to put into operation a maintenance programme for the monument. In that year PREMA (Prevention in the Museums of Africa) was commenced, in collaboration with the Government of Benin. A three-year-long research project financed by the Italian Ministry for Foreign Affairs and UNESCO produced roughly 2,500 pages of documentation concerning the architecture of the site, covering a period that began in 1731 and runs up to the present day. The material gathered was copied, bound, and included in the libraries of Benin, as well as in France, Italy, and the United States of America.

After visiting Abomey in 1993, a mission from the Getty Conservation Institute launched a campaign for the restoration of the bas-reliefs that decorated the palaces. In the course of this project, which lasted four years, fifty of the fifty-six original bas-reliefs that decorated the walls of the palace of Glèlè were replaced on the monument and the functionaries of the Cultural Heritage of Benin were trained in the planning functions and other practical aspects of the conservation programme. The authorities in Benin have collected more funds to carry on the conservation programme by increasing the museum's resources, improving the training and education of the staff of the cultural centre, and by creating a digital documentation programme in order to move this area off the Endangered Heritage List.

The Palace of the Queen is one of the best-preserved complexes.

The Temples
of Abu Simbel

The temporal subdivision of Egyptian history into dynasties was already used by ancient historians, who identified long periods punctuated by transitional periods caused by political and economic difficulties. With the eighteenth dynasty (1550–1307 B.C.) the New Kingdom began, the third historic period of great expansion towards the territories of Palestine and the Sinai and a period of great artistic endeavours. 'Thebes existed before any other city' is written in a papyrus dated between 1290 and 1224 B.C., and it was Thebes, *Ta-ipet*, that became the capital, with the majestic temples in present-day Karnak and Luxor, while in the surrounding areas, on the western bank of the Nile, there was a proliferation of royal tombs in the areas now known by the names of Valley of the Kings and Valley of the Queens.

The nineteenth dynasty was the period during which the Pharaoh Ramesses II (who ruled from 1279 to 1213 B.C.) lived, commissioning the two spectacular and magnificent temples at Abu Simbel. Carved directly out of the rocky cliff and closely adjoining one another, the temples were bathed by the waters of the left bank of the Nile in Lower Nubia, near the present-day Sudanese border. The temples were discovered by J. L. Burckhardt in 1813, while he was sailing on the Nile to return to Cairo, and from there to England. From this point on, campaigns were conducted to clean the monuments, which were almost completely buried in sand. When the decision was made to build an immense dam upstream from Aswan in order to control the flooding of the river for the general benefit of the entire Egyptian region, the temples ran the risk of being entirely submerged by the rising waters. Credit goes to UNESCO, in collaboration with various countries, for having organized and implemented a massive rescue effort. The exceedingly difficult operation

was successfully carried out over the course of a few years, from 1963 to 1968, by carving the monuments up into 1,036 blocks weighing approximately 30 metric tons each, transporting them to the site where they are now located, and reassembling them as they originally were, covering them with a dome of reinforced concrete. Since 1979 the temples have been inscribed on the World Heritage List.

Ramesses II chose to build the two temples dedicated to him on the site where there existed two grottoes consecrated to the cult of the local divinities. In this way, the sovereign reaffirmed the fact that Nubia belonged to the Egyptian Empire. In order to construct the two façades, the mountain was cut sheer. In the case of the Great Temple, the height extended to 33 metres and the width to 36 metres. Four colossal statues were carved out of the living rock, fastened to the cliff wall, and depicting Ramesses II, seated, with the nemes and the uraeus on his forehead, the double crown of Lower and Upper Egypt, the fake beard, and his hands resting on his thighs. Standing between and on either side of the pharaoh's legs were depicted princes, princesses, and the Queen Nefertari, much smaller in size, and standing erect. Between the two central colossi, the portal is surmounted by the figure of Ra-Harakhte, recognizable by the hawk-like features of the face crowned by the sun disk. This deity, a manifestation of the rising sun, was created by merging Ra, the Sun God, Lord of the Heavens, possessor of wisdom and the creative force, with Horus (*Hor*, 'the distant one'). Harakhte means 'Horus of the two horizons', the unifier of Lower and Upper Egypt, and therefore the progenitor and protector of all the pharaohs. The façade is concluded on the top by a row of statues of baboons, considered the protectors of the element that was indispensable to life: water. Nowadays, these animals still live

View of the façade of the Great Temple of Ramesses II.

On pages 328–29
Panoramic view of the temples dedicated to Ramesses II along the banks of the Nile.

On the facing page
Detail of the face of one of the colossi depicting the seated pharaoh, set so as to guard the entrance to the Great Temple.

around the springs from which the Nile originates.

Inside the temple there is, in succession, a great hall, whose ceiling is supported by eight colossal pillars in the shape of statues of the king, a smaller hall with simple pillars, a vestibule and a sanctuary. In the sanctuary, which was accessible only to the pharaoh and the high priest, there were four seated statues depicting a deified Ramesses II, Amon-Ra, the Sun God and king of all the gods, Harakhte and Ptah. In order to render more distant and therefore more majestic the sacred sacellum, an illusionistic layout with false perspective was created by gradually raising the floor and lowering the ceiling. Twice a year, on 20 February and 20 October, the rays of the sun penetrated from the entrance, illuminating the first three statues, but never the statue of Ptah, who was not a solar deity. This conclusion was reached through careful and refined astronomical calculations concerning the orientation of the temple and distance from the Tropic of Cancer. The repositioning of the temple was done in consideration of this particular factor, which was thus preserved.

The importance of the Great Temple is documented by the reliefs that adorn the walls of the halls. In the first hall, Ramesses II, in immense proportions, wearing the double crown of Lower and Upper Egypt, is depicted as he destroys a group of enemies. On the northern wall is depicted the battle of Qadesh, fought by the pharaoh against the Hittites. The military event is narrated on two levels without any specific order. High up, Ramesses II has just fired an arrow at his enemies who, dying, wind up crushed under the wheels of his chariot; all around, soldiers in chariots or on foot lay siege to a city, represented by five towers enclosed in an oval surrounded by the waters of the River Orontes. On the right, the Hittite King Muwatalli orders a retreat. At the bot-

THE BATTLE OF QADESH

The sources concerning this military event are
the bulletins recorded on the walls of no fewer
than five temples of the Egyptian Kingdom – at Abu
Simbel, Luxor, Karnak, in the Ramesseum and
at Abydos – and the poem of Pentaur, a papyrus
now preserved at the British Museum in London,
drawn up by the scribe Pentaur in Memphis during
the reign of the successor to Ramesses II,
Merenptah (1224–14 B.C.). In the fifth year of his
reign, in 1275 B.C., Ramesses II declared war upon
the Hittite Kingdom of Muwatalli in order to regain
control of Syria, which had been lost during the reign
of Amenophis IV (1350–33 B.C.). Qadesh was one
of the most important kingdoms of central Syria
and the forwardmost point for successive invasions
to the north. The pharaoh marched with four military
corps, the armies of Amon, R a, Ptah, and Seth,
crossing the territories of what is now Israel,
and stopping at Megiddo, to the south of the lake
of Tiberias. From that point an expeditionary corps
set out, the Naharin, whose task was to reach
Qadesh by proceeding along the coast. The pharaoh
marched inland through the Bekaa Valley and forded
the River Orontes on a line with the present-day Nahr
el Asi. It was here that the Hittites made a surprise
attack upon the Ra division, separating it from the
army of Amon which had already established itself
on the other bank of the river, and destroying it
entirely. This was a harsh blow, but Ramesses II
decided to attack the city with the army that remained
to him while awaiting reinforcements from the north.
And so he did, and after a day of hard fighting both
armies had suffered serious losses. Despite the
crushing victory proclaimed in the temples and
acclaimed by the populace, the result of the clash
was an agreed truce. Many years later, in the face
of the common danger presented by the expansion
of the Assyrian Empire, the two peoples signed
a peace treaty, the first international treaty in history.

*Depiction of the Pharaoh
Ramesses II while
he destroys his enemies,
on the southern wall of
the first hall of the Great
Temple of Abu Simbel.*

On the facing page
*View of the interior of
the Little Temple
dedicated to Queen
Nefertari: you can make
out the pillars decorated
with stylized depictions of
the goddess Hathor and
the god of writing, Toth,
with the head of Ibis,
painted on the left wall.*

THE TOMBS OF RAMESSES II AND NEFERTARI

While the Pharaoh Ramesses II lived much longer than his wife Nefertari, sixty-seven years as opposed to forty-six years, their life after death was far more pleasant for the queen than for the king. The tomb of the great pharaoh, in fact, is still being excavated today, while the queen's tomb has been completely restructured and is open to the public.

The KV7 (KV for King Valley), where Ramesses II was buried, is located at the mouth of the valley, a position that was unfortunate in that it was most often exposed and most brutally subject to the flooding that resulted from the torrential rains that were common in this region of Egypt. The tomb, carved into living rock, presents a series of corridors subdivided by stairs, upon which two successive vestibules open out. The first leads to two secondary halls, while the second precedes a great hall supported by eight pillars. From the 'Hall of the Sarcophagus', you enter two small chambers situated in the two side walls, while in the far wall two hypostyle rooms have been carved out, one of which possesses two further annexes. On the lower part of the right door jamb that separates the third and fourth corridors we find the mention of 'Nefertari, great royal wife', contained within a cartouche. The tomb was first broken into in ancient times, leaving only a few fragments of the magnificent funereal dowry buried with the sovereign; for that reason, the priests decided to protect the mummy by moving it to the hiding place of Deir el-Bahari, where it was discovered in 1881. The same fate was visited upon the tomb of Nefertari, but her mummy was not saved. Only two pieces survive from that tomb, now preserved in the Egyptian Museum of Turin. The open-air access staircase leads to an antechamber that is connected to a vestibule and an annex on the eastern side. On the far wall, there is an internal staircase that leads to the funerary chamber. On either side and at the far end, small rooms were carved out in which the funerary furnishings were to be stored.

On the facing page
*Detail of Queen
Nefertari in the splendid
and newly restored
paintings that adorn
the underground tomb
in the Valley of
the Queens near Thebes.*

*The painted ceiling
of the first hall
of the Great Temple,
supported by the colossi of
the Pharaoh Ramesses II.*

tom, on the left is depicted the walled encampment with the soldiers in frantic activity as they prepare for war, checking their chariots and horses; further off the attack of the enemy triggers a defensive battle. On the right we see the war council: the pharaoh sits in a throne, larger than all the others, and is surrounded by the royal guard of the Shardana, characterized by their circular shields and their helmets with round caps and horns. All around the scene, hieroglyphics describe the battle.

Not far off stands the Little Temple dedicated to the goddess Hathor in memory of the king's wife Nefertari, 'beauty among the beauties'. Hathor means 'house of Horus'; in the beginning she was the mother of Horus and therefore of all pharaohs; she was later venerated as the goddess of love and fertility. In the façade six statues in standing positions, about 10 metres tall, are carved into the rock. They represent the pharaoh and his wife, assimilated to the divinity and therefore depicted with the divinity's attributes, that is, a sun disk between the horns of a cow. The interior is subdivided into a hall held up by pillars decorated with reliefs depicting the goddess, a vestibule with side rooms and the sanctuary, which contained the statue of the goddess in the form of a cow in the act of protecting Ramesses II. Here too the interior walls of the halls are decorated with magnificent reliefs showing the presentation of offerings and festive processions in honour of the pharaoh and his wife Nefertari. The queen, with her slender figure and her fine profile, is assimilated now to the goddess Hathor, now to the goddess Sothi, evoking the renewal of the Nile's floods. All of this alludes to the queen's function as symbol of the female principle, an element of certainty alongside her husband, ensuring the perpetuation of the cosmic order. The texts designate her as 'the beloved of the king, the sweetness of love, splendid in her face'.

The imposing façade of the Great Temple, embellished by statues of the sovereign on his throne.

Overall view of the façade of the Little Temple, dedicated to the goddess Hathor, in memory of the king's wife Nefertari.

On the facing page
A picture taken during the difficult reassembly process organized by UNESCO, which made it possible to save the temples from the encroaching waters of the Aswan Dam.

The Pyramids
from Giza to Dashur

The three thousand years of Egyptian history before Christ are punctuated by the list of the thirty-one dynasties that ruled over the country. The first of these dynasties, between 2920 and 2770 B.C., created the Egyptian Empire by unifying the territories that include the Nile delta, Lower Egypt and the desert as far as the present-day Aswan Dam, Upper Egypt. The first sovereign of the unified kingdom, Menes or Narmer, ordered the construction of a new capital in the area around the Nile delta, at the point where the two kingdoms bordered: 'the city of Menes', Mennufer, also known as Hut-Ka-Pta, or 'dwelling of the Ka of Pta', the most important sanctuary dedicated to the god of the creative force, depicting as a ram-headed artisan working intently to shape humanity with his potter's wheel. It is from this latter name that the Greek word *Aigyptos* derives, hence the Latin name, *Aegyptus*, and then the English name, Egypt. Of the grandeur of Memphis, as the ancient Greeks called it, there survive today a few ruins of the sanctuary to Pta, from which come numerous votive statues depicting pharaohs and dignitaries, and monumental necropolises, since 1979 a World Heritage Site protected by UNESCO.

In the necropolis of Saqqara, the closest to the capital and the largest in all the land, stands the first great stone pyramid. It was built as a mausoleum, for himself and for his family, by Djoser (2630–11 B.C.), the founder of the Third Dynasty. This was a transformation of the earlier tombs, shaped like great brick rectangles, with the walls sloping inward and a flat roof, commonly referred to as a *mastaba* from a similar word for 'counter' that the Arabs used to describe them. For the first time, the bricks were replaced by stone: blocks of siliceous limestone joined with mortar and sheathed in limestone from Tura, a place on the far bank of the Nile; the limestone sheath ranged in thickness from 1.6 to 2.5 metres. Atop a first *mastaba*, 8 metres tall and 63 metres long on each side, others were stacked to a height of 60 metres. This resulted in an imposing step construction, the forerunner of all later pyramids. Stones that had been carved with one sloping side, recently discovered at the foot of the pyramid, allow us to venture that the final plan had called for the construction of a genuine pyramid, like the pyramids of Giza. Approximately in the centre of the construction, in a great shaft 28 metres deep and 7 metres wide, was the royal burial chamber. On the base of a statue of Djoser and on the interior of the enclosure wall surrounding the pyramid, near the entry colonnade, the name of the architect has been discovered: Imhotep, vizier to the king, chief of all government administration, high priest, and physician. His name was so famous that he was deified by the ancient Greeks and identified with the figure of Aesculapius. The pyramid is located inside a funerary complex enclosed by a curtain wall rising to a height of 10 metres and consisting of a fine-grain limestone facing with jutting areas and niches corresponding to pilaster strips, a style that echoes the façades of the residential palaces, since the tomb is nothing less than the residence of the spirit. In the enclosure wall are fourteen false stone doors and a monumental entrance consisting of a corridor and hall flanked by columns. The entry path leads to a plaza known as the 'Courtyard of the Jubilee', where one can see a depiction of the ceremony of coronation during the jubilee rituals intended to rejuvenate the powers of the king. One side of the courtyard is occupied by a great stepped podium upon which were arranged the thrones of the pharaoh, as King of both Lower and Upper Egypt. To the east and to the west of the podium were built sanctuaries with rectangular plans, with flat or arched roofs, their façades either flat or enlivened by

Panoramic view of the City of the Dead, over which loom the masses of the Pyramids of Cheops (2551–28 B.C.) and Chephren (2520-2494 B.C.) at Giza.

On the facing page
The houses on the outskirts of Cairo run up against the edges of the archaeological area of Giza.

slender tapered columns, probably containing the images of the gods who witnessed the coronation of the sovereign. The complex included other religious buildings, such as the 'House of the North' and the 'House of the South', in imitation of the palaces of Djoser as the King of the North and the South; on the western side underground chambers and halls were built at ground level to contain the countless offerings that were donated daily to the royal dead. As if each of the kingdoms had dedicated a funerary structure to its own monarch, there are also two tombs: on the southern side of the complex stands a simple *mastaba* construction which is associated with a chapel decorated by a crowning frieze depicting cobras, symbols of Lower Egypt. In the *serdab* ('cella') was a statue of Djoser which could see, through two holes driven through the wall, the Pole Star and the various constellations, eternal destinations of his journey into the world beyond. This statue is the first instance known of life-sized sculpture in the round.

The founder of the Fourth Dynasty, Snefru (2575–51 B.C.), transformed once and for all the structure of the tomb by choosing the now familiar pyramid shape with a square base. In the necropolis of Dashur, only 2 kilometres away from Saqqara, stands the 'Red Pyramid', named after the reddish hue of the limestone that was used to build it; it seems very low and flattened in shape because of the relationship between its large base of 213 metres square and its relatively low height of 99 metres. To the south of this pyramid is the 'Rhomboid Pyramid', with its double slope on each of the four faces, apparently an intermediate form from the step pyramid to the pyramid with oblique sides. With Snefru we also find for the first time the annex constructions, which became characteristic features of all funerary complexes of this type. The entrance to the

Southern view of the Rhomboid Pyramid built at the behest of Snefru (2575–51 B.C.) in the necropolis of Dashur, accompanied by the small pyramidal cenotaph from the Kingdom of Upper Egypt.

Panoramic view of the Pyramid of Mycerinus at Giza (2490–72 B.C.), accompanied by the smaller pyramids in which his wives were buried.

On the facing page
Detail of the oldest Egyptian pyramid, the Tomb of Djoser, conceived by Imhotep in the first half of the third millennium B.C. in the necropolis of Saqqara.

339

One of the entrances in the enclosure walls that surround the funerary structures of the Tomb of Djoser, over which looms the bulk of the step pyramid.

The mastaba *and the decorated chapel that constitute the Tomb of the Pharaoh Djoser, dedicated by the subjects of Lower Egypt.*

tomb was located on the north side, facing the Pole Star; to the east, a funerary temple was linked by an elevated road to a temple in the valley; to the south, a secondary pyramid represented the cenotaph of the Kingdom of Upper Egypt. The best preserved valley temple from the necropolis of Dashur is the one linked to the Rhomboid Pyramid. The plan is rectangular and the entrance is on the south. A corridor divides two halls meant to receive offerings and leads to an open courtyard, enclosed on the northern side by a wall with a double colonnade of five pillars with square bases. The decoration called for figures of Snefru on the pillars against the northern wall and personifications of his qualities in the form of female figures bearing votive trays, with water and bread, along the walls of the corridor.

Credit goes to the son of Snefru, Khufu or Cheops (2551–28 B.C.), and to his successors Rakhaef, or Chephren (2520–2494 B.C.) and Menkaure, or Mycerinus (2490–72 B.C.), for the construction of the great pyramids of Giza, considered one of the seven wonders of the

world ever since the classical era. The pyramid is a symbol of the sun, the great god Ra, whose cult became pre-eminent from the Fourth Dynasty on, when the pharaohs began to claim that they were his children. The *Pyramid Texts,* found in the funerary chambers of the tombs dating from the end of the Old Kingdom, speak of the transformation of the dead king into the Sun: the Horus-king was therefore associated with Ra, whose principal cult was in the city that the Greeks called – and it was no coincidence – Heliopolis. The shape, with its four corners sloping from top to bottom and from the centre towards the corners is similar to the depiction of the rays of the sun: they start from the one, in the sky, and they branch out towards the manifold, on earth, and vice-versa; from the multiplicity and the haphazard nature of the earth they lead up towards divine unity, which is where the sovereign will return.

'The Horizon of Cheops' was the name of the pharaoh's tomb, because in ancient Egyptian there was no hieroglyphic corresponding to the term pyramid. It is the oldest and the largest, standing 146.59 metres tall. Though nowadays the surface is rough and irregular because of the removal of the outer rock covering during the Middle Ages, it still presents an absolute geometric perfection. The entrance is located in the middle of the north side, just above the base. In the interior, the narrow passageway splits in two: heading down you reach a chamber carved into the rock beneath the monument; heading up you reach a small room called the 'Chamber of the Queen', and then an inclined corridor, the 'Great Gallery', in turn connected to the large 'Chamber of the King', where the royal sarcophagus was housed. Higher up, six cavities have been identified, clearly intended to lighten the enormous weight bearing up on it. Smaller, but equally perfect, are the other two pyramids: 'Great is Chephren', 136.5 metres high, and 'Divine is Mycerinus', 66 metres high.

The faces of the pyramid are always oriented towards the four cardinal points of the compass in order to signify that the Ka of the ruler can choose to travel anywhere on earth.

Each tomb forms part of the classical funerary complex first built at the behest of Snefru: transported by ship, the dead king reached the valley temple from the Nile riverbank or else along a canal running alongside the river. Then he climbed along a covered road as far as the tomb in the funerary chamber of which he was finally deposited, enclosed in a series of sarcophagi, one within another. At the foot of the Pyramid of Cheops on the south side, a large boat was uncovered, probably the 'sun boat' for the king's voyage into the world beyond. The valley temple connected with the Pyramid of Chephren is a severe rectangular construction in limestone blocks, slightly inclined, covered by a flat roof, and completely sheathed – inside and out – with granite slabs. The two entrances are flanked by a pair of sphinxes and by lions, and are decorated along the exterior by a string of hieroglyphics bearing the name and titles of the king. The internal corridor leads to a room with alabaster floors, subdivided into cellae by massive architraved pillars. In each cella were statues of green diorite depicting Chephren enthroned.

Detail of the crowning frieze on the chapel, decorated with cobras, symbols of Lower Egypt.

Panoramic view of the temples of the Courtyard of the Jubilee, the area at the foot of the step pyramid where the Pharaoh Djoser would observe celebrations held in his honour during his reign.

The Royal Hill of Ambohimanga

The Island of Madagascar was first sighted at the end of the fifteenth century by Portuguese mariners who named it the Island of San Lorenzo. Its present-day name was mistakenly given it by the German cosmographer Martin Behaim who, in his globe of 1492, confused it, based on information gathered from Marco Polo, with Madagosho or Madagascar, which is further north.

The present-day population is the result of various migratory waves of Australo-Melanesian and Indonesian groups. Belonging to the first group are the Bara and the Sakalava, who may have arrived in the second millennium B.C., followed by the Betsileo and the Tsimihety. More recent migrations introduced to the island the Merina, who may have originally come from the Indonesian island of Java: they form the group that is now dominant, settled on the central highland, in the land that is named after them: Imerina. This new tribe introduced its own culture, the cultivation of rice, and the use of the zebu in working the fields. Even the social structure is typical of the rice-growing peoples of monsoonal Asia, with a sovereign and a noble class of free men, the *hova*, a name that is also used to describe the Merina at large. Beginning in the seventeenth century, the Kingdom of the Merina developed, at the behest of King Adrianjaka, in the heart of the highlands, where they built the strongholds of their power, the citadels, or *rova*. After a period of civil wars and anarchy, the island found a renewed unity under King Andrianampoinimerina (1787–1810), acquiring control over the central region with the annexation of the land of the Betsileo and the Sihanaka. Further expansions took place under his son and successor Radama I (1810–28) who, having obtained weapons from the English, conquered two-thirds of the island.

A site of the mingling of Asian and African cultures, then, Madagascar has managed to combine the shared characteristics of its populations in the cultural symbol of the Royal Hill of Ambohimanga. In the document drawn up at the end of the assembly that approved its addition to the UNESCO World Heritage List in 2001, there is a description of the criteria that led to this decision: 'The Royal Hill of Ambohimanga is the most significant symbol of the cultural identity of the people of Madagascar. The traditional design, materials, and layout of the Royal Hill of Ambohimanga are representative of the social and political structure of Malagasy society from at least the 16th century. The Royal Hill of Ambohimanga is an exceptional example of a place where, over centuries, common human experience has been focused in memory, ritual, and prayer'.

The Royal Hill of Ambohimanga, 1,468 metres high, is located in the area around the capital, Antananarivo. The Royal City is surrounded with a ring of walls, in which there are fourteen fortified stone portals. Inside are sacred groves and fig orchards, a fruit reserved for the higher nobility, who surrounded the royal suites in simple wooden houses. The site includes a sacred spring which gushes out of living rock, forming the sacred pond of Amparihy: here, the viscera of dead kings were ritually washed, with the goal of purifying the city before placing them in the tombs that formed the necropolises on the slopes of the hill.

After the transfer of the Royal Palace to the new capital of Antananarivo, Ambohimanga continued to house the relics of the former sovereigns. They rested in a wooden mortuary house, the Tranomanara, before being transported to the tomb where the king, having become an ancestor, continued to exert protection and judgement over the living. Eleven kings rested there until March of 1897, when the French authorities who had colonized the island decided to move it to Antananarivo.

The Stone Gate, one of the fourteen entrances through which one can enter from the plain to the citadel, or rova.

On the facing page Panoramic view of one of the steep roads that separate the palace complexes.

An historical and sacred site associated with the cult of ancestors and kings, the hill is also a document of traditional agricultural practices, in particular of rice paddies arranged on irrigated terraces. Even now it remains the object of pilgrimages from among local populations and even from the African continent.

The entrance gates are often covered with straw roofs to provide some shelter against the harsh sunlight for the guards who scrutinized all who entered.

Detail of one of the gates, with the large blocks of hewn stone, used to support the walls of the fortification.

Panoramic view of the courtyards that separate the simple and rustic royal palaces.

AFRICAN CULTS

Every population that inhabits the African continent possesses a mythology of its own and its own pantheon of deities, each with its own name. All the same, a general characteristic of African cults is a belief in a cosmic vital force, emanated jointly by the spirits of nature and by ancestors, tribal chiefs, and priests: this force is assimilated, first and foremost, to fecundity, and then to the reproductive act of men, animals, and plants. According to this conception, the positive and the good can be found in everything that is favourable to fecundity, while anything that hinders or prevents fecundity is negative and evil. The cults and rituals serve the development of the vital force and are intended to ward off all efforts to undermine it. In order to give energy to life it is indispensable to maintain a continual and close link with the mythical origins of one's family and tribe and to respect established traditions. Priests, warriors, and heroes are considered messengers of the will of the gods or ancestors. Through them, men discovered the secrets of procreation, the use of fire, the practice of agriculture, and various vocations useful to survival. Prayer, sacrifice and dance are the principal forms of ritual. Dance, in particular, is the depiction of the struggle between the creative principle and the destructive act, so it must be performed while wearing masks.

The circular retaining wall and parapet of the tribune in the Square of Justice, where the king would proclaim his decrees.

Detail of the decoration on the wooden verandas that surround the royal residences.

USA

CANADA

UNITED STATES

New York

Taos

MEXICO

BAHAMAS

Guadalajara

CUBA

DOMINICAN REP.

JAMAICA

GUATEMALA BELIZE

HAITI

HONDURAS

EL SALVADOR NICARAGUA

COSTA RICA

VENEZUELA GUYANA

PANAMA

SURINAME

FRENCH GUYANA

COLOMBIA

ECUADOR

PERÚ

BRAZIL

BOLIVIA

Congonhas

PARAGUAY

CHILE

ARGENTINA

URUGUAY

AMERICA America

The Sanctuary of Bom Jesus do Matosinhos at Congonhas do Campo

Inland from the former Brazilian capital of Rio de Janeiro, separated by the Serra de Mantiqueira, extends the State of Minas Gerais, the El Dorado of the Portuguese thanks to the abundant presence of mines yielding the precious metal. To the south of Belo Horizonte, at Congonhas do Campo, the Portuguese colonist Feliciano Mendes ordered the beginning of construction in 1757 of the Sanctuary of Bom Jesus do Matosinhos, in fulfilment of a vow that he had made when in the painful throes of a serious illness contracted while working in the mines. Inspired by the Sanctuaries of Bom Jesus do Matosinhos, not far from Oporto, and Bom Jesus de Braga, both in Portugal, the complex was completed in a little more than sixty years of hard work, and constituted an original creation, unique in its style, of the best known Brazilian artists and artisans of the time.

Immersed in the still-luxuriant nature of the Brazilian highlands, the sanctuary is an integral part of the landscape, constituting a full attainment of the union of nature, man, and deity of Brazilian culture. Built on the peak of the Morro do Maranhão, it consists of seven square chapels covered by a pyramidal little dome with slightly curving corners; since 1974 the chapels have been connected to each other and to the church by a cobblestone path shaded by palm trees and other forest trees typical of South America. Along this path extends the Via Crucis. In fact, inside each chapel are displayed scenes of the Passion, created with life-sized figures carved in wood and painted before being installed in their respective positions. The cruelty of the centurion, the compassion of the pious women, the courage and the resignation of Christ can be read on the intense and realistic features of the faces. This magnificent work, begun in 1796 and completed in 1799, is attributed to the Brazilian artist Antonio Francisco Lisboa, known as 'Aleijadinho'. The sculptor, assisted by colleagues and apprentices, produced no fewer than sixty-six statues. The scenes of *The Last Supper*, the *Prayer in the Garden of Gethsemane*, and *Jesus's Arrest* were all painted by another skilful artisan, Manoel da Costa Athayde, between 1808 and 1819.

The church courtyard was constructed by raising the ground around the church, which was built first, and thus creating a terrace with a basement in a curving outline, reached via a double two-ramp staircase. The staircase was the creation of Thomaz de Maia Brito and it was completed between 1777 and 1790. The statues of the twelve prophets of the Old Testament who announced the events depicted in the chapels, carved life-sized in soapstone and arranged symmetrically along the parapet, were also the work of Aleijadinho, who executed them between 1800 and 1805.

The church was designed by the architect Francisco Lima Cerqueira and the master builders Domingos Antonio Dantas and Antonio Rodrigues Falcado who completed the building in 1773. Cerqueira was responsible, in particular, for the remarkable innovations present in

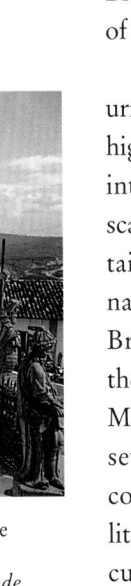

Detail of the entrance staircase of the church, adorned with statues of the prophets, carved between 1800 and 1805.

The prophet Ezekiel is depicted with papyrus scrolls, symbols of their wisdom.

On the facing page
Overall view of the elegant façade of the sanctuary, built between 1773 and 1790.

ANTONIO FRANCISCO LISBOA, ARCHITECT, PAINTER, AND SCULPTOR

Practically unknown in the Western world, Antonio Francisco Lisboa was the most important Brazilian artist of the modern age, comparable to the Italian Gian Lorenzo Bernini. He was born around 1730 in Ouro Preto, to an artisan of Portuguese origin and a black slave woman. In about 1770 he contracted a debilitating disease that left him lame. His nickname, Aleijadinho, in fact, translates as 'the little lame one'. Probably, the disease in question was either syphilis or leprosy, and it worsened over time until he was unable to use his fingers and practically unable to walk. Despite the fact that he was physically disabled, he was a prolific and talented artist, the creator of the finest Baroque art in Brazil, known as the Barroco Mineiro because it developed in the mining state of Minas Gerais.

When he reached Rio de Janeiro, Lisboa was exposed to images and books on European art, and he managed to incorporate in his own traditional art Baroque and Rococo with hints of classical and Gothic styles, utilizing however only such native materials as Brazilian woods and soapstone.

His most important creations were the Church of São Francisco de Assis in 1766 at Ouro Preto, the Church of São Francisco de Assis at São João del Rei in 1774, and the marvellous sculptures in the Sanctuary of Congonhas do Campo. The two churches, characterized by a skilful use of symmetry, express equilibrium and harmony. In contrast, the statues, among his latest works, possess considerable expressive power, probably inspired by the sufferings caused by disease. The artist died in 1814.

On the facing page
*Detail of the apse
and altar, done in Rococo
style, in the interior
of the church.*

*Detail of the face
of one of the prophets.*

*Built on a hilltop,
the sanctuary is the final
destination of a long
itinerary, even now
visited by pilgrims.*

*View of the façade and
the church courtyard
that opens out as
a terrace, enlivened by
the statues of prophets.*

Life-size depiction of The Last Supper: *made up of wooden statues carved by Antonio Francisco Lisboa and painted by Manoel da Costa Athayde.*

Christ Carrying the Cross, *in one of the most moving scenes reconstructed in the seven chapels that stand before the church itself.*

the architecture of the church, sufficient to create a regional school of architecture in its own right. The plan of the building develops along a single and broad aisle, terminating in a principal chapel where the altar is located. On either side of the central structure stand two tall bell towers, recessed from the main line of the façade, and covered with domes similar to those on the other chapels, but smaller in size. The façade is a simple square opened by a portal with its jambs finely adorned, as well as by two windows. The upper part terminates in a pediment with an undulating silhouette. Externally, the complex is plastered a bright white, broken only by the reliefs in soapstone that mark its profiles along the parapet of the staircase, the corners of the towers, the jutting consoles that divide the main part of the façade from the pediment, the reliefs of the portal, and the pediment itself. The motifs are repeated in slightly simpler form for the chapels.

While the exterior represents the Brazilian Baroque style, the interior harkens back to Italian culture with the decoration in a luxuriant Rococo style that covers the walls and ceilings and clearly informs the carvings on the altar, the statues, and the paintings that cover the walls of the hall and the principal tribune.

In 1985, following a thorough study developed and encouraged by Myriam Andrade Ribeiro de Oliveira, UNESCO recognized the Sanctuary of Bom Jesus as a significant document of the artistic and religious culture of Brazil, and added it to the World Heritage List.

On the facing page
The prophet Daniel, carved personally by Lisboa, who was also known as Aleijadinho.

The Hospicio Cabañas at Guadalajara

The name of the city of Guadalajara comes from the Arabic term *Wad-al-hidjara*, which means 'river that runs among the rocks'. A native of this Castilian city in Spain was Nuño Beltrán de Guzmán, the conqueror of the American territories overlooking the Pacific Ocean to the west of Mexico City. The region became the Kingdom of Nueva Galicia, and its capital was the new settlement of Guadalajara, built in the fertile valley of the Rio Grande de Santiago. Upon the establishment of the new federated Mexican nation, on 27 May 1824, Guadalajara became the capital of the new State of Jalisco.

The Hospicio Cabañas is one of the most important monuments in the city. In 1786, in conjunction with a famine so serious that the year is known as the 'year of hunger', a hospice was improvised in the Casa del Beaterio Viejo to help the victims of hunger. After this experience, a charitable organization decided in 1790 to create a hospice for the poor. Four years later, the Catalonian merchant José Llores y Comelles died; in 1767 he had written a will ordering that upon his death a hospital and a home for abandoned children should be built, to be administered by the diocese. With the funds donated by the Catalonian philanthropist and the royal sponsorship of Charles IV, between 1796 and 1797, orders were given for the construction of a new home for the protection of abandoned minors. All the same, work did not begin until 1801, with the supervision of Bishop Don Juan Cruz Ruiz de Cabañas y Crespo, who was actively engaged with continual requests for a home with workshops where the young children could learn a trade, an indispensable experience if they were to have a worthy future. The grading of the land and the construction of the water pipes and sewage drains were done by Pedro and José Ciprés, artisans from Mezquitán. Finally, in 1805, with a plan by the Valencian archi-

tect Manuel Tolsá, director of the sculptural department at the Academy of Fine Arts of San Carlos, the cornerstone was laid for the new building under the supervision of José Gutiérrez, director of the department of architecture at the same institution.

In 1810, the Casa de la Misericordia (House of Mercy), or Hospicio Cabañas, housed the first children, despite the absence of a roof over the main chapel. Sadly, that same year, the outbreak of the first events that led to the war of independence caused it to shut down until 1829, and the building was used as a headquarters and prison at the command of the first leader of the insurrections, Miguel Hidalgo y Costilla. In 1836, the project was assigned to the architect Manuel Gómez Ibarra who completed the chapel in 1845.

The architecture designed by Manuel Tolsá developed out of a symmetrical Greek-cross plan. The centre culminates in the large chapel covered with a dome set on a tambour, surrounded on the exterior by a colonnade. The austerity of the external facings is mitigated by the elegant rhythm of columns and arcades, which limit without enclosing the twenty-three courtyards, overlooked by 160 rooms. The façade presents a Tuscan-style portico with tympanum, inspired by European neo-classical architecture.

The Casa de la Misericordia offered shelter to orphans, beggars, the elderly, widows, and the penniless. Its schools and artisan workshops encouraged for almost two centuries the training and work of countless inhabitants of the State of Jalisco. The print shop and the bookstore were major sources for the diffusion of culture during the nineteenth century. Among the many historic events that took place within this structure, we should mention the disavowal of the office of the last superintendent of the Audiencia de Guadalajara, a functionary of the Spanish monarchy, and

Panoramic view of one of the sides of the Hospicio Cabañas, with a secondary entrance in the European neo-classical style.

On the facing page
The arcades of the entrance portico to the Main Chapel, over which looms the bulk of the tambour of the dome.

The main courtyard, opened by an arched portico, directly behind the Main Chapel.

The main façade of the Hospicio, with the entrance framed by Tuscan-style columns.

On the facing page
The fresco of the Man of Fire, which decorates the dome of the Main Chapel.

the ensuing triumph of independence in 1821, the disavowal of the President of Mexico, Antonio López de Santa Ana, in 1834, and the signature of the 'Plan of the Hospicio' by López de Santa Ana himself in a bid to regain power in 1852.

From 1937 to 1939, the central chapel was decorated with paintings by the Jalisco-born artist José Clemente Orozco (1883–1949). His work represents one of the most important creations by the exponent of the Mexican Muralism movement. He belonged to the group of post-revolutionary artists who supported new ideals of liberty, whose belief was that art should be accessible to persons from every walk of life. For this reason, he devoted himself to the creation of monumental artworks in public places. Thanks to his work, the Hospicio Cabañas was placed on the UNESCO World Heritage List on 4 December 1997.

In the spare and carefully defined space made up of vertical walls, barrel vaults, lunettes, and domes, Orozco painted a total of 1,250 square metres with his own personal vision of the history of Mexico, at the same time a reflection on the history and life of man and the world at large. There are depictions on the indigenous world and the ways in which it was repressed, the savagery and barbarianism of Cortés's conquest, the challenges of building a new state through a bloody revolution and, finally, on the walls of the central rings, the works of man, with his religion, arts, and industries. The striving of humanity is summarized in the great symbolic figure painted on the vault of the dome: a man burning in the fire of a yearning towards the transcendental. Despite the division created by the architecture, the work maintains its own consistency and unity in the forms and opaque colours with grey tones, enlivened in some sections of the scenes and in the central dome with the yellow, orange, and red colours of the flames.

Today the structure houses the Secretariat of Culture of the State of Jalisco, a museum of the monument, and the historical archives. It houses national and international art exhibitions and an art school, operating as a driving force in the cultural life of the Mexican state. The Cabañas Institute continues its humanitarian activity by educating invalid children in a separate, newly constructed building.

The Statue of Liberty in New York

The Statue of Liberty, the best known symbol of the United States of America, was a gift to the American people from France and the French republican *fronde*. An allegorical depiction of 'Liberty Lighting the World', it had in fact been executed in Paris in 1876, on the occasion of the first centennial of the American Declaration of Independence, by the sculptor Frédéric-Auguste Bartholdi. But the original idea for that monument had been conceived by Édouard de Laboulaye, who wanted 'his' Liberty to be marked by a confident pacifism, alien to the many bloody Liberties of the past. He wrote, perhaps alluding to the painting by Delacroix *Liberty Leading the People on the Barricades*, set in the 'glorious' Three Days of Paris in 1830: 'This Liberty would not be the one that wears a Phrygian bonnet and carries a pike, rather it would be the American Liberty, who does not brandish an incendiary torch, but rather holds up a torch that illuminates'.

The execution of the statue, in fact, was not merely the work of the conceptualist and the sculptor. Its 46 metres of height posed substantial structural problems, which Bartholdi solved by turning to the engineer Alexandre Gustave Eiffel, who would later build the tower in Paris that still bears his name. Together, the artist and the engineer designed an immense iron and steel framework that would serve as the load-bearing structure, and upon it the figure was modelled with the application of repoussé sheets of copper, 2.5 millimetres thick. This metallic skeleton presented a sufficient degree of elasticity to withstand the wind pressure to which the vast surface of the statue was exposed.

For this official artwork, intended to express 'high ideals', Bartholdi took a decidedly conservative approach, evident in the classical references in the drapery and the pose of the statue, and in its monumental nature, clearly derived from Michelangelo. The figure, in fact, is dressed in the ancient style, and holds up its right arm bearing the torch, while in its left hand it holds a tablet bearing the inscription 'July IV, MDCCLXXVI'; its head is covered with a seven-pointed crown, symbolizing the seven seas of the world; in the crown are twenty-five windows. According to tradition, however, the sculptor made use of real models: his future bride for the figure, and his mother for the austere features of the face.

The immense cost of the project was covered by the French through a public subscription, while the Americans launched a public subscription of their own to gather the funds needed for the construction of the pedestal. The pedestal, completed in 1875, was designed by Richard Morris Hunt, who called for a block of reinforced concrete with a series of sober socles, shaped to look like rusticated ashlars, surmounted by a neo-classical loggia made of cement and granite. The pedestal stood at the star-shaped enclosure of Fort Wood, built in 1812 at the entrance to New York harbour.

Before it was sent to America, the statue was on view for a certain period in Paris. Already, during the Exposition Universelle of Paris in 1878, visitors could enter a full-sized model of the head. Later, and for another limited period of time, Liberty rose over the rooftops of Paris, and for 50 centimes it was possible to climb up to the crown and to the torch. Even though the Parisians, Victor Hugo among them, did not want to relinquish their statue, in 1885 it was disassembled into 350 pieces, packed into 214 shipping crates, and shipped off to America in the French frigate *Isère*.

Once it reached its destination, it was mounted on its pedestal in the course of just

The Statue of Liberty, standing at the entrance to New York harbour, in the middle of the star-shaped enclosure of Fort Wood.

On the facing page
The Statue of Liberty stands on a high pedestal made of reinforced concrete and granite, built in 1875 to plans by Richard Morris Hunt.

four months and inaugurated in a solemn ceremony on 28 October 1886. Placed at the entrance to New York harbour, at the southern tip of Manhattan, its torch raised in its upstretched arm, it began to serve its function as a lighthouse. Visitors can climb 354 steps to look out of the windows in the statue's crown. On the second floor of the pedestal is a museum devoted to the history of the monument and its popularity, documented by its exploitation in advertising. In fact, the Statue of Liberty has been immortalised by photographers, draftsmen, and artists: in particular, Andy Warhol executed a number of renowned multiples. The movies have been attracted by the image as well: the Statue of Liberty had memorable cameos in such films as Hitchcock's *Saboteur* (1942), and *Planet of the Apes* by Schaffner (1967).

In 1986, on the occasion of the centennial of its arrival in New York, the Statue of Liberty was lovingly restored by a French-Canadian group, which renovated the copper garb, replacing the old torch with a new one whose flame is laminated with gold, and reinforced the right arm and the head, which were not aligned on their axis because of an initial error in assembly.

On the facing page
Paul Joseph Victor Dargaud, The Statue of Liberty, Executed by Frédéric-Auguste Bartholdi in the Studio of the Founder Gayet Near the Boulevard de Courcelles in 1883. *Paris, Musée Carnavalet.*

The austere face of the allegorical figure of Liberty is surmounted by a seven-pointed crown, symbolizing the seven seas of the world.

The Pueblo of Taos

The State of New Mexico is located in the south-west of the vast territory that comprises the United States of America. The region consists of a number of chains of the geological complex known as the Rocky Mountains, separated by river valleys with rushing mountain streams. The most important river is the Rio Grande, and along one of its tributaries grew up the village of Taos.

The settlement dates back roughly to 1130–80; the earliest constructions of the Hlauuma (House of the North) and the Hlaukwima (House of the South), religious in nature, date back to this period, when a calamity of unknown origins – possibly climate-related, since the farming was done on lands that are now entirely non-productive – forced the populations of prehistoric origins, such as the Anasazi Indians, to abandon the fertile zones of Mesa Verde and Chaco. The history of the settlement of the region, reconstructed through archaeological researches, involved the disappearance of the great Indian communities with the subsequent proliferation of little villages in the valleys of the Rio Grande and its tributaries. These were modest rural settlements, organized according to common social and religious structures, with extremely sophisticated agricultural practices, such as the irrigation system for the cultivation of maize.

The occupation of the territory through this type of settlement was so particular that the first Spanish expedition – led between 1540 and 1542 by Francisco Vázquez de Coronado, in that period the Governor of Nueva Galicia, the present-day State of Jalisco in Mexico – called the inhabitants of the region simply *pueblos*, which means, in Spanish, roughly 'villages'. In reality, the name groups together various tribes, each with a language of its own (Tewa, Tiwa, Towa, Keresan, Zunian), settling in distinct regions around the Rio Grande: the Hopi, the Keres, the Tano, and the Zuñi.

The social organization of the community tended to be matriarchal and matrilineal, since the woman owned the lands and the home. The decision-making roles within the clan, on the other hand, were often assigned to the priests. The religion venerated the Sun as the supreme being, accompanied by the principal deities of the Earth and the Moon. In the *kivas*, ceremonial centres with a circular plan, meetings were held to decide on the actions of the tribe, as were purely religious ceremonies. Almost all the *kivas* – there are six in the Pueblo of Taos – feature certain elements: a stone erected between the fire pit and the external exhaust, used as a flue, and a hole in the ground to allow the Earth gods to take part in the rite.

The village is built entirely in clay bricks made of earth, water, and straw, moulded and sun-dried. The flat roofs are made of wooden beams, or *vigas*, covered with tiles that are also made of wood. On the exterior, the houses were plastered with a mud that had a distinctive reddish-brown colour, while the interior was coated with a white hue, made with natural earths. The constructions stand beside one another on different levels. In the past, there were no streets dividing the houses: the entrance was through the roof.

The Spanish conquest was resisted by the Indians. The introduction of new breeds of livestock and new grains, purely for the consumption of the colonists, did little to modify their traditions. Beginning in 1613 the inhabitants of Taos refused to pay the cash tributes, or *encomiendas*, demanded by the Spanish Crown in favour of its subjects. Every village was given the name of a Christian saint, and yet Christianity was not happily tolerated, and even now most of the holidays are based on the native religion. In 1634 the missionary Alonso de Benavides complained to the Pope about the behaviour of the Indians, who were indifferent to his attempts to convert them. In 1680,

Panoramic view of the village of Taos, founded by Pueblo Indians along the Rio Grande Valley.

On the facing page
Detail of the houses made with clay bricks and arranged in stacked levels.

THE AMERICAN INDIANS

Upon the arrival of the Europeans, the native Americans were called by one of two names: 'Indians', because of Christopher Columbus's mistaken belief that he had reached the East Indies, and 'redskins', because of their custom of painting their face during religious ceremonies.

In North America, the Indian tribes spread out over immense natural stretches, differing greatly in climate and resources. The result was a great variety of ways of life and cultural elements which gave rise to over 200 different languages. The hunter tribes of the plains and the prairies between the Mississippi and the Rocky Mountains, such as the Comanche, the Arapaho, the Cheyenne, the Blackfeet, and the Sioux were, for the most part, nomadic. These tribes preserved their traditions and their lifestyles for many years, even after the arrival of the Europeans on the continent.

The first contacts with the colonists actually proved beneficial to them: the Spaniards had brought horses with them, and they spread and multiplied in America, where horses had been unknown. The new animal was bred and raised by a number of tribes and became a way of improving their hunting methods and facilitating their mobility.

In the eastern regions, from the Great Lakes to the Atlantic coast, lived the Huron and the Algonquin, who hunted and undertook a limited degree of farming. The real farmers were the Creek, the Cherokee, and the Seminole, who lived between the Appalachians and the Florida Peninsula.

In the south-west, from Arizona to New Mexico, the Apache, Hopi, Navajo, and Yuma had settled. Influenced by cultural contacts with the civilizations of the Mexican highlands, their way of life, based on farming (maize and legumes), was tied to settlement in stable villages which consisted of clay and mud houses, the *pueblos*. Despite the differences, there were certain cultural elements that were common to the various groups.

The leadership of the tribe was entrusted to councils of heads of families or clans, alongside the shaman who, as the religious authority, preserved the oral traditions and the cult of the 'Great Spirit'. The exploitation of natural resources aimed at obtaining the bare necessities for survival. Bison were hunted with a view to reducing their numbers as little as possible. In farming communities, there was no private ownership of land, which was considered a collective resource and the very foundation of life.

The numerous attempts to coexist peacefully with the Europeans were undermined by breaches of promise and expanding colonization which, especially in the central plains, deprived the Indians of their lands; the most numerous tribes therefore attempted to organize an armed defence. One of the last episodes in this struggle was the Battle of the Little Big Horn (1876), in Montana, in which Colonel George Custer and hundreds of soldiers died, encircled by Sioux and Cheyenne.

The problem of Indian settlements was addressed in 1871 with a Federal law that did not recognize the Indian tribes as 'independent nations', and allowed them to live on special reservations located, for the most part, on the interior, in isolated western sections. In these territories half of the descendants of the original Indians now live, roughly 1.5 million individuals. Some reservation communities, such as the Hopi and Navajo tribes in Arizona and New Mexico, have preserved a minimum of community life and traditions. A few groups have been able to exploit the natural resources found on their territory, such as the timber and mineral products, and have been able to build businesses. Overall, however, Indians have much lower incomes than average, are largely unemployed, have average life expectancies of forty years, in contrast with the seventy-four years of the whites, and their condition is substantially still that of alienated outsiders. On some reservations, the infant mortality rate is close to 100 per thousand, as against the 5 per thousand of the white population.

On the facing page
Detail of the method of construction of the residences, with clay bricks and wooden cores.

Detail of one of the little windows bordered with light blue that enliven the yellow clay walls.

Colours and shapes enliven these deceptively simple structures.

the first Christian church was burned down; it had been built in 1619 and was dedicated to Saint Jerome. The struggle continued in the years that followed, despite changes in the 'enemy' administration. Indeed, in 1821 New Spain became independent, taking the name of Mexico, after bloody revolts led first by the Indios and later by the Creole aristocracy. The weakness of Mexican administration led to the secession of Texas, and the war that followed, from 1846 to 1848, led to the annexation of New Mexico by the United States (Treaty of Hidalgo Guadalupe).

The inhabitants of Taos obtained the recovery of their lands in 1970; in particular, they were able to return once again to the sacred territory of the Blue Lake. In 1906, in fact, 48,000 acres of land had been entrusted to the United States Forest Service and declared off-limits to the Indians who wished to practise the ancient rites of their religion there; today, instead, the area is off-limits to tourists.

The Taos Pueblo was placed on the UNESCO World Heritage List in 1992.

The simple entrance
to one of the churches
that constitute the centres
of village life.

The yellow houses
of Taos stand out against
the bright blue sky
of New Mexico.

On the facing page
Quaint view of the kiln
where the lively ceramic
native vases are fired.

UNESCO

Unesco

World Heritage Sites

Africa

EGYPT

Saint Catherine Area

The Orthodox Monastery of Saint Catherine stands at the foot of the Mount Horeb of the Old Testament, where Moses received the Tablets of the Law. The mountain is known and revered by Muslims as Jebel Musa. The entire area is sacred to three world religions: Christianity, Islam, and Judaism. The monastery, founded in the sixth century, is the oldest Christian monastery still in use for its initial function. Its walls and buildings are very significant in the study of Byzantine architecture and the monastery houses outstanding collections of early Christian manuscripts and icons. The rugged mountainous landscape, containing numerous archaeological and religious sites and monuments, forms a perfect backdrop for the monastery. UNESCO added the site to the World Heritage List in 2002.

SOUTH AFRICA

Robben Island

Robben Island was used at various times between the seventeeth and twentieth centuries as a prison, a hospital for socially unacceptable groups and a military base. Its buildings, particularly those of the late twentieth century such as the maximum security prison for political prisoners, witness the triumph of democracy and freedom over oppression and racism. UNESCO added the site to the World Heritage List in 1999.

TUNISIA

Amphitheatre of El Djem

The impressive ruins of the largest coliseum in North Africa, a huge amphitheatre which could hold up to 35,000 spectators, can be found in the small village of El Jem. This third-century construction illustrates the extent and grandeur of Imperial Rome. UNESCO added the site to the World Heritage List in 1979.

America

ARGENTINA

Jesuit Block and Estancias of Córdoba

The Jesuit Block in Córdoba, heart of the former Jesuit Province of Paraguay, contains the core buildings of the Jesuit system: the university, the church and residence of the Society of Jesus, and the college. Along with the five *estancias*, or farming estates, they contain religious and secular buildings which illustrate the unique religious, social and economic experiment carried out in the world for a period of over 150 years in the seventeenth and eighteenth centuries. UNESCO added the site to the World Heritage List in 2000.

CUBA

San Pedro de la Roca Castle, Santiago de Cuba

Commercial and political rivalries in the Caribbean region in the seventeenth century resulted in the construction of this massive series of fortifications on a rocky promontory, in order to protect the important port of Santiago. This intricate complex of forts, magazines, bastions and batteries is the most complete and best preserved example of Spanish-American military architecture, based on Italian and Renaissance design principles. UNESCO added the site to the World Heritage List in 1997.

MEXICO

Earliest Sixteenth-Century Monasteries on the slopes of Popocatepetl

These fourteen monasteries stand on the slopes of Popocatepetl, to the south-east of Mexico City. They are in an excellent state of conservation and are good examples of the architectural style adopted by the first missionaries – Franciscans, Dominicans and Augustinians – who converted the indigenous populations to Christianity in the early sixteenth century. UNESCO added the site to the World Heritage List in 1994.

SAINT CHRISTOPHER AND NEVIS

Brimstone Hill Fortress National Park

Brimstone Hill Fortress National Park is an outstanding, well-preserved example of seventeenth- and eigteenth-century military architecture in a Caribbean context. Designed by the British and built by African slave labour, the fortress is testimony to European colonial expansion, the African slave trade and the emergence of new societies in the Caribbean. UNESCO added the site to the World Heritage List in 1999.

UNITED STATES OF AMERICA

Mesa Verde

A great concentration of ancestral Pueblo Indian dwellings, built from the sixth to the twelfth century, can be found on the Mesa Verde plateau in south-west Colorado at an altitude of more than 2,600 metres. Some 4,400 sites have been recorded, including villages built on the Mesa top. There are also imposing cliff dwellings, built of stone and comprising more than 100 rooms. UNESCO added the site to the World Heritage List in 1978.

Independence Hall

The Declaration of Independence and the Constitution were signed in this hall in the heart of Philadelphia, in 1776 and 1787 respectively. Since then, the universal principles set forth in these two documents of fundamental importance to American history have continued to guide lawmakers all over the world. UNESCO added the site to the World Heritage List in 1979.

Asia

AFGHANISTAN

Minaret and Archaeological Remains of Jam

The 65 metre-tall Minaret of Jam is a graceful, soaring structure, dating back to the twelfth century. Covered in elaborate brickwork with a blue tile inscription at the top, it is noteworthy for the quality of its architecture and decoration, which represent the culmination of an architectural and artistic tradition in this region. Its impact is heightened by its dramatic setting, a deep river valley between towering mountains in the heart of the Ghur Province. UNESCO added the site to the World Heritage List in 2002.

ARMENIA

Monastery of Geghard and the Upper Azat Valley

The Monastery of Geghard contains a number of churches and tombs, most of them cut into the rock, which illustrate the very peak of Armenian Middle Ages architecture. The complex of medieval buildings is set in a landscape of great natural beauty, surrounded by towering cliffs at the entrance to the Azat Valley. UNESCO added the site to the World Heritage List in 2000.

BANGLADESH

Ruins of the Buddhist Vihara at Paharpur

Evidence of the rise of Mahayana Buddhism in Bengal from the seventh century onwards, Somapura Mahavira, or the Great Monastery, was a renowned intellectual centre until the twelfth century. Its layout perfectly adapted to its religious function, this monastery-city represents a unique artistic achievement. With its simple, harmonious lines and its profusion of carved decoration, it influenced Buddhist architecture as far away as Cambodia. UNESCO added the site to the World Heritage List in 1985.

CHINA

Summer Palace: an Imperial Garden in Beijing

The Summer Palace in Beijing – first built in 1750, largely destroyed in the war of 1860 and restored on its original foundations in 1886 – is a masterpiece of Chinese landscape garden design. The natural landscape of hills and open water is combined with artificial features such as pavilions, halls, palaces, temples and bridges to form a harmonious ensemble of outstanding aesthetic value. UNESCO added the site to the World Heritage List in 1998.

Temple of Heaven: an Imperial Sacrificial Altar in Beijing

The Temple of Heaven, founded in the first half of the fifteenth century, is a dignified complex of fine cult buildings set in gardens and surrounded by historic pine woods. In its overall layout and that of its individual buildings, it symbolizes the relationship between earth and heaven – the human world and God's world – which stands at the heart of Chinese cosmogony, and also the special role played by the emperors within that relationship. UNESCO added the site to the World Heritage List in 1998.

CYPRUS

Painted Churches in the Troodos Region

This region is characterized by one of the largest groups of churches and monasteries of the former Byzantine Empire. The complex of ten monuments included on the World Heritage List, all richly decorated with murals, provides an overview of Byzantine and post-Byzantine painting in Cyprus. They range from small churches whose rural architectural style is in stark contrast to their highly refined decoration, to monasteries such as that of Saint John Lampadistis. UNESCO added the site to the World Heritage List in 1985–2001.

GEORGIA

Bagrati Cathedral and Gelati

The construction of Bagrati Cathedral, named after Bagrat III, the first King of united Georgia, started at the end of the tenth century and was completed in the early years of the eleventh century. Although partly destroyed by the Turks in 1691, its ruins still lie in the centre of Kutaisi. The Gelati Monastery, whose main buildings were erected between the twelfth and seventeenth centuries, is a well-preserved complex, with wonderful mosaics and wall paintings. The cathedral and monastery represent the flowering of medieval architecture in Georgia. UNESCO added the site to the World Heritage List in 1994.

INDIA

Brihadisvara Temple, Thanjavur

The great Temple of Tanjore (Thanjavur) was built between 1003 and 1010 in the reign of the great King Rajaraja, founder of the Chola Empire which stretched over all of South India and the neighbouring islands. Surrounded by two rectangular enclosures, the Brihadisvara Temple (built from blocks of granite and, in part, from bricks) is crowned with a pyramidal thirteen-storey tower, the *vimana*, standing 61 metres high and topped with a bulb-shaped monolith. The walls of the temple are covered with rich sculptural decoration. UNESCO added the site to the World Heritage List in 1987.

Humayun's Tomb

This tomb, built in 1570, is of particular cultural significance as it was the first garden-tomb on the Indian subcontinent. It inspired several major architectural innovations, culminating in the construction of the Taj Mahal. UNESCO added the site to the World Heritage List in 1993.

Mahabodhi Temple Complex at Bodh Gaya

The Mahabodhi Temple Complex is one of the four holy sites related to the life of the Lord Buddha, and particularly to the attainment of enlightenment. The first temple was built by Emperor Asoka in the third century B.C., and the present temple dates from the fifth or sixth centuries. It is one of the earliest Buddhist temples built entirely in brick still standing in India from the late Gupta period. UNESCO added the site to the World Heritage List in 2002.

INDONESIA

Prambanan Temple Compounds

Built in the tenth century, this is the largest temple compound dedicated to Shiva in Indonesia. Rising above the centre of the last of these concentric squares are three temples decorated with reliefs illustrating the epic of the *Ramayana*, dedicated to the three great Hindu divinities (Shiva, Vishnu and Brahma), and three temples dedicated to the animals who serve them. UNESCO added the site to the World Heritage List in 1991.

JAPAN

Hiroshima Peace Memorial (Genbaku Dome)

The Hiroshima Peace Memorial, Genbaku Dome, is a stark and powerful symbol of the achievement of world peace for more than half a century following the unleashing of the most destructive force ever created by humankind. UNESCO added the site to the World Heritage List in 1996.

Itsukushima Shinto Shrine

The island of Itsukushima, in the Seto inland sea, has been a holy place of Shintoism since the earliest times. The first shrine buildings here were probably erected in the sixth century. The present shrine dates from the thirteenth century and its harmoniously arranged buildings reveal great artistic and technical skill. The shrine plays on the contrasts in colour and form between mountains and sea and illustrates the Japanese concept of scenic beauty, which combines nature and human creativity. UNESCO added the site to the World Heritage List in 1996.

PAKISTAN

Fort and Shalamar Gardens in Lahore

These are two masterpieces from the time of the brilliant Moghul civilization, which reached its height during the reign of the Emperor Shah Jahan. The fort contains marble palaces and mosques decorated with mosaics and gilt. Near the city of Lahore, the elegance of the splendid gardens, built on three terraces with lodges, waterfalls and large ornamental ponds, is unequalled. UNESCO added the site to the World Heritage List in 1981.

Rohtas Fort

Following his defeat of the Moghul Emperor Humayun in 1541, Sher Shah Suri built a strong fortified complex at Rohtas, a strategic site in the north of what is now Pakistan. It was never taken by storm and has survived intact to the present day. The main fortifications consist of the massive walls, which extend for more than 4 kilometres; they are lined with bastions and pierced by monumental gateways. Rohtas Fort, or Qila Rohtas, is an exceptional example of early Muslim military architecture in Central and South Asia. UNESCO added the site to the World Heritage List in 1997.

REPUBLIC OF KOREA

Jongmyo Shrine

Jongmyo is the oldest and most authentic of the Confucian royal shrines to have been preserved. Dedicated to the forefathers of the Choson Dynasty (1392–1910), the shrine has existed in its present form since the sixteenth century and houses tablets bearing the teachings of members of the former royal family. Ritual ceremonies linking music, song and dance still take place there, perpetuating a tradition that goes back to the fourteenth century. UNESCO added the site to the World Heritage List in 1995.

Hwaseong Fortress

When the Choson Emperor Chongjo moved his father's tomb to Suwon at the end of the eighteenth century, he surrounded it with strong defensive works, laid out according to the precepts of an influential military architect of the period, who brought together the latest developments in the field from both East and West. The massive walls, extending for nearly 6 kilometres, still survive; they are pierced by four gates and equipped with bastions, artillery towers and other features. UNESCO added the site to the World Heritage List in 1997.

TURKEY

Great Mosque and Hospital of Divrigi

In this region of Anatolia, conquered by the Turks at the beginning of the eleventh century, Emir Ahmet Shah founded a mosque in 1228–29 containing a single prayer room and crowned by two cupolas, with a hospital adjoining it. A highly elaborate technique of vault construction, and a creative, imaginative type of decorative sculpture – particularly on the three doors, in contrast to the unadorned walls of the interior – are the unique features of this masterpiece of Islamic architecture. UNESCO added the site to the World Heritage List in 1985.

Europe

BELARUS

Mir Castle Complex

The construction of this castle began at the end of the fifteenth century, in Gothic style. It was subsequently extended and reconstructed, first in the Renaissance and then in the Baroque style. After being abandoned for nearly a century and suffering severe damage during the Napoleonic period, the castle was restored at the end of the nineteenth century, with the addition of a number of other elements and the landscaping of the surrounding area as a park. Its present form is testimony to its often turbulent history. UNESCO added the site to the World Heritage List in 2000.

BELGIUM

Grand-Place, Brussels

La Grand-Place in Brussels is a remarkably homogeneous body of public and private buildings, dating mainly from the late seventeenth century. The architecture provides a vivid illustration of the level of social and cultural life of the period in this important political and commercial centre. UNESCO added the site to the World Heritage List in 1998.

Notre-Dame Cathedral in Tournai

The Cathedral of Notre-Dame in Tournai was built in the first half of the twelfth century. It is especially distinguished by a Romanesque nave of extraordinary dimensions, a wealth of sculpture on its capitals and a transept topped by five towers, all precursors of the Gothic style. The choir, rebuilt in the thirteenth century, is in the pure Gothic style. UNESCO added the site to the World Heritage List in 2000.

BULGARIA

Boyana Church

Located on the outskirts of Sofia, Boyana Church consists of three buildings. The eastern church was built in the tenth century, then enlarged at the beginning of the thirteenth century by Sebastocrator Kaloyan, who ordered a second two-storey building to be erected next to it. The frescoes in this second church, painted in 1259, make it one of the most important collections of medieval paintings. The ensemble is completed by a third church, built at the beginning of the nineteenth century. This site is one of the most complete and perfectly preserved monuments of eastern European medieval art. UNESCO added the site to the World Heritage List in 1979.

Madara Rider

The Madara Rider, representing the figure of a knight triumphing over a lion, is carved into a 100 metre-high cliff near the village of Madara in north-east Bulgaria. Madara was the principal sacred place of the First Bulgarian Empire before Bulgaria's conversion to Christianity in the ninth century. The inscriptions beside the sculpture tell of events that occurred between A.D. 705 and 801. UNESCO added the site to the World Heritage List in 1979.

Rock-hewn Churches of Ivanovo

In the valley of the Roussenski Lom River, in north-east Bulgaria, a complex of rock-hewn churches, chapels, monasteries and cells developed in the vicinity of the village of Ivanovo. This is where the first hermits had dug out their cells and churches during the twelfth century. The fourteenth-century murals testify to the exceptional skill of the artists belonging to the Tarnovo School of painting. UNESCO added the site to the World Heritage List in 1979.

Thracian Tomb of Kazanlak

Discovered in 1944, this tomb dates from the Hellenistic period, around the end of the fourth century B.C. It is located near Seutopolis, the capital city of the Thracian King Seutes III, and is part of a large Thracian necropolis. The *tholos* has a narrow corridor and a round burial chamber, both decorated with murals representing Thracian burial rituals and culture. These paintings are Bulgaria's best-preserved artistic masterpieces from the Hellenistic period. UNESCO added the site to the World Heritage List in 1979.

Thracian Tomb of Sveshtari

Discovered in 1982 near the village of Sveshtari, this third-century B.C. Thracian tomb reflects the fundamental structural principles of Thracian cult buildings. The tomb has a unique architectural decor, with polychrome half-human, half-plant caryatids and painted murals. The ten female figures carved in high relief on the walls of the central chamber and the decoration of the lunette in its vault are the only examples of this type found so far in the Thracian lands. It is a remarkable reminder of the culture of the Getes, a Thracian people who were in contact with the Hellenistic and Hyperborean worlds, according to ancient geographers. UNESCO added the site to the World Heritage List in 1985.

CROATIA

The Episcopal Complex of the Euphrasian Basilica in the Historic Centre of Porec

The group of religious monuments in Porec, where Christianity was established as early as the fourth century, constitutes the most complete surviving complex of its type. The basilica, atrium, baptistery and episcopal palace are outstanding examples of religious architecture, while the basilica itself combines classical and Byzantine elements in an exceptional manner. UNESCO added the site to the World Heritage List in 1997.

Cathedral of Saint James in Šibenik

The Cathedral of Saint James in Šibenik (1431–1535), on the Dalmatian coast, bears witness to the considerable exchanges in the field of monumental arts between Northern Italy, Dalmatia and Tuscany in the fifteenth and sixteenth centuries. The three architects who succeeded one an-

other in the construction of the cathedral – Francesco di Giacomo, Georgius Mathei Dalmaticus and Niccolò di Giovanni Fiorentino – developed a structure built entirely from stone and using unique construction techniques for the vaulting and the dome of the cathedral. The form and the decorative elements of the cathedral, such as a remarkable frieze decorated with seventy-one sculptured faces of men, women, and children, also illustrate the successful fusion of Gothic and Renaissance art. UNESCO added the site to the World Heritage List in 2000.

CZECH REPUBLIC

Pilgrimage Church of Saint John of Nepomuk at Zelena Hora

This pilgrimage church, built in honour of Saint John of Nepomuk, stands at Zelena Hora, not far from Zdar nad Sazavou in Moravia. Constructed at the beginning of the eighteenth century on a star-shaped plan, it is the most unusual work by the great architect Jan Blazej Santini, whose highly original style falls between neo–Gothic and Baroque. UNESCO added the site to the World Heritage List in 1994.

The Lednice-Valtice Cultural Landscape

Between the seventeenth and twentieth centuries, the ruling dukes of Liechtenstein transformed their domains in southern Moravia into a striking landscape. It married Baroque architecture (mainly the work of Johann Bernhard Fischer von Erlach) and the classical and neo-Gothic style of the Castles of Lednice and Valtice with countryside fashioned according to English romantic principles of landscape architecture. With its 200 square kilometres, it is one of the largest artificial landscapes in Europe. UNESCO added the site to the World Heritage List in 1996.

Litomysl Castle

Litomysl Castle was originally a Renaissance arcade-castle of the type first developed in Italy and

then adopted and greatly developed in central Europe in the sixteenth century. Its design and decoration are particularly fine, including the later High- Baroque features added in the eighteenth century. It preserves intact the range of ancillary buildings associated with an aristocratic residence of this type. UNESCO added the site to the World Heritage List in 1999.

Holy Trinity Column in Olomouc

This memorial column, erected in the early years of the eighteenth century, is the most outstanding example of a type of monument specific to central Europe. In the characteristic regional style known as Olomouc Baroque and rising to a height of 35 metres, it is decorated with many fine religious sculptures, the work of the distinguished Moravian artist Ondrej Zahner. UNESCO added the site to the World Heritage List in 2000.

Tugendhat Villa in Brno

The Tugendhat Villa in Brno, designed by the architect Mies van der Rohe, is an outstanding example of the international style in the modern movement in architecture as it developed in Europe in the 1920s. Its particular value lies in the application of innovative spatial and aesthetic concepts that aim to satisfy new lifestyle needs by taking advantage of the opportunities afforded by modern industrial production. UNESCO added the site to the World Heritage List in 2001.

DENMARK

Roskilde Cathedral

Built in the course of the twelfth and thirteenth centuries, this was Scandinavia's first Gothic cathedral to be built of brick and it encouraged the spread of this style throughout northern Europe. It has been the mausoleum of the Danish royal family since the fifteenth century. Porches and side chapels were added up to the end of the nineteenth century. Thus the cathedral provides a clear overview of the development of European religious architecture. UNESCO added the site to the World Heritage List in 1995.

FINLAND

Fortress of Suomenlinna
Built in the second half of the eighteenth century by Sweden on a group of islands located at the entrance of Helsinki's harbour, this fortress is an especially interesting example of European military architecture of the time. UNESCO added the site to the World Heritage List in 1991.

Petäjävesi Old Church
Petäjävesi Old Church, in central Finland, was built of logs between 1763 and 1765. This Lutheran country church is a typical example of an architectural tradition that is unique to eastern Scandinavia. It combines the Renaissance conception of a centrally planned church with older forms deriving from Gothic groin vaults. UNESCO added the site to the World Heritage List in 1994.

Verla Groundwood and Board Mill
The Verla groundwood and board mill and its associated residential area is an outstanding, remarkably well-preserved example of the small-scale rural industrial settlements associated with pulp, paper and board production that flourished in northern Europe and North America in the nineteenth and early twentieth centuries. Only a handful of such settlements survives to the present day. UNESCO added the site to the World Heritage List in 1996.

FRANCE

Mont-Saint-Michel and its Bay
Perched on a rocky islet in the midst of vast sandbanks exposed to powerful tides between Normandy and Brittany, stands the 'Wonder of the West', a Gothic–style Benedictine abbey dedicated to the archangel Saint Michael, and the village that grew up in the shadow of its great walls. Built between the eleventh and sixteenth centuries, the abbey is a technical and artistic *tour de force*, having had to adapt to the problems posed by this unique natural site. UNESCO added the site to the World Heritage List in 1979.

Amiens Cathedral
Amiens Cathedral, in the heart of Picardy, is one of the largest 'classic' Gothic churches of the thirteenth century. The coherence of its plan, the beauty of its three-tier interior elevation and the arrangement of an extremely scholarly sculptural programme on its principal façade and on the wing of the southern transept are striking. UNESCO added the site to the World Heritage List in 1981.

Cistercian Abbey of Fontenay
This stark Burgundian monastery was founded by Saint Bernard in 1119. With its church, cloister, refectory, sleeping quarters, bakery and ironworks, it is an excellent illustration of the ideal of self-sufficiency as practised by the earliest communities of Cistercian monks. UNESCO added the site to the World Heritage List in 1981.

Church of Saint-Savin-sur Gartempe
Known as the 'Romanesque Sistine Chapel', the Abbey Church of Saint-Savin contains many beautiful eleventh- and twelfth-century murals which are still in a remarkable state of preservation. UNESCO added the site to the World Heritage List in 1983.

Pont du Gard, Roman Aqueduct
The Pont du Gard was built shortly before the Christian era to allow the aqueduct of Nîmes (which is almost 50 kilometres long) to cross the Gard River. The Roman architects and hydraulic engineers who designed this bridge, which stands almost 50 metres high and is on three levels – the longest measuring 275 metres – created a technical as well as an artistic masterpiece. UNESCO added the site to the World Heritage List in 1985.

Bourges Cathedral
The Cathedral of Saint Etienne of Bourges, built between the late twelfth and late thirteenth centuries, is one of the great masterpieces of Gothic art and is admired for its proportions and the unity of its design. The tympanum, sculptures and stained glass windows are particularly striking. Apart from the beauty of the architecture, it attests to the power of Christianity in medieval France. UNESCO added the site to the World Heritage List in 1992.

GERMANY

Speyer Cathedral
Speyer Cathedral, a basilica with four towers and two domes, was founded by Conrad II in 1030 and remodelled at the end of the eleventh century. It is one of the most important Romanesque monuments from the time of the Holy Roman Empire. The cathedral was the burial place of the German emperors for almost 300 years. UNESCO added the site to the World Heritage List in 1981.

Castles of Augustusburg and Falkenlust at Brühl
Set in an idyllic garden landscape, Augustusburg Castle (the sumptuous residence of the prince-archbishops of Cologne) and the Falkenlust hunting lodge (a small rural folly) are among the earliest examples of Rococo architecture in eighteenth-century Germany. UNESCO added the site to the World Heritage List in 1984.

Abbey and Altenmünster of Lorsch
The abbey, together with its monumental entrance, the famous 'Torhalle', are a rare architectural vestige of the Carolingian era. The sculptures and paintings from this period have remained in remarkably good condition. UNESCO added the site to the World Heritage List in 1991.

Maulbronn Monastery Complex
Founded in 1147, the Cistercian Maulbronn Monastery is considered the most complete and

best-preserved medieval monastic complex north of the Alps. Surrounded by fortified walls, the main buildings were constructed between the twelfth and sixteenth centuries. The monastery's church, mainly in Transitional Gothic style, had a major influence in the spread of Gothic architecture over much of northern and central Europe. The water-management system at Maulbronn, with its elaborate network of drains, irrigation canals and reservoirs, is of exceptional interest. UNESCO added the site to the World Heritage List in 1993.

Cologne Cathedral

Begun in 1248, the construction of this Gothic masterpiece took place in several stages and was not completed until 1880. Over seven centuries, successive builders were inspired by the same faith and a spirit of absolute fidelity to the original plans. Apart from its exceptional intrinsic value and the artistic masterpieces it contains, Cologne Cathedral testifies to the enduring strength of European Christianity. UNESCO added the site to the World Heritage List in 1996.

Wartburg Castle

Wartburg Castle blends superbly into its forest surroundings and is in many ways 'the ideal castle'. Although it has retained some original sections from the feudal period, the form it acquired during the nineteenth-century reconstitution gives a good idea of what this fortress might have been at the height of its military and seigneurial power. It was during his exile at Wartburg Castle that Martin Luther translated the New Testament into German. UNESCO added the site to the World Heritage List in 1999.

Monastic Island of Reichenau

The island of Reichenau on Lake Constance preserves the traces of the Benedictine monastery, founded in 724, which exercised remarkable spiritual, intellectual and artistic influence. The Churches of Saint Mary and Marcus, Saint Peter and Saint Paul, and Saint George, mainly built between the

ninth and eleventh centuries, provide a panorama of early medieval monastic architecture in central Europe. Their wall paintings bear witness to impressive artistic activity. UNESCO added the site to the World Heritage List in 2000.

GREECE

Temple of Apollo Epicurius at Bassae

This famous temple to the god of healing and the sun was built towards the middle of the fifth century B.C. in the lonely heights of the Arcadian mountains. The temple, which has the oldest Corinthian capital yet found, combines the Archaic style and the serenity of the Doric style with some daring architectural features. UNESCO added the site to the World Heritage List in 1986.

HUNGARY

Millenary Benedictine Abbey of Pannonhalma and its Natural Environment

The first Benedictine monks settled here in 996. They went on to convert the Hungarians, to found the country's first school and, in 1055, to write the first document in Hungarian. From the time of its founding, this monastic community has promoted culture throughout central Europe. Its 1,000-year history can be seen in the succession of architectural styles of the monastic buildings (the oldest dating from 1224), which still today house a school and the monastic community. UNESCO added the site to the World Heritage List in 1996.

IRELAND

Skellig Michael

This monastic complex, perched since about the seventh century on the steep sides of the rocky Island of Skellig Michael, some 12 kilometres off the coast of south-west Ireland, illustrates the very spartan existence of the first Irish Christians. Since the extreme remoteness of Skellig Michael has un-

til recently discouraged visitors, the site is exceptionally well preserved. UNESCO added the site to the World Heritage List in 1996.

ITALY

Crespi d'Adda

Crespi d'Adda in Capriate San Gervasio in Lombardy is an outstanding example of the nineteenth- and early twentieth–century 'company towns' built in Europe and North America by enlightened industrialists to meet the workers' needs. The site is still remarkably intact and is partly used for industrial purposes, although changing economic and social conditions now threaten its survival. UNESCO added the site to the World Heritage List in 1995.

Turin, Residences of the Royal House of Savoy

When Emmanuel-Philibert, Duke of Savoy, moved his capital to Turin in 1562, he began a vast series of building projects (continued by his successors) to demonstrate the power of the ruling house. This outstanding complex of buildings, designed and embellished by the leading architects and artists of the time, radiates out into the surrounding countryside from the Royal Palace in the 'Command Area' of Turin to include many country residences and hunting lodges. UNESCO added the site to the World Heritage List in 1997.

Botanical Garden, Padua

The world's first botanical garden was created in Padua in 1545. It still preserves its original layout: a circular central plot, symbolizing the world, surrounded by a ring of water. Other elements were added later, some architectural (ornamental entrances and balustrades) and some practical (pumping installations and greenhouses). It continues to serve its original purpose as a centre for scientific research. UNESCO added the site to the World Heritage List in 1997.

Piazza Armerina, Villa Romana del Casale

Roman exploitation of the countryside is symbolized by the villa, the centre of the large estate upon which the rural economy of the Western Empire was based. In its fourth century A.D. form, the Villa, Romana del Casale is one of the most luxurious examples of this type of monument. It is especially noteworthy for the wealth and quality of the mosaics which decorate almost every room, and which are the finest still *in situ* anywhere in the Roman world. UNESCO added the site to the World Heritage List in 1997.

Villa Adriana, Tivoli

Villa Adriana, an exceptional complex of classical buildings created in the second century A.D. by the Roman Emperor Hadrian, reproduces the best elements of the material cultures of Egypt, Greece, and Rome in the form of an 'ideal city'. UNESCO added the site to the World Heritage List in 1999.

MALTA

Hal Saflieni Hypogeum

The Hypogeum is an enormous subterranean structure excavated *c.* 2500 B.C., using cyclopean rigging to lift huge blocks of coralline limestone. Perhaps originally a sanctuary, it became a necropolis in prehistoric times. UNESCO added the site to the World Heritage List in 1980.

NETHERLANDS

D.F. Wouda Steam Pumping Station

The Wouda Pumping Station at Lemmer in the Province of Friesland opened in 1920. It is the largest steam-pumping station ever built and is still in operation. It represents the apogee of the contribution made by Dutch engineers and architects to the protection of people and their lands against the natural forces of water. UNESCO added the site to the World Heritage List in 1998.

Rietveld Schröder House

The Rietveld Schröder House in Utrecht was commissioned by Ms Truus Schröder-Schräder, designed by the architect Gerrit Thomas Rietveld, and built in 1924. This small one-family house, with its interior, the flexible spatial arrangement, and the visual and formal qualities, was a manifesto of the ideals of the De Stijl group of artists and architects in the Netherlands in the 1920s, and has since been considered one of the icons of the modern movement in architecture. UNESCO added the site to the World Heritage List in 2000.

NORWAY

Urnes Stave Church

Set in the natural landscape of Sogn og Fjordane, the Church of Urnes (the *stavkirke*), built during the twelfth and thirteenth centuries, is an exceptional vestige of Scandinavian wooden architecture. It brings together traces of Celtic art, Viking traditions and Romanesque spatial structures. UNESCO added the site to the World Heritage List in 1979.

POLAND

Auschwitz Concentration Camp

The fortified walls, the barbed wire, the platforms, the barracks, the gallows, the gas chambers and the cremation ovens all bear witness to the conditions within which the Hitlerian genocide took place in the former concentration and extermination camp of Auschwitz-Birkenau, the most extensive of the Third Reich. Millions of persons, among them a great number of Jews, were systematically starved, tortured and assassinated in this camp, symbol of the cruelty of man to his fellow men in the twentieth century. UNESCO added the site to the World Heritage List in 1979.

Castle of the Teutonic Order in Malbork

When the seat of the Grand Master of the Teutonic Order moved from Venice to what was then known as Marienburg, the earlier castle was greatly enlarged and embellished. It became the supreme example of the medieval brick castle. It fell into decay later, but in the nineteenth and early twentieth centuries was meticulously restored; it was here that many of the conservation techniques now accepted as standard were evolved. Following severe damage in World War II, it was once again restored, using the detailed documentation prepared by the earlier conservators. UNESCO added the site to the World Heritage List in 1997.

Churches of Peace in Jawor and Swidnica

The Churches of Peace in Jawor and Swidnica, the largest timber-framed religious buildings in Europe, were built in the former Silesia in the mid-seventeenth century, at a time of religious strife following the Peace of Westphalia. Constrained by the physical and political conditions, the Churches of Peace bear testimony to the quest for religious freedom and are a rare expression of Lutheran ideology in an idiom generally associated with the Catholic Church. UNESCO added the site to the World Heritage List in 2001.

PORTUGAL

Monastery of the Hieronymites and Tower of Belém, Lisbon

Standing at the entrance to Lisbon's harbour, the Monastery of the Hieronymites – on which construction began in 1502 – exemplifies Portuguese art at its best, while the nearby Tower of Belém, built to commemorate Vasco de Gama's expedition, is a reminder of the great maritime discoveries that laid the foundations of the modern world. UNESCO added the site to the World Heritage List in 1983.

Monastery of Batalha

Built to commemorate the victory of the Portuguese over the Castilians in the Battle of Aljubarrota in 1385, the Monastery of the Dominicans of Batalha remained for two more centuries the main workshop of the Portuguese monarchy in which an original, national Gothic style was formed, profoundly influenced by Manueline art, as the masterpiece, the Royal Cloister, demonstrates. UNESCO added the site to the World Heritage List in 1983.

Monastery of Alcobaça

The Monastery of Santa Maria d'Alcobaça, north of Lisbon, was founded in the twenth century by King Alfonso I. Its size, the clarity of its architectural style, the beauty of the materials used and the care with which it was built make it a masterpiece of Gothic Cistercian art. UNESCO added the site to the World Heritage List in 1989.

ROMANIA

Monastery of Horezu

Founded in 1690 by Prince Constantin Brancovan, the Monastery of Horezu, in Walachia, is a masterpiece of 'Brancovan' style, known for its architectural purity and balance, the richness of its sculpted detail, its treatment of religious compositions, its votive portraits and its painted decorative works. The school of mural and icon painting established at the monastery of Horezu in the eighteenth century was very well-known throughout the Balkan region. UNESCO added the site to the World Heritage List in 1993.

RUSSIAN FEDERATION

Khizi Pogost

The *pogost* of Kizhi–the Kizhi enclosure–is located on one of the many islands on Lake Onega, in Karelia. Two wooden eighteenth-century churches, and an octogonal clock tower, also in wood, made in 1862, can be seen there. These unusual constructions, in which the science of carpentry led to a bold visionary architecture, perpetuate an ancient model of parish space and are in total harmony with the surrounding landscape. UNESCO added the site to the World Heritage List in 1990.

Architectural Ensemble of The Trinity-Sergius Lavra in Sergiev Posad

This is a fine example of a working Orthodox monastery, with military features that are typical of the period during which it developed, from the fifteenth to the eighteenth centuries. The main church of the Lavra, the Cathedral of the Assumption (echoing the Kremlin Cathedral of the same name), contains the tomb of Boris Godunov. Among the treasures of the Lavra is the famous icon, *The Trinity*, by Andrei Rublev. UNESCO added the site to the World Heritage List in 1993.

Church of the Ascension, Kolomenskoye

The Church of the Ascension was built in 1532, in the Imperial estate of Kolomenskoye, near Moscow, to celebrate the birth of the prince who was to become Czar Ivan IV "the Terrible". One of the earliest examples of traditional wooden tent-roofed churches on a stone and brick substructure, it has had a great influence on the development of Russian ecclesiastical architecture. UNESCO added the site to the World Heritage List in 1994.

Ensemble of the Ferapontov Monastery

The Ferapontov Monastery is an exceptionally well-preserved and complete example of a Russian Orthodox monastic complex from the fifteenth to seventeenth centuries, a period of great significance in the development of the unified Russian state and its culture. The architecture of the monastery is outstanding in its inventiveness and purity and it is graced by the magnificent wall paintings of Dionisy, the greatest Russian artist from the end of the fifteenth century. UNESCO added the site to the World Heritage List in 2000.

Historic and Architectural Complex of the Kazan Kremlin

Built on an ancient site, the Kazan Kremlin originates from the Muslim period of the Kazan Khanate Golden Horde, and was then conquered by Ivan the Terrible in 1552 to become the Chris-

tian see of the Volga Land. The only surviving Tatar fortress in Russia and an important pilgrimage place, the Kazan Kremlin consists of an outstanding group of historic buildings dating from the sixteenth to the nineteenth centuries, integrating remains of earlier structures of the tenth to the sixteenth centuries. UNESCO added the site to the World Heritage List in 2000.

SPAIN

Burgos Cathedral

Begun in the thirteenth century, at the same time as the great cathedrals of the Île-de-France, and completed in the fifteenth and sixteenth centuries, Our Lady of Burgos sums up Gothic architecture in all its beauty with a unique collection of reredos, tombs, choir, stalls, stained glass, etc. UNESCO added the site to the World Heritage List in 1984.

Cathedral, Alcázar and Archivo de Indias in Seville

Together these three buildings form a remarkable monumental complex in the heart of Seville. The cathedral and the Alcázar – dating from the Reconquest of 1248 to the sixteenth century and imbued with Moorish influences – are an exceptional testimony to the civilization of the Almohads as well as that of Christian Andalusia. The Giralda minaret is the masterpiece of Almohad architecture. It stands next to the cathedral with its five naves; the largest Gothic building in Europe, it houses the tomb of Christopher Columbus. The ancient Lonja (exchange), which became the Archivo de Indias, contains valuable documents from the archives of the colonies in the Americas. UNESCO added the site to the World Heritage List in 1987.

Poblet Monastery

Located in Catalonia, this Cistercian abbey, one of the largest in Spain, surrounds its twelfth-century church. The majestic severity of the monastery, which is associated with a fortified royal residence and contains the pantheon of the kings of Catalonia and Aragon, is an impressive sight. UNESCO added the site to the World Heritage List in 1991.

Royal Monastery of Santa Maria de Guadalupe

The monastery, an exceptional illustration of four centuries of Spanish religious architecture, symbolizes two significant events in world history that occurred in 1492: the reconquest of the Iberian Peninsula by the Catholic kings and Christopher Columbus's arrival in the Americas. Its famous statue of the Virgin became a powerful symbol of the Christianization of much of the New World. UNESCO added the site to the World Heritage List in 1993.

The Palau de la Música Catalana and the Hospital de Sant Pau, Barcelona

These are two of the finest contributions to the architecture of Barcelona by the Catalan *Art Nouveau* architect Lluís Domènech i Montaner. The Palau de la Música Catalana is an exuberant steel-framed structure full of light and space, and decorated by many of the leading designers of the day. The Hospital de Sant Pau is equally bold in its design and decoration, while at the same time perfectly adapted for the needs of the sick. UNESCO added the site to the World Heritage List in 1997.

San Millán Yuso and Suso Monasteries

The monastic community founded by Saint Millán in the mid-sixth century became a place of pilgrimage. A fine Romanesque church built in honour of the holy man still stands at the site of Suso. It was here that the first literature was produced in Castilian, from which one of the most widely spoken languages in the world today is derived. In the early sixteenth century the community was housed in the fine new monastery of Yuso, below the older complex; it is still a thriving community today. UNESCO added the site to the World Heritage List in 1997.

University and Historic Precinct of Alcalá de Henares

Alcalá de Henares was the first planned university city in the world, founded by Cardinal Ximénez de Cisneros in the early sixteenth century. It was the original model for the *Civitas Dei* (City of God), the ideal urban community which Spanish missionaries brought to the Americas, and also for universities in Europe and beyond. UNESCO added the site to the World Heritage List in 1998.

Roman Walls of Lugo

The walls of Lugo were built in the latter half of the second century to defend the Roman town of Lucus. The entire circuit survives intact and is the finest example of late Roman fortifications in western Europe. UNESCO added the site to the World Heritage List in 2000.

Aranjuez Cultural Landscape

The Aranjuez cultural landscape is an entity of complex relationships: between nature and human activity, between sinuous watercourses and geometric landscape design, between the rural and the urban, between forest landscape and the delicately modulated architecture of its palatial buildings. Three hundred years of royal attention to the development and care of this landscape have seen it express an evolution of concepts from humanism and political centralization, to characteristics such as those found in its eighteenth-century French-style Baroque garden, to the urban lifestyle which developed alongside the sciences of plant acclimatization and stockbreeding during the Age of Enlightenment. UNESCO added the site to the World Heritage List in 2001.

SWEDEN

Skogskyrkogården

This Stockholm cemetery was created between 1917 and 1920 by two young architects, Asplund and Lewerentz, on the site of former gravel pits overgrown with pine trees. The design blends vegetation and architectural elements, taking advantage of irregularities in the site to create a landscape that is finely adapted to its function. It has had a profound influence in many countries of the world. UNESCO added the site to the World Heritage List in 1994.

SWITZERLAND

Convent of Saint Gall

The perfect example of a great Carolingian monastery, this convent, rebuilt during the period of Abbot Gozbert (816–837), contains precious manuscripts in its Baroque library, including the earliest-known architectural plan drawn on parchment. UNESCO added the site to the World Heritage List in 1983.

UKRAINE

Kiev: Saint Sophia Cathedral and Related Monastic Buildings, the Kiev-Pechersk Lavra

Designed to rival Hagia Sophia in Constantinople, Kiev's Saint-Sophia Cathedral symbolizes the 'new Constantinople', capital of the Christian principality of Kiev, which was created in the eleventh century in a region evangelized after the baptism of Saint Vladimir in 988. The spiritual and intellectual influence of Kiev-Pechersk Lavra contributed to the spread of Orthodox thought and faith in the Russian world from the seventeenth to the nineteenth centuries. UNESCO added the site to the World Heritage List in 1990.

UNITED KINGDOM

Studley Royal Park including the Ruins of Fountains Abbey

A striking landscape was created around the ruins of the Cistercian Fountains Abbey and Fountains Hall Castle, in Yorkshire. The eighteenth-century landscaping, gardens and canal, the nineteenth-century plantations and vistas, and the neo-Gothic Castle of Studley Royal Park, make this an outstanding site. UNESCO added the site to the World Heritage List in 1986.

Blenheim Palace

Near Oxford, in a romantic park created by the well-known landscape gardener "Capability" Brown, is Blenheim Palace, given by the English nation to John Churchill, first Duke of Marlborough, in recognition of his victory in 1704 over French and Bavarian troops. Built between 1705 and 1722, characterized by eclectic inspiration and a return to national roots, it is a perfect example of an eighteenth-century princely home. UNESCO added the site to the World Heritage List in 1987.

New Lanark

New Lanark is a small eighteenth-century village set in a sublime Scottish landscape where the philanthropist and Utopian idealist Robert Owen moulded a model industrial community in the early nineteenth century. The imposing cotton mill buildings, the spacious and well-designed workers' housing, and the dignified educational institute and school still testify to Owen's humanism. UNESCO added the site to the World Heritage List in 2001.

The Derwent Valley Mills

The Derwent Valley in central England contains a series of eighteenth- and nineteenth-century cotton mills and an industrial landscape of high historical and technological interest. The modern factory owes its origins to the mills at Cromford, where Richard Arkwright's inventions were first put into industrial-scale production. The workers' housing associated with this and other mills are intact and illustrate the socio-economic development of the area. UNESCO added the site to the World Heritage List in 2001.

YUGOSLAVIA

Studenica Monastery

Founded in the late twelfth century shortly after the abdication of Stevan Nemanja, creator of the medieval Serb State, the Studenica Monastery is the largest and richest of the Orthodox monasteries in Serbia. Its two main monuments, the Church of the Virgin and the Church of the King, constructed out of white marble, make up a veritable conservatory of thirteenth- and fourteenth-century Byzantine painting. UNESCO added the site to the World Heritage List in 1988.

Photographic credits

Agenzia Fotografica Luisa Ricciarini, Milan: pp. 5, 6, 8-9, 10, 11, 12, 13, 14, 15, 16, 17, 24, 25, 26, 27, 28, 29, 30, 31, 32, 33, 37, 38, 39, 42, 43, 44, 46, 48-49, 50, 51, 52, 53, 54, 55, 56 bottom, 57, 60, 61, 62, 63, 64, 65, 66, 67, 68, 69, 70 left, 71, 72, 73, 74 up, 75, 78 right, 79 up, 81, 83, 86, 87, 88 bottom, 90, 95 up, 96, 97, 101, 102, 108 up, 110, 111, 112, 115 bottom, 116, 117, 118, 119, 120, 121, 122, 123, 124, 125, 126, 127, 128, 129, 130, 144 right, 154 left, 155, 156 bottom, 157, 158, 162, 163 up, 164-165, 166, 167, 169, 170 bottom, 172, 173, 174, 175, 177, 178, 179, 182, 183 bottom, 184, 185, 186, 188, 189, 190, 191, 192, 193, 194, 198, 199, 200, 202, 204, 205, 208, 209, 210, 212, 214, 215, 217, 218, 219, 220, 221, 223 bottom, 224, 225, 226, 227, 228, 229, 230, 231, 234, 235, 236, 237, 238, 239, 240, 241, 242, 243, 244, 245, 246, 247, 248, 250, 251, 252, 253, 254, 255, 256, 257, 258, 260, 261, 274, 275, 276-277, 278, 279, 280, 282, 283 up, 284, 286 up, 288, 289, 290, 291, 292, 293, 294, 295, 296, 297, 298, 299, 300, 301, 302, 303, 304, 305, 306, 307, 308, 309, 310, 311, 312, 313, 314, 315, 316, 317, 318, 319, 327, 330, 333, 334, 335, 336, 337, 338, 339, 340, 341, 351 up, 352 bottom, 358, 359, 360, 361

Archivio Eric Lessing/Contrasto: pp. 7, 47, 82, 89, 91, 92, 93, 94, 95 bottom, 187, 326, 331

Archivio Scala, Florence: pp. 4, 6 up, 17 right, 36, 40, 41, 45, 56 left, 70 bottom, 74 bottom, 78 left, 79 bottom, 84, 85, 98, 99, 100, 103 bottom, 104, 105, 106, 107, 108 up, 114, 115 up, 118, 131, 132-133, 134, 135, 136, 137, 168, 170 up, 171 left, 176, 180,181, 183 up, 198 centre, 201, 203, 206, 207, 211, 213, 216, 222, 223 up, 281, 283 bottom, 285, 286 bottom, 287, 353

Archivio Fotografico Unesco: pp. 265 bottom, 266 bottom, 268, 325, 348 left, 349, 350, 364

The Image Bank/Guido Alberto Rossi: pp. 34-35; /Bertrand: pp. 58-59; /H. Sund: pp. 196-197; /Giuliano Colliva: pp. 328-329

San Marcos/A.Vázquez: pp.18, 20; /G.M. Azumendi: pp. 354, 355, 356, 357; /C. Redondo: pp. 270, 271, 272, 273; /J. Giró: pp. 262, 263, 264, 265 up, 266 bottom, 267, 269; /S. Janini: pp. 342, 343, 344, 345; /J.A. Fernández: pp. 322, 323, 324; /T. Vives: p. 259

Archivio Iconografico, S.A./CORBIS: pp. 76, 352 up

Tom Bean/CORBIS: p. 366 up

Gianni Dagli Orti/CORBIS: p. 80

Michael Freeman/CORBIS: pp. 363, 365 bottom

Dave G. Houser/CORBIS: p. 365 up

Wolfgang Kaehler/CORBIS: pp. 362, 367

Michael Nicholson/CORBIS: p. 77

Kevin Schafer/CORBIS: p. 366 bottom

Julia Waterlow, Eye Ubiguitours/CORBIS: pp. 348 right, 351 bottom

Massimo Zanella: pp. 86 right, 99 left